# Effective Perl Programming

## Writing Better Programs with Perl

Joseph N. Hall
with
Randal L. Schwartz

**ADDISON-WESLEY**

**An imprint of Addison Wesley Longman, Inc.**
Reading, Massachusetts • Harlow, England • Menlo Park, California
Berkeley, California • Don Mills, Ontario • Sydney
Bonn • Amsterdam • Tokyo • Mexico City

The publisher offers discounts on this book when ordered in quantity for special sales. For more information, please contact:

Addison Wesley Longman, Inc.
One Jacob Way
Reading, Massachusetts 01867

Library of Congress Cataloging-in-Publication Data

Hall, Joseph, 1966-
Effective Perl programming: writing better programs with
Perl / Joseph Hall, with Randal Schwartz.
   p.  cm.
Includes bibliographical references and index.
ISBN 0-201-41975-0  (alk. paper)
1. Perl  (Computer program language)   I. Schwartz, Randal L.
II. Title.
QA76.73.P22H35   1998
005.13'3—dc21                                    97-45837
                                                  CIP

ISBN 0-201-41975-0

Text printed on recycled and acid-free paper.
  2 3 4 5 6 7 8 9 10-MA-01009998

Second Printing, March 1998

2386707

For my mother, Judy, with love—All
those books were good for something.


And for Donna—
Awaiting many more Volcano Days.

# Contents

# Foreword

I didn't learn English by reading the dictionary, or by stopping after I had read the "See Dick Run" primers. In the same way, I don't learn a new computer language by merely sitting down with the reference materials or any available tutorials. To really *know* a computer language, and be fluent in its usage, I have to get to the next level of proficiency. This requires learning how people use it when they're using it in the best and most efficient way.

*Effective Perl Programming* represents a good solid cross-section of the best and most efficient ways to use the wildly popular Perl language, captured and organized in readily digestible pieces. This book nicely complements my two best-selling Perl books—the authoritative reference manual and the highly acclaimed tutorial guide—by filling in this "next level" of information. You will find that the material here is easy to read and neatly lays out what you need to know to get beyond the basics with Perl.

Joseph Hall has worked with me as a successful Perl instructor and a developer of quality course materials. With this book, he also proves himself to be a competent and fun-to-read author, and I'm honored to be working with him. I wish you many productive hours with Perl, hopefully enhanced by your reading of this book.

RANDAL L. SCHWARTZ                                          PORTLAND, OREGON
CO-AUTHOR, *PROGRAMMING PERL* AND *LEARNING PERL*

# Preface

I used to write a lot of C and C++. My last major project before stepping into the world of Perl full time was an interpreted language that, among other things, drew diagrams, computed probabilities, and generated entire FrameMaker books. It comprised over 50,000 lines of platform-independent C++, and it had all kinds of interesting internal features. It was a fun project. It also took two years to write.

It seems to me that most interesting projects in C and/or C++ take months or years to complete. But it also seems to me that a whole lot of ideas that start out being mundane and uninteresting *become* interesting three-month projects when they are expressed in an ordinary high-level language.

This is one of the reasons why I originally became interested in Perl. I had heard that Perl was an excellent scripting language with powerful string handling, regular expression, and process control features. I learned Perl, and learned to like it, when I was thrown into a project in which most of my work involved slinging around text files. I quickly found myself spending hours writing Perl programs that would have taken me days or weeks to write in a different language.

## Who should read this book

*Effective Perl Programming* is a book of advice and examples. It derives from my experience as a Perl programmer and—especially—as a Perl instructor. The book is suitable for readers who have a basic understanding of Perl and a few months of practical experience programming in it. Because *Effective Perl Programming* is a guidebook, not a manual, readers will need access to a comprehensive reference. I recommend either the Perl man pages (freely available in many forms, including Unix man and HTML) or *Programming Perl*.

Although I use a lot of Unix-derived examples in this book, most of what appears here is not specific to Unix. I thought about including Win32 Perl and MacPerl examples but eventually decided that the book would have more integrity and consistency if it didn't stray from Perl's "native" operating system. I do encourage non-Unix developers to read *Effective Perl Programming*, or at least to give it a careful look.

## How and why I wrote this book

I've always wanted to be a writer. In childhood I was obsessed with science fiction. I read constantly, sometimes three paperbacks a day, and every so often, wrote some (bad) stories myself. In 1985, I attended the Clarion Science Fiction Writers' workshop in East Lansing, Michigan. Afterward, I spent a year or so occasionally working on short story manuscripts, but never published any fiction. (Not yet, anyway!)

Later on, when I had settled down into a career in software, I met Randal Schwartz. I hired him as a contractor on an engineering project and worked with him for over a year. Eventually he left to pursue teaching Perl full time. After a while, so did I.

In May 1996, I had a conversation with Keith Wollman at a developer's conference in San Jose. When we drifted onto the topic of Perl, he asked me what I would think of a book called *Effective Perl*. I liked the idea. Scott Meyers's *Effective C++* was one of my favorite books on C++, and extending the series to cover Perl would obviously be useful. I couldn't get Keith's idea out of my head. With some help from Randal, I worked out a proposal for the book, and Addison-Wesley accepted it.

The rest—well, that was the fun part. I spent many 12-hour days and nights with FrameMaker in front of the computer screen, asked lots of annoying questions on the Perl 5 Porters list, posted many bug reports to the same list, looked through dozens of books and manuals, wrote many, many little snippets of Perl code, and drank many, many cans of Diet Coke and Diet Pepsi. I even had an occasional epiphany as I discovered very basic things about Perl I had never realized I was missing. After a while, a manuscript emerged.

This book is my attempt to share with the rest of you some of the fun and stimulation I experienced while learning the power of Perl. I certainly appreciate you taking the time to read it, and I hope you will find it useful and enjoyable.

JOSEPH N. HALL                                        CHANDLER, ARIZONA

# Acknowledgements

This book was hard to write. I think mostly I made it hard on myself, but it would have been a lot harder if I had not had help from a large cast of programmers, authors, editors, and other professionals, many of whom contributed their time for free or at grossly inadequate rates that might as well have been for free. Everyone who supported me in this effort has my appreciation and heartfelt thanks.

Chip Salzenberg and Andreas "MakeMaker" König provided a number of helpful and timely fixes to Perl bugs and misbehaviors that would have complicated the manuscript. It's hard to say enough about Chip. I've spent a little time mucking about in the Perl source code. I hold him in awe.

Many other members of the Perl 5 Porters list contributed in one way or another, either directly or indirectly. Among the most obviously helpful and insightful were Jeffrey Friedl, Chaim Frenkel, Tom Phoenix, Jon Orwant, Charlie Stross, and Tom Christiansen.

Randal Schwartz, author, instructor, and "Just Another Perl Hacker," contributed passages to the book and was my primary technical reviewer. If you find any mistakes, e-mail *him*. (Just kidding.) Working with Randal has taught me an enormous amount about Perl, and his books and USENET postings have taught countless programmers how to write cool things in Perl. Many thanks to Randal for lending his time and thought to this book.

Many thanks, also, to Larry Wall, the gracious and literate creator of Perl, who has answered questions and provided comments on many topics.

I've been very lucky to work with Addison-Wesley on this project. Everyone I've had contact with has been friendly and has contributed in some significant way to the book's forward progress. I would like to extend particular thanks to Kim Fryer, Ben Ryan, Carol Nelson, Keith Wollman, Elizabeth Spainhour, Tracy Russ, and Mike Hendrickson. Many thanks also to the excellent production staff, including Ann Knight, Regina Knox, and Roberta Clark, who finished a complex task in a short time and meanwhile proved to me that copyediting and proofreading need not be overly traumatic.

A number of other people have contributed comments, inspiration, and/or moral support. My friends Nick Orlans, Chris Ice, and Alan Piszcz trudged through several revisions of the incomplete manuscript. My current and former employers—Charlie Horton, Patrick Reilly, and Larry Zimmerman—have been a constant source of stimulation and encouragement.

Although I wrote this book from scratch, some of it by necessity parallels the description of Perl in the Perl man pages as well as *Programming Perl*. There are only so many ways to skin a cat. I have tried to be original and creative, but in a few cases it was hard to stray from the original description of the language.

Many thanks to Jeff Gong, for harrassing The Phone Company [1] and keeping the T-1 alive. Jeff really knows how to keep his customers happy.

Many thanks to the sport of golf for keeping me sane and providing an outlet for my frustrations. It's fun to make the little ball go. Thanks to *Master of Orion* and *Civilization II* for much the same reasons.

Most of all, though, I have to thank Donna, my soulmate, fiancee, and also one heck of a programmer. This book would not have come into being without her inexhaustible support, patience, and love.

---

1. Go see the movie *The President's Analyst* if you don't get this.

# Introduction

"Learning the fundamentals of a programming language is one thing: learning how to design and write effective programs in that language is something else entirely." What Scott Meyers wrote in the Introduction to *Effective C++* is just as true for Perl.

Perl is a very high level language—a VHLL for the acronym-aware. It incorporates high-level functionality like regular expressions, networking, and process management into a context-sensitive grammar that is more "human," in a way, than that of other programming languages. Perl is a better text processing language than any other widely used computer language, or perhaps any other computer language, period. Perl is an incredibly effective scripting tool for Unix administrators, and it is the first choice of most Unix CGI scripters worldwide. Perl also supports object-oriented programming, modular software, cross-platform development, embedding, and extensibility.

There is a lot to learn about Perl.

Once you have worked your way through an introductory book or class on Perl, you have learned to write what Larry Wall, Perl's creator, fondly refers to as "baby talk." Perl baby talk is plain, direct, and verbose. It's not bad—you are *allowed and encouraged* to write Perl in whatever style works for you.

You may reach a point at which you want to move beyond plain, direct, and verbose Perl toward something more succinct and individualistic. This book is written for people who are setting off down that path. *Effective Perl Programming* endeavors to teach you what you need to know to become a fluent and expressive Perl programmer. This book will provide you several different kinds of advice to help you on your way.

- **Knowledge, or perhaps, "Perl trivia."** Many different complex tasks in Perl have been or can be reduced to extremely simple statements. A lot of learning to program effectively in Perl is acquiring an adequate reservoir of experience and knowledge about the "right" ways to do things. Once you know good solutions, you can apply them to your own problems. Furthermore, once you know what good solutions look like, you can invent your own and judge their "rightness" accurately.

- **How to solve problems.** You may already have good analytical and/or debugging skills from your work in another programming language. This book will teach you how to beat your problems using Perl, by showing you a lot of problems and their solutions in Perl. It will also teach you how to beat the problems that Perl gives you, by showing you how to efficiently debug and improve your programs.

- **Style.** This book will teach you idiomatic Perl style, primarily by example. You will learn to write Perl more succinctly and elegantly. If succinctness isn't your goal, you will at least learn to avoid certain awkward constructs. You will also learn to evaluate your efforts and those of others.

- **How to grow further.** This book is a little less than three hundred pages long. Although it purports to be a book on intermediate to advanced Perl, not a whole lot of advanced Perl will actually fit between its covers. A real compendium of advanced Perl would require thousands of pages. What this book is really about is how you can make yourself an advanced Perl *programmer*—how you can find the resources you need to grow, how to structure your learning and experiments, and how to recognize that you have grown.

This is intended to be a thought-provoking book. There are subtleties to many of the examples. Anything really tricky will be explained, but a lot of other things that are simple but not always obvious will be left to stand on their own. Don't be alarmed if you find yourself puzzling something out for a while. Perl is an idiosyncratic language and in many ways is very different from other programming languages. Remember that fluency and style only come through practice and reflection, and that while learning is hard work, it is also enjoyable and rewarding.

## The world of Perl

Perl is a remarkable language. It is, in my opinion, the most successful modular programming environment to date. In fact, Perl modules are the closest thing to the fabled "Software ICs"[1] that the software world has seen. There are many reasons for this, one of the most important being that there is a centralized, coordinated module repository, the Comprehensive Perl Archive Network (CPAN), which reduces the amount of energy

---

1. The term coined by Brad Cox and Lamar Ledbetter in their classic June 1985 *Byte* article of the same name.

wasted on competing, incompatible implementations of functionality (see Appendix B, "Resources").

Perl has a minimalistic but sufficient modular and object-oriented programming framework. The lack of extensive access control features in the language makes it possible to write code with unusual characteristics in a natural, succinct form. It seems to be a natural law of software that the most useful features are also the ones that fit existing frameworks most poorly. I believe that Perl's skeletal approach to "rules and regulations" effectively subverts this law.

Perl provides excellent cross-platform compatibility. It excels as a systems administration scripting tool on Unix because it hides the differences between different versions of Unix to the greatest extent possible. Can you write cross-platform shell scripts? Yes, but with extreme difficulty. Most mere mortals should not attempt such things. Can you write cross-platform Perl scripts? Yes, easily. Perl also ports reasonably well between its Unix birthplace and other platforms, such as the Macintosh, Windows 9x, and Windows NT.

As a Perl programmer, you have some of the best support in the world. You have complete access to the source code for all the modules you use, as well as the complete source code to the language itself. If picking through the code for bugs isn't your speed, you have on-line support available via USENET on the Internet 24 hours a day, 7 days a week. If free support isn't your style, you can also buy commercial support.

Finally, you have a language that dares to be different. In a day and time when most programming languages are designed to be rigorous, Perl is fluid. At its best, in the presence of several alternative interpretations, Perl does what you *mean*. A scary thought, perhaps, but I believe it is an indication of true progress in computing, something that reaches beyond mere cycles, disk space, and RAM.

## Terminology

In general, the terminology used in Perl isn't that different from that used to describe other programming languages. However, there are a few terms with slightly peculiar meanings. In addition, as Perl has evolved, some terminology has faded from fashion and some new terminology has been added. Here, I will explain a few of the more nitpicky entries in the Perl glossary.

The terms *array* and *list* have precise meanings in Perl. However, those meanings are really only clear to people who are somewhat familiar with the internals of Perl, and it is not often that the differences are evident. Basically, an array is a Perl data structure with more or less permanently allocated storage, which may or may not have a name associated with it. A list, on the other hand, is a bunch of values on the run-time stack. Perl converts lists and arrays back and forth with indifference. An array used in a list context becomes a list of values; a list assigned to an array variable becomes an array. The difference is apparent only in a limited number of circumstances. You cannot, for example, pop from a list.

*Associative array* is an obsolete pre-Perl 5 term. Around the advent of Perl 5, the Perl Illuminati tired of this elaborate seven-syllable compound word and replaced it with the much more succinct *hash*. There is no difference in meaning.

An *operator* in Perl is a parentheses-less syntactic construct. (But the arguments to an operator may, of course, be contained in parentheses.) A *list operator* is an identifier followed by a list of elements separated by commas:

```
print "Hello", chr(44)," world!\n";        print is a list operator.
```

A *function* in Perl is an identifier followed by a pair of parentheses that completely enclose the arguments:

```
print ("Hello", chr(44), " world!\n");     print is also a function.
```

Now, you may have just noticed a certain similarity between list operators and functions. In Perl, there is no difference other than the syntax used. I will generally use the term "operator" when I refer to Perl built-ins like `print` and `open`, but may use "function" occasionally. There is no particular difference in meaning.

The proper way to refer to a subroutine written in Perl is, well, *subroutine*. Of course, "function," "operator," and even "procedure" will make acceptable literary stand-ins.

Although the term *method* is dealt with thoroughly in Item 49, I should discuss it briefly here. Perl methods are really subroutines written to conform to certain conventions, which are neither required nor recognized by Perl. However, Perl does have a special *method call syntax* that is used to support object-oriented programming. A good way of defining the (somewhat elusive) difference is by stating that a method is a subroutine that is intended to be called via method call syntax.

A Perl *identifier* is a "C symbol"—a letter or underscore followed by zero or more letters, digits, or underscores. Identifiers are used to name Perl *variables*. Perl variables are identifiers combined with the appropriate punctuation, for example, $a or &func.

Although this is not strictly in keeping with the usage in the internals of Perl, I will use the term *keyword* to refer to the small number of identifiers in Perl that have distinctive syntactic meanings, for example, `if` and `while`. Other identifiers like `print` and `oct` that have ordinary function or operator syntax will be called *built-ins*, if anything.

An *lvalue* (pronounced "ell value") is a value that can appear on the left hand side of an assignment statement. This is the customary meaning of the term; however, there are some unusual constructs that act as lvalues in Perl, for example, the `substr` operator.

*Localizing* a variable means creating a separate scope for it that applies through the end of the enclosing block or file. Special variables must be localized with the `local` operator.[2] Ordinary variables can be localized with either `my` or `local` (see Item 23). I will say "localize with `my`" when it makes a difference.

## Notation

In this book I use my "PEGS" (PErl Graphical Structures) notation to illustrate data structures. It should be mostly self-explanatory, but here is a brief overview.

Scalar values are represented with a single rectangular box:

| 3.1416 |
|:---:|

Variables are values with names. Names go in a sideways "picket" above the value. Boxes can be adorned with the internal Perl type[3] and with the access syntax for the value:

GV ▸ a ⟩
SV ▸ 3.1416 $a

Arrays and lists have the same graphical representation. They look like a stack of values with a thick bar on top:

| H |
|:---:|
| He |
| Li |

---

2. Future versions of Perl may add the ability to localize special variables in a different way, probably with `my`.

3. For example, GV or SV. If you don't know what these mean, you probably don't need to worry about them.

Hashes look like a stack of names next to a stack of values:

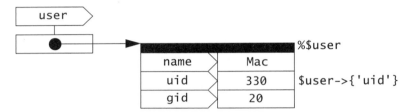

References are drawn with dots and arrows like those LISP diagrams from days of yore:

That's all there is to the basics. PEGS is really not very complicated, but if you want to know more, you can take a look at the official PEGS web page, located at `http://www.effectiveperl.com/pegs/`.

## Perl style

Part of what you should learn from this book is a sense of good Perl style. Style is, of course, a matter of preference and debate. I won't pretend to know or demonstrate The One True Style, but I hope to show readers one example of contemporary, efficient, "effective" Perl style.

The fact that the code appears in a book affects its style somewhat. Examples can't be too verbose or boring—each one has to make one or two specific points without unnecessary clutter. Therefore, you will find the following:

- I don't use `English`. It's just too verbose for this little book. Furthermore, `English` is not common practice among Perl programmers, and scripts that `use English` suffer a speed penalty. This is not to say that `English` is not useful, just that you won't see it here.

- Not everything runs cleanly under -w or use strict (see Item 36). I advise *all* Perl programmers to make use of both -w and use strict regularly. However, starting off all the examples with my($this, $that) isn't going to make them more readable, and it's readability that's important here.

- I generally minimize punctuation (see Item 10). Veteran Perl 4 programmers may find the lack of parentheses unnerving, but it grows on you.

- Finally, I try to make the examples meaningful. Not every example can be a useful snippet, but I've tried to include as many pieces of real-world code as possible.

## Organization

The first two chapters generally present material in order of increasing complexity. Otherwise, the book jumps around a lot. Use the table of contents and the index, and keep a good Perl reference (the man pages or *Programming Perl*) handy.

The way the examples in this book are formatted isn't particularly mysterious, but I should mention a few things. Snippets of code and short examples appear inlined in the text:

```
print "This is an example.\n";          This is a comment.
```

Longer or especially significant examples appear in boxes:

■ **Important examples appear in boxes.**

| *Pay attention to the code below.* |
|---|
| print "This is an important example!\n";          *This is another comment.* |

Square bullets ■ indicate boxes that demonstrate good practices or *do*s. Inverted triangles ▼ indicate boxes that demonstrate poor practices or *don't*s. Circular bullets ● indicate boxes containing material of a more general nature.

In some cases, I suggest running an example program. If I don't specify a name, the program is called tryme. Keyboard input (the stuff you're supposed to type) appears in **bold typewriter** font. Command lines begin with a % prompt:

```
print "Enter the magic number: ";
if (<> == 7) {
  print "Magic mode on!\n";
} else {
  print "Nothing happens.\n";
}
```

```
% tryme
Enter the magic number: 7
Magic mode on!
```

## How to contact us

Although I think this has turned out to be a pretty good book, I'm sure there are ways it could be made better. If you find errors, I'd appreciate it if you would report them to me at bookbugs@effectiveperl.com. Suggestions for enhancements, new material, or different ways of treating topics (for a later edition or perhaps another book) can be sent to suggestions@effectiveperl.com. The next edition will acknowledge, by name, all contributors who were the first to find a particular bug or who were the first to suggest new material.

Errata and other material of interest will be published on the *Effective Perl Programming* web site at http://www.effectiveperl.com.

# Basics

If you are experienced in other languages but new to Perl, you are probably still discovering Perl's idiosyncracies. This section deals with some of those idiosyncracies. In particular, it addresses those that can bedevil newly minted Perl programmers who are still attuned to other languages.

For example, you should already know that Perl's variables are generally made up of some piece of punctuation like $ or @ followed by an identifier. But do you know whether different types of variables with the same name, such as $a and @a, are completely independent of one another? They are—see Item 1.

You should know that @a is an array, but do you know the difference between $a[$i] and @a[$i]? The latter is a *slice*—see Item 2.

You should know that the number 0 is false, and that the empty string, "", is false, but do you know whether the string consisting of a single space, " ", is false? It's *true*—see Item 5.

If you are a more experienced Perl programmer, these first few Items will be mostly review for you. However, you may find some interesting details toward the end of some Items in this section.

## Item 1:   Know your namespaces.

There are seven separate kinds of variables or variable-like things in Perl: scalar variables, array variables, hash variables, subroutine names, format names, filehandles, and directory handles.

Each of these different kinds of variables has its own *namespace*. Changing the value of one kind of variable does not in any way affect the value of another kind of variable with the same name. For example, the scalar variable $a is independent of the array variable @a:

```
$a = 42;                              Set scalar $a = 42.
```

```
@a = (1, 2, 3);
```
@a = (1,2,3), *but* $a *is still* 42.

Also, each package (see Item 42) in a Perl program defines its own set of namespaces. For example, $a in package main is independent of $a in package foo:

```
$a = 1;
```
*Assuming we start in package* main, *set scalar* $main::a = 1.

```
package foo;
```
*Default package is now* foo.

```
$a = 3.1416;
```
$foo::a *is* 3.1416; $main::a *is still* 1.

You have to look to the right as well as the left of an identifier, as Perl does, to determine what kind of variable the identifier refers to. For example, the syntax for accessing elements of arrays and hashes begins with $, not @ or %. The $ means that the result is a scalar value, not that you are refer-ring to a scalar variable:

```
$a = 1;
@a = (1, 2, 3);
%a = ('a' => 97, 'b' => 98);
```
*Set scalar* $a = 1.
*Set array* @a = (1,2,3).
*Set hash* %a.

```
$a[3] = 4;
$a{'c'} = 99;
```
$a *is still* 1; @a *is* (1,2,3,4) *now.*
$a, @a *still the same;* %a *has three key-value pairs now.*

Not all variable-like things in Perl are prefixed with punctuation charac-ters. Subroutine names can be prefixed with an ampersand, but the ampersand is generally optional. In some cases, parentheses around the subroutine arguments can also be omitted:

```
sub hi {
  $name = shift; "hi, $name\n"
}
```
*A subroutine named* hi.

```
print &hi("Fred");
```
*The "old-style" syntax.*

```
print hi("Fred");
```
*Parens following* hi *cause it to be recognized as a sub name.*

```
print hi "Fred";
```
*Parens can also be omitted if* hi *is defined in the source code before it is used (see Item 10).*

Filehandles, format names, and directory handles are not prefixed with punctuation characters, but are recognized in context:

*The filehandle, format name, and dirhandle below are independent of one another, even though they are all named* TEST.

```
open TEST, ">$$.test";
print TEST "test data\n";

format TEST =
@<<<<<<<<<<<<< @<<<< @<<<<
$name, $lo, $hi
.

opendir TEST, ".";
```

*Open filehandle named* TEST.
*Print to filehandle* TEST.

*Format named* TEST.

*Directory handle named* TEST.

It's not necessarily bad programming style to take advantage of Perl's independent namespaces by giving two different *kinds* of variables the same name. Sometimes it even seems like the sensible thing to do:

```
@who =
  grep { /\bjoebloe\b/ } `who`;

foreach $who (@who) {
  # ... do something with $who
}
```

@who *contains output from* who *command, one line per element.*

*Iterate over each line of output using variable* $who.

## Item 2:    Avoid using a slice when you want an element.

Is @a[1] an array element? Or an array slice?

It's a *slice*.

One of the counterintuitive things encountered by people just beginning to learn Perl is the difference between array elements and array slices. Even after you know the difference, it's not hard to type @ instead of $.

An introductory book or course about Perl will typically begin by telling you that scalar variable names begin with $, and array variable names begin with @. This is, of course, an oversimplification, which is corrected in the next step of the introduction, where you learn that to access element $n of array @a, you use the syntax $a[$n], not @a[$n]. This may seem peculiar. However, it *is* a consistent syntax. Scalar *values*, not variables, begin with $, even when those values come from an array or hash.

Therefore, @a[$n] doesn't mean element $n of array @a. Rather, it is something different, called a slice. A slice is a shortcut way of writing a list of elements:

```
@giant = qw(fee fie foe fum);
```

@giant *is* ('fee', 'fie', 'foe', 'fum').

```
@queue = ($giant[1], $giant[2]);        @queue is ('fie', 'foe').
@queue = @giant[1, 2];                  Same thing, using a slice.

@fifo = (1, 2);                         Same thing again, using a list of
@queue = @giant[@fifo];                 values in an array.
```

A slice has all the characteristics of a list of variable names. You can even use it on the left-hand side of an assignment expression, or in other places where an lvalue is required:

```
($giant[1], $giant[2]) =                @giant is ('fee', 'tweedle',
  ("tweedle", "dee");                   'dee', 'fum').

@giant[1, 2] = ("tweedle", "dee");      Same thing, assigning to a slice.
```

Now, @a[1] is as much a slice as are @a[1, 2], @a[2, 10], @a[5, 3, 1], @a[3..7], and so on. @a[1] is a *list*, not a scalar value. It is a list of one element.

These *single-element slices* are something you should watch out for. They are dangerous critters if not used properly. A slice used in a scalar context returns the last value in the slice, which makes single-element slices work like scalar values, *in some cases*. For example:

```
$jolly = @giant[3];                     $jolly = 'fum', but for the
                                        wrong reason.
```

Probably what was intended here was $jolly = $giant[3]. The single-element slice @giant[3] is still OK, sort of, since @giant[3] in a scalar context evaluates to its last (and in this case only) element, $giant[3].

Although single-element slices work somewhat like array elements on the right side of assignments, they behave very differently on the left-hand side of assignments. Because a single-element slice is a list, an assignment to a single-element slice is a list assignment, and thus the right-hand side of the assignment is evaluated *in a list context*. Unintentionally evaluating an operator in a list context can produce dramatic (and unfortunate) results. A good example is the line input operator, *<filehandle>*:

▼ **Don't use a single-element slice as the left-hand side of an assignment.**

| | |
|---|---|
| *What was intended was* $info[0] = <STDIN>. | |
| @info[0] = <STDIN>; | *OOPS! <STDIN> in a list context!* |
| ($info[0]) = <STDIN>; | *Same problem w/o slice.* |

This reads all the lines from standard input, assigns the first one to element 0 of @info, and ignores the rest! Assigning <STDIN> to @info[3] evaluates <STDIN> in a list context. In a list context, <STDIN> reads all the lines from standard input and returns them as a list.

One more difference between slices and elements is that the expression in the brackets of an element access is evaluated in a scalar context, whereas for slices it is evaluated in a list context. This leads to another example of bizarre behavior that is more difficult to explain:

▼ **Don't confuse slices and elements.**

*Suppose you want to add an additional line containing* 'EOF' *to the end of the array* @text. *You could write this as* $text[@text] = 'EOF'. *But don't write* @text[@text] *instead.*

```
chomp (@text = <STDIN>);
```
*Read lines into* @text. *So far, so good.*

```
@text[@text] = 'EOF';
```
*Seriously wrong! See below.*

The array @text inside the brackets above is interpreted in a list context. In a scalar context it returns the number of elements in @text, but in a list context it returns the contents of the array itself. The result is a slice with as many elements as there are lines.

The contents of the lines are interpreted as integer indices—if they're text they will likely all turn out to be zero, so the slice will look like @text[0, 0, 0, 0, 0, ...]. Then 'EOF' is assigned to the first element of the slice, and undef to all the rest, which means that this will probably just over-write the first element of @text with undef, leaving everything else alone.

What a mess!

Get in the habit of looking for single-element slices like @a[0] in your pro-grams. Single-element slices are generally not what you want (though they're handy for tricks now and then), and a single-element slice on the left-hand side of an assignment is almost certainly wrong. The -w com-mand line option (see Item 36) will flag many suspect uses of slices.

## Slicing for fun and profit

Beginning Perl programmers generally do not (intentionally) use slices, except to select elements from a result:

```
($uid, $gid) = (stat $file)[4, 5];
```
*Get user and group id from result of* stat $file.

```
$last = (sort @list)[-1];
```
*Find the element of* @list *that comes last in ASCII order (inefficient for long* @list).

```
$field_two = (split /:/)[1];
```
*Get the second element from the result of splitting $_ on :.*

However, slices can be put to some pretty interesting (and weird) uses. For example:

```
@list[5..9] = reverse @list[5..9];
```
*Reverse elements 5 through 9 of @list.*

```
@list[reverse 5..9] = @list[5..9];
```
*There's more than one way to do it.*

They make a handy way to swap two elements:

```
@a[$n, $m] = @a[$m, $n];
```
*Swap $a[$m] and $a[$n].*

```
@item{'old', 'new'} =
  @item{'new', 'old'};
```
*Swap $item{old} and $item{new}.*

Slices are also used in sorting (see Item 14):

■ **Use slices to reorder arrays.**

| | |
|---|---|
| *Given two parallel arrays @uid and @name, this example sorts @name according to the numerical contents of @uid.* | |
| `@name = @name[`<br>`  sort {$uid[$a] <=> $uid[$b]} 0..$#name`<br>`];` | *Sort indices 0..$#name according to @uid, then use the result to reorder @name.* |

You can use hash slices to create hashes from two lists, to overlay the contents of one hash onto another, and to "subtract" one hash from another:

■ **Use slices to create and manipulate hashes.**

| | |
|---|---|
| `@char_num{'A'..'Z'} = 1..26;` | *Create a hash from the keys 'A'..'Z' and values 1..26.* |
| `@old{keys %new} = values %new;` | *Overlay the contents of %new on %old.* |
| `%old = (%old, %new);` | *Another (probably less efficient) way of writing the above.* |
| `delete @name{keys %invalid};` | *"Subtract" elements in %invalid from %name.* |
| `foreach $key (keys %invalid) {`<br>`  delete $name{$key};`<br>`}` | *Another more verbose way of writing the above.* |

## Item 3:   Don't assign undef when you want an empty list.

Uninitialized scalar variables in Perl have the value undef. You can reset scalar variables to their "pristine" state by assigning undef to them, or by using the undef operator:

```
$toast = undef;
```
*It's toast.*

```
undef $history;
```
*It's history.*

Uninitialized array variables, however, have the value (), the empty list. If you assign undef to an array variable, what you actually get is a list of one element containing undef:

▼ **Don't assign undef to an array variable.**

```
@still_going = undef;

if (@still_going) { ... }
```
*WRONG—@still_going = (undef).*
*Therefore this is TRUE.*

The simplest way to avoid this is to assign the empty list () to array variables when you want to clear them. You can also use the undef verb:

```
@going_gone = ();
if (@going_gone) { ... }
```
*@going_gone = empty list, so scalar(@going_gone) = 0 = FALSE.*

```
undef @going_gone;
if (defined(@going_gone)) { ... }
```
*Now it's really gone.*
*FALSE*

The defined operator is the only way to distinguish undef from 0 and the empty string ''. The defined operator will work on any value—in earlier versions of Perl it would work only on lvalues, but that is no longer the case.

```
if (defined($a)) { ... }
if (defined(0)) { ... }
```
*TRUE if $a is not undef.*
*TRUE; error in Perl 4.*

```
if (defined(@a)) { ... }
if (defined(())) { ... }
```
*TRUE if @a is initialized.*
*TRUE; error in Perl 4.*

You can assign undef to an element of an array:

```
$puka[3] = undef;
@puka[1, 5, 7] = ();
@puka[0..99] = ();
```
*"Puka" is Hawaiian for "hole."*
*Create more holes.*
*100 copies of undef.*

Note that `undef` is a perfectly reasonable element value. You cannot shorten an array by assigning `undef` values to elements at the end of the array. To actually shorten an array without assigning a whole new value to it, you must assign to `$#array_name` or use one of the array operators like `splice` or `pop`.

```
@a = 1 .. 10;                    @a has 10 elements.
$a[9] = undef;                   @a still has 10.
print scalar(@a), "\n";          "10"—(1..9, undef)

$val = pop @a;                   @a now has 9 elements: (1..9).
print scalar(@a), "\n";          "9"—(1..9)

splice @a, -2;                   Splice off the last 2 elements.
print scalar(@a), "\n";          "7"—(1..7)

$#a = 4;                         Shorten @a to 5 elements.
print scalar(@a), "\n";          "5"—(1..5)
```

### Hashes and `undef`

The remarks above also apply to hashes. As with arrays, you cannot `undef` a hash by assigning `undef` to it. In fact, assigning any list with an odd number of elements to a hash results in a warning message (at least in newer versions of Perl). You can assign the empty list `()` to create an empty hash, or you can use the `undef` operator to reset the hash to a pristine state.

```
%gone = ();                           %gone now contains no keys.
if (keys %gone) { ... }               FALSE

%nuked = (U => '235', Pu => 238);     %nuked has two key-value pairs.
undef %nuked;                         "Nuked" it—completely gone.
if (keys %nuked) { ... }              FALSE
if (defined %nuked) { ... }           Also FALSE, because %nuked is
                                      completely gone.
```

As with arrays, you cannot shorten or remove elements from a hash by assigning `undef` values to them. In order to remove elements from a hash you must use the `delete` operator. The `delete` operator can be used on hash slices as well as single elements:

■ **Use `delete` to remove key-value pairs from hashes.**

```
%spacers = (                          Some sample data.
  husband => "george", wife => "jane",
  daughter => "judy", son => "elroy"
);
```

■ Use `delete` to remove key-value pairs from hashes. (cont'd)

```
delete $spacers{'husband'};                    husband/george is gone.
if (exists $spacers{'husband'}) { ... }        FALSE

delete @spacers{'daughter', 'son'};            daughter/judy and son/elroy
                                               are gone.
```

## Item 4: String and numeric comparisons are different.

Perl has two completely different sets of comparison operators, one for comparing strings and one for comparing numbers. It's worthwhile to know the difference and to keep them straight, because using the wrong comparison operator can be the source of hard-to-find bugs.

The operators used to compare strings are made up of letters and look like words, or like FORTRAN. Strings are compared "ASCIIbetically"—that is, by comparing the ASCII values of the characters in the strings, including case, spaces, and the like:

```
'a' lt 'b'                     TRUE
'a' eq 'A'                     FALSE—capitalization.
"joseph" eq "joseph "          FALSE—spaces count.
"H" cmp "He"                   -1—cmp operator.
```

The `cmp` operator does a string comparison and returns -1, 0, or 1, depending on whether its left argument is less than, equal to, or greater than its right argument, respectively. It is particularly useful for sorting (see Item 14).

Numeric comparison operators are made up of punctuation and look like algebra, or like C:

```
0 < 5                          TRUE
10 == 10.0                     TRUE
10 <=> 9.5                     1—"spaceship" operator.
```

The *spaceship operator* $<=>$[1] is like `cmp`, except that it compares its arguments numerically.

String comparison operators should not be used for comparing numbers, because they don't compare numbers properly. (Unless your definition of "properly" puts "10" before "2".) The same applies for numeric operators used to compare strings:

---

1. Is it Darth Vader's fighter? Or a starbase from the old character-based Star Trek games? You decide.

```
'10' gt '2'                    FALSE—'1' sorts before '2'.
"10.0" eq "10"                 FALSE—different strings.
'abc' == 'def'                 TRUE—both look like 0 to ==.
```

The kind of mistake this leads to is:

▼ **Don't compare strings with numeric operators, or vice versa.**

```
$hacker = 'joebloe';
if ($user == $hacker) {        WRONG—== used on strings.
  deny_access();               Oops—most strings look like 0
}                              to ==, so nobody gets on.
```

Perl's `sort` operator uses string comparisons by default. Don't use string comparisons to sort numbers! See Item 14 for more about sorting.

## Item 5:   Remember that 0 and "" are false.

Because numeric and string data in Perl have the same scalar type, and because Boolean operations can be applied to any scalar value, Perl's test for logical truth has to work for both numbers and strings.

The basic test is this: *0 and the empty string are false*. Everything else is true.

More precisely, when a quantity is used in a "Boolean context" (a term sometimes used to refer to conditionals in control expressions, the `?:` operator, `||`, `&&`, etc.), it is first converted to a string (see Item 6). The string result is then tested. If the result is the empty string, or a string consisting exactly of the single character `"0"`, the result is "false." Otherwise, the result is "true." Note that this rule means that `undef` will evaluate as false, because it always looks like the number 0 or the empty string to everything except the `defined` operator. This generally works very well. If problems do arise, they are usually the result of testing a quantity to see if it is false when really it should be tested to see if it is `undef`:

▼ **Don't test for falsehood when you should be testing for `undef`.**

```
while ($file = <*>) {          WRONG—what about a file
  do_something($file);         named "0"?
}
```

The code in this example works well *almost* all of the time. Each time through the loop, the fileglob `<*>` produces another filename from the current directory, which goes into `$file`. Once all the filenames in the directory have been enumerated, `<*>` returns `undef`, which appears to be the empty string and therefore false, causing the `while` loop to terminate.

There is one problem, though. If there is a file named 0 in the current directory, it also appears to be false, causing the loop to terminate early. To avoid this, use the `defined` operator to test specifically for `undef`:

■ Use the `defined` operator to test for `undef`.

```
while (defined($file = <*>)) {                 CORRECT—loop now
   do_something($file);                        terminates only when <*>
}                                              returns undef.
```

You may also need to use a different strategy when testing to see if an element is present inside a hash. `undef` is a perfectly acceptable value in a hash:

*Suppose %hash is undefined to start.*

```
if ($hash{'foo'}) { ... }                 FALSE
if (defined($hash{'foo'})) { ... }        Also FALSE.

$hash{'foo'} = undef;                     Assign an undef value.
if (defined($hash{'foo'})) { ... }        Still FALSE.
print keys %hash;                         ('foo')
```

The `exists` operator can determine whether a particular key is present, even if the corresponding value in the hash is `undef`:

*Continued from above:*

```
if (exists($hash{'foo'})) { ... }     TRUE
```

## Item 6:   Understand conversions between strings and numbers.

Perl's scalar variables can contain either string or numeric data. They can also contain both at the same time, usually as the result of converting string data to a number, or vice versa.

Perl automatically converts values from numeric to string representation, or vice versa, as required. For example, if a string appears next to a numeric operator like +, Perl converts the string value to a number before proceeding with the arithmetic. Or, if a number is the object of a pattern match, Perl first converts the number to a string. Places where strings are expected are referred to as *string contexts*, and places where numbers are expected are referred to as *numeric contexts*. These are nice terms to know, but we won't use them very often in this book, since it rarely makes any real difference.

The function used for converting numbers to strings is the C standard library's `sprintf()`, with a format of "%.15g" or something similar.[2] You can change this format by changing the special variable $#, but the use of $# is deprecated. If you need to use a particular format, use Perl's `sprintf`:

```
$n = sprintf "%10.4e", 3.1415927;    "3.1416e+00"
```

The function used for converting strings to numbers is the C standard library's `atof()`. Any leading white space is ignored. Conversion uses whatever leading part of the string appears number-like, and the rest is ignored. Anything that doesn't look like a number is converted to zero. For example:

```
$n = 0 + "123";              123
$n = 0 + "123abc";           Also 123—trailing stuff ignored.
$n = 0 + "\n123";            Also 123—leading whitespace.
$n = 0 + "a123";             0—no number at beginning.
```

The conversion process *does not* recognize octal or hexadecimal. Use the oct operator to convert octal or hexadecimal strings:

```
$n = 0 + "0x123";            0—looks like number 0.
$n = 0 + oct("0x123");       291—oct converts octal and hex
                             strings to decimal.

print "mode (octal): ";      Prompt for file mode.
chmod <STDIN>, $file;        WRONG—string from STDIN
                             converted to decimal, not octal.

print "mode (octal): ";      Prompt for file mode.
chmod oct(<STDIN>), $file;   RIGHT—mode string converted
                             to octal.
```

When a number is automatically converted to a string, or vice versa, both representations remain. They will persist until the value of the variable is changed.

Usually, it does not matter whether a variable contains a string or a numeric value, but there are a few occasions when it does. For example, the bitwise numeric operators act on the whole numeric value if applied to a number, but characterwise if applied to a string:

---

2. Well, sort of. Perl prefers to use `gconvert()`. This is one of the reasons you shouldn't mess with $# any more.

```
$a = 123;
$b = 234;
$c = $a & $b;                          number 106

$a = "$a";
$b = "$b";
$d = $a & $b;                          string "020"
```

Finally, the error variable `$!` is an example of a variable with a "magic" property. It returns the value of the system variable `errno` when it is used in a numeric context, but it returns the string from the `perror()` function (or some equivalent for your system) in a string context:

```
open FH, "";                           Invalid filename; should produce
                                       an error.

print "$!\n";                          "No such file or directory"

print 0 + $!, "\n";                    "2" (or whatever)
```

# Idiomatic Perl

Perl is a language designed by a linguist, and as much as any human language, Perl is a language of idioms.

What I call *idiomatic Perl* is the mixture of elegance and custom that comes naturally to Perl programmers, or, at least hopefully, to the majority of them, after experience and experimentation. Exactly what is idiomatic and what is purely a matter of style or opinion is debatable. There are many different ways to express both simple and complex algorithms in Perl. Some ways, however, are clearly more "right" than others.

Perl is hardly ever a programmer's first language. Newly minted Perl programmers are usually familiar with the C programming language, or shell scripting, or both. They may also be familiar with other languages. Because Perl derives much of its distinctive syntax and functionality from other well-known languages, the first temptation of a beginning programmer is to write Perl in a way that resembles something from a familiar environment:

```
$n = $#ary;                          Add up all the elements of @ary
for ($i = 0; $i <= $n; $i++) {       using subscripts—as in C.
  $sum += $ary[$i];
}
```

Or, perhaps:

```
while ($val = shift @ary) {          Add up all the elements of
  $sum += $val;                      @ary—a shell-ish approach that
}                                    leaves @ary empty.
```

Both of the above will work, but neither is particularly succinct or efficient. The subscripting operation in the first example is slow and unnecessary, and the second version leaves @ary empty, which may not be desirable. The idiomatic way is:

```
foreach (@ary) {                        Add up all the elements of
  $sum += $_;                           @ary—the Perl way.
}
```

Idiom and convention are very important in Perl. They are less important in simple languages like C and Bourne or C shell. There are not too many tricks to be learned in C programming. (You may think I'm crazy to say that, but if you take a look at your local bookstore's programming section, you will see that all the books on how to do clever things in C are fairly skinny. It's the books on C++ that are thick.) And although there are a lot of details to be learned in support of shell programming, a thorough how-to book on shell programming is a slim volume.

Not so with Perl.

Perl is an expressive language and often a succinct one. The language has been designed to allow frequently used constructs to be coded very compactly. Perl's very high level features like <>, regular expressions, and grep are particularly potent. For example:

```
($a, $b) = ($b, $a);                    Swap $a and $b.

print sort <>;                          Read lines from files or
                                        standard input and print them
                                        out in sorted order.

print grep /\bjoebloe\b/, <>;           Print all the lines containing
                                        the word joebloe.

@div5 = grep { not $_ % 5 } @n;         Copy all the numbers in @n
                                        evenly divisible by 5 into @div5.

$bin_addr = pack 'C4',                  One way of turning
  split /\./, $str_addr;                "123.234.0.1" into the integer
                                        0x7bea0001.
```

All of these examples can be coded in other ways, but when written in the style of some other language, the result will be longer and less efficient. You could, say, reproduce the functionality of <> explicitly in Perl, but the result would be a fairly long Perl program that would obscure the "interesting" part of the program. The resulting program would also be harder to debug and to maintain, simply because of its greater length and complexity.

To a certain extent, idiom and style overlap. Some idioms, like print sort <>, are inarguable, but there are certainly gray areas:

```
foreach $key (sort keys %h) {
  print "$key: $h{$key}\n";
}
```
*Print key-value pairs from %h one per line.*

```
print map "$_: $h{$_}\n",
  sort keys %h;
```
*Another way to print key-value pairs.*

The first example above is very plain Perl. It is efficient and readable and uses only basic features of the language. The second example is shorter and, some might argue, has a higher "cool factor" because it uses the nifty map operator and a list context in place of the mundane foreach loop in the first. However, you should consider yourself and your potential audience before leaving code like the second example for posterity, because it is definitely more obscure (but not *that* obscure) and might even be less efficient.

Every Perl programmer needs to master a number of basic idioms and should at least learn to recognize a number of others. Programmers should always use those idioms that produce efficient, succinct, and readable code. Other more complex idioms may or may not be appropriate, depending on the programmer, audience, and nature of the program being written.

In this section (were you wondering when it would ever really get started?), we'll look at a number of Perl idioms. You will definitely want to learn and use the simpler ones. Beyond that, you will have to consider the trade-offs between "plain" and "nifty."

How your Perl looks is up to you. You can write very plain Perl if you like. Writing plain Perl is like building a house and choosing to build as much as possible out of masonry blocks. It works, it's simple, it's a little dull, and it's hard to create intricate shapes.

On the other hand, you may want to try using all the nifty features that Perl gives you. Continuing the analogy, you may be the kind of builder who spends more time at Home Depot looking at power tools than he does pounding nails on the job. You may like to build all kinds of cool features using the latest technology. This is fine, so long as you realize that sometimes a hammer is all you need.

Or, maybe after a while you will wind up somewhere in between.

Sometimes you need s/\G0/ /g,[1] and sometimes you just need $a = $b.

---

1. This little jewel is discussed in Item 60.

## Item 7:   Use $_ for elegance.

"Dollar underscore," or $_: you may love it, or you may hate it. But either way, if you're going to be a proficient Perl programmer, you've got to understand it.

$_ is a default argument for many operators, and also for some control structures. Here are some examples:

● **$_ as a default argument**

```
print $_;                                      print
print;                                         Same thing.

print "found it" if $_ =~ /Rosebud/;           Matches and substitutions.
print "found it" if /Rosebud/;                 Same thing.

$mod_time = -M $_;                             Most filehandle tests.
$mod_time = -M;                               Same thing.

foreach $_ (@list) { &do_something($_) }       foreach
foreach (@list) { &do_something($_) }          Same thing.

while (defined($_ = <STDIN>)) { print $_ }     while; a special case.
while (<STDIN>) { print }                      Same thing.
```

The last example illustrates the special case in which using the line input operator *<filehandle>* alone as the condition of a while loop is a shortcut for reading a line from the file into $_ until the end of file is reached.

This is by no means an exhaustive list. Consult the on-line documentation or your favorite comprehensive Perl reference for more information.

$_ is a normal scalar variable—mostly. You can use it, print it, change its value, and so on, just as if it were an ordinary scalar. There are a couple of things to watch out for, though.

### $_ and the main package

$_ is always in the package main. This applies even, or especially, if you are in some other package:

```
package foo;
$_ = "OK\n";                                   This still means $main::_.
package main;
print;                                         Prints OK.
```

In fact, all special variables ($-punctuation) have this property. You can use a variable like $foo::_ if you like, but it has no special properties and isn't "the" $_.

## Localizing $_

$_ can only be localized using local. You cannot use my. The following won't work, no matter where or how you try it:

```
my $_;                                      ILLEGAL
```

## Programming style and $_

Oddly enough, when you use $_, you may not see much of it:

```
while (<>) {                          Count all the 5-letter words.
  for (split) {
    $w5++ if /^\w{5}$/
  }
}

@small_txt = grep              Find files ending in .txt and
  { /\.txt$/ and (-s) < 5000 }   less than 5,000 bytes long.
    @files;
```

Some Perl programmers may feel that $_ is more an aid to obfuscation than elegance. I have a book on my shelf that opines: "Many Perl programmers write programs that have references to $_ running like an invisible thread through their programs. Programs that overuse $_ are hard to read and are easier to break than programs that explicitly reference scalar variables you have named youself." I find this hard to accept. Is:

```
while (defined ($line = <STDIN>)) {
  print $line if $line =~ /Perl/
}
```

really superior to:

```
while (<STDIN>) { print if /Perl/ }
```

You'll have to decide.

## Item 8:    Know the other default arguments: @_, @ARGV, STDIN.

$_ is not the one and only default argument in Perl. There are several others.

### @_ as a default

Inside a subroutine, shift uses @_ as a default argument:

```
sub foo {                                $x gets the first argument.
  my $x = shift;
```

One interesting quirk in Perl syntax shows up when you try to shift an array argument passed by reference:

```
bar(\@bletch);                           Pass ref to @bletch to sub &bar.

sub bar {                                OOPS! This is the variable
  my @a = @{shift};                      @shift.
```

You have to put something else inside the braces to let Perl know that the identifier isn't a variable name:

```
my @a = @{shift()};                      My preferred form.

my @a = @{+shift};                       Works, but looks weird to me.
```

### @ARGV as a default

On the other hand, outside a subroutine, shift uses @ARGV as a default:

```
while ($_ = shift) {                     Shifting @ARGV by default.
  if (/^-(.*)/) {
    process_option($1);                  Process opt if starts with -.
  } else {
    process_file($_);                    Otherwise it's a file.
  }
}
```

The shift operator always uses the main @_ or @ARGV even if your default package is something other than main.

### STDIN as a default

Unlike the rest of the file test operators, which use $_ as a default, the -t operator uses the filehandle STDIN as a default. -t tests a filehandle in the manner of the Unix isatty() function to determine whether the filehandle is interactive, that is, whether input is coming from a human typing at a keyboard:

```
print "You're alive!" if -t STDIN;       Are we talking to a human?
print "You're alive!" if -t;             Same thing.
```

Use the -t operator to help modify the behavior of a program, depending on whether it is running interactively. For example, you could use -t in a CGI script to start it up in a special debugging mode if the script is being run from the command line.

## Item 9:  Know common shorthands and syntax quirks.

Perl is a "human" language in that it has a very context-dependent syntax. You can take advantage of this by omitting things that are assumed by the interpreter, for example, default arguments, $_, and optional punctuation. Perl figures out what you really mean from the context. (Usually.)

Perl is also a very high level language with an extremely rich and diverse syntax, but sometimes the various syntactic features don't fit together as well as they might. In some cases, you may have to help Perl along by resorting to a syntactic gimmick of one kind or another. Along these lines, here are some suggestions and some things to watch out for.

### Use for instead of foreach

The keyword for is actually a synonym for the keyword foreach, and vice versa. The two are completely interchangeable. Thus we have the commonly seen:

```
for (<*.c>) {                        Really a foreach loop, adding
    $bytes += -s                     up sizes of the .c files.
}
```

And, conversely:

```
foreach ($i = 0; $i < 10; $i++) {    Strange, but really a for loop,
    print $i * $i, "\n";             printing first 10 squares.
}
```

Perl determines which kind of loop you have written by looking at something other than the keyword. (I guess that's kind of obvious.) Substituting for in place of foreach is a fairly innocuous and frequently used shorthand among more worldly Perl programmers—I've done it here and there in this book.

### Swap values with list assignments

Perl doesn't have a special "swap" operator, but you can always use a list assignment to the same effect:

```
($b, $a) = ($a, $b);                    Swap $a and $b.

($c, $a, $b) = ($a, $b, $c);            Rotate through $a, $b, and $c.
```

Slices give you a convenient syntax for permuting the contents of an array:

```
@a[1, 3, 5] = @a[5, 3, 1];              Shuffle some elements.

@a[map { $_ * 2 + 1, $_ * 2 }          Swap odd- and even-numbered
  0 .. ($#a / 2)] = @a;                 elements of @a.
```

## Force a list context with [...] or (...) [...] if you have to

In some cases you may need to force an expression to be evaluated in a list context. For example, if you want to split a string captured by a regular expression memory, you might first write:

```
($str) = /([^:]*)/;                     Split $_ on + up to :.
@words = split /\+/, $str;
```

To write this in a single expression without the use of the temporary $str, you have to resort to trickery, because the pattern match would not return the right kind of value in the scalar context imposed by split:

```
@words =                                The inside of a literal slice is
  split /\+/, (/([^:]*)/)[0];          an array context, so this works.

@words =                                Another approach that works.
  split /\+/, join '', /([^:]*)/;
```

If you want to take a reference to a list literal in a single step, use the anonymous array constructor [...]. The reference operator \ applied to a list literal actually creates a list of references, not a reference to a list. (Don't ask me why—this one never made much sense to me. Also see Item 32.)

```
$wordlist_ref =                         WRONG—creates a scalar ref
  \(split /\+/, $str);                  to last fragment from split.

$wordlist_ref =                         CORRECT—returns an array
  [split /\+/, $str];                   ref.
```

## Use => to make initializers, and some function calls, prettier

The => operator is a synonym for the comma operator. There is one minor difference in functionality, which is that if the left-hand argument to => is an identifier by itself, it is always treated as a string. It will *not* be interpreted as a function call. Thus you can use things like `print` to the left of `=>` without fear:

```
@a = (time => 'flies');                 time is taken literally.
print "@a\n";                           "time flies"

@b = (time, 'flies');                   time operator.
print "@b\n";                           "862891055 flies"
```

Use `=>` to make initializers prettier, if you like. This is especially appropriate when creating initializers for hashes:

■ **Use the => operator to beautify initializers.**

```
%a = (
  'Ag' => 47, 'Au' => 79, 'Pt' => 78       Use arrows to pair up keys and
);                                          values in hash initializers.

%a = (
  Ag => 47, Au => 79, Pt => 78              You can omit quotes around
);                                          identifiers to the left (still
                                            passes strict subs).
```

You can simulate named parameters for function calls. Here is one simple way to do it:

■ **Use the => operator to simulate named parameters.**

```
sub img {
  my %param = ( align => 'middle' );      Default args.
  my %param_in = @_;                      Read params in as a hash.

  @param{keys %param_in} =                Overwrite defaults with
    values %param_in;                     %param_in.

  # or, just use:
  # my %param = ( align => 'middle', @_ );  Another way to handle defaults.

  print "<img ",                          Write out the keys and values
    (join ' ',                            of the hash as an HTML tag.
      map { "$_=\"$param{$_}\"" }
        keys %param),
    ">";
}
img(src => 'icon.gif', align => 'top');   Yields <img src="icon.gif"
                                          align="top">.
```

This is discussed further in Item 27.

Finally, here's another interesting use of => as syntactic sugar:

```
rename "$file.c" => "$file.c.old";
```

Don't confuse => with ->, which is used for subscripting references (see Item 30) and method calls (see Item 50).

## Watch what you put inside {...}

Parentheses, square brackets, angle brackets, and braces all have multiple meanings in Perl. Perl uses the contents of the braces (or whatever) and the surrounding context to figure out what to do with them. Usually the result makes sense, but at times it may surprise you.

Be especially careful with braces. Braces are used to enclose blocks, delimit variable names, create anonymous hashes, *and* as hash element and dereferencing syntax. It's dizzying if you think about it too hard. It's pretty scary that the interpreter can tell the difference between an anonymous hash constructor and a block!

If you see a plus sign inside braces for no apparent reason, there probably *is* a reason for it. Perl's unary plus has no effect on its argument, but it does provide a fix for some syntactic problems:

> *Suppose we want to dereference a function returning an array ref.*

```
@a = @{func_returning_aryref};
```
*WRONG—refers to variable @func_returning_aryref.*

```
@a = @{func_returning_aryref()};
```
*OK—parentheses force interpretation as a function.*

```
@a = @{&func_returning_aryref};
```
*OK—ampersand forces interpretation as a function.*

```
@a = @{+func_returning_aryref};
```
*OK—another strange use of the plus sign.*

If you're unlucky, you might also run into a situation in which an anonymous hash constructor is confused with a block:

> *Suppose we have a function that returns a list of key-value pairs that we want to use in an anonymous hash constructor.*

```
$hashref = eval {
  { key_value_pairs() }
};
```
*WRONG—innermost set of braces looks like a block.*

```
$hashref = eval {                    OK—it's a hash constructor
  +{ key_value_pairs() }             when it's part of an expression.
};

$hashref = eval {                    OK—explicit return also makes
  return { key_value_pairs() }       it an expression.
};
```

And, finally, you should be aware that an identifier appearing all alone (possibly surrounded by whitespace) inside braces is taken literally as a string.[2] If it is the name of a function, the function is *not* called unless there is something other than just an identifier present:

```
${shift} = 10;                       Sets $shift = 10.

sub soft { ${+shift} = 10; }         Calls shift and uses it as a
                                     variable name—soft reference.

soft 'a';                            Sets $a = 10.
```

## Use @{[...]} or eval {...} to make a copy of a list

Sometimes you may want to perform a destructive operation on a copy of a list, rather than the original:

*Find .h files that are missing.*

```
@cfiles_copy = @cfiles;
@missing_h = grep { s/\.c$/\.h/ and not -e } @cfiles_copy;
```

Perl doesn't give you a function for making copies of things, but if you need to make an unnamed copy of a list, you can put the list inside the anonymous array constructor [...], then dereference it:

*Find .h files that are missing, but without making an explicit copy.*

```
@missing_h = grep { s/\.c$/\.h/ and !-e } @{[@cfiles]};
```

Another way to make a copy of something is to put it inside an eval block:

```
@missing_h = grep { s/\.c$/\.h/ and !-e } eval {@cfiles};
```

Use the block form of eval in situations like this, not the string form, since the block form is much more efficient (see Item 54).

---

2. This is not strictly true—it applies only to braces used as part of reference or variable syntax, so "block" braces like those in while ($_ = shift @lines) { print } will work fine.

## Item 10: Avoid excessive punctuation.

Perl programs tend to be filled with punctuation. Excessive punctuation makes programs less readable, and wise programmers will take advantage of features that make it possible to write programs with considerably less punctuation. For example, Perl allows user-written functions to use the same ampersand-less syntax that built-in functions do:

● **Different kinds of function call syntax**

```
sub myfunc { ... };

&myfunc(1, 2, 3);                      Old-style, explicit ampersand.

myfunc(1, 2, 3);                       No ampersand.

myfunc 1, 2, 3;                        Works if myfunc has already
                                       been declared.
```

The traditional & syntax has its uses—it's the only way to call a subroutine whose name is a keyword, for example, &for. The list operator syntax, without ampersand or parentheses, works if the definition or declaration of the function appears lexically before the function call. This is generally fine, but there are some pitfalls:

```
myfunc 1, 2, 3;                        ERROR—can't use as list
sub myfunc { };                        operator before definition.

myfunc 1, 2, 3;                        ERROR—definition must
BEGIN { sub myfunc { } };              lexically precede use.

eval "sub myfunc {}";                  ERROR—and it must also be
myfunc 1, 2, 3;                        present at compile time.

BEGIN { eval "sub myfunc {}" }         OK—but strange.
myfunc 1, 2, 3;
```

Another helpful feature is the addition of the super-low precedence short-circuit logical operators and and or. (There's also the less exciting not and the generally useless xor.) These allow you to get rid of parentheses in a variety of situations:

■  **Use and and or instead of && and ||.**

*The* and *and* or *operators allow you to omit parentheses around list operators, assignment, and binding.*

```
print "hello, " && print "goodbye.";   WRONG—goodbye.1
print "hello, " and print "goodbye.";  OK—hello, goodbye.
```

■ **Use and and or instead of && and ||. (cont'd)**

| | |
|---|---|
| `$size = -s $file or`<br>`  die "$file has zero size.\n";` | die *if file has zero size.* |
| `$word =~ /magic/ or $mode = 'peon';` | `$mode = 'peon' unless $word`<br>`=~ /magic/;` |

Remember that you can always eliminate a semicolon preceding a closing brace. This is probably a good idea in blocks that consist of a single statement, especially when such a block is used as an argument to map, grep, do, eval, or the like:

| | |
|---|---|
| `@caps = map { uc $_; } @words;` | *Unnecessary semicolon.* |
| `@caps = map { uc $_ } @words;` | *Looks cleaner.* |

One more way to get rid of extra parentheses and braces is to use the statement modifier, or "backwards conditional," syntax. It's handy once you get used to it:

| | |
|---|---|
| `if (/^END$/) { last }` | *Mundane.* |
| `last if /^END$/;` | *Doesn't this look better?* |

## Item 11: Consider different ways of reading from a stream.

The line input operator *<filehandle>* can be used to read either a single line from a stream in a scalar context, or the entire contents of a stream in a list context. Which method you should use depends on your need for efficiency, access to the lines read, and other factors like syntactic convenience.

The line-at-a-time method is the most efficient in terms of memory, and is as fast as "ordinary" alternatives. The implicit while (<>) form is equivalent in speed to the corresponding explicit code:

| | |
|---|---|
| `while (<FH>) {`<br>`  # do something with $_`<br>`}` | *The usual implicit line-at-a-time loop using <FH> inside while.* |
| `while (defined($line = <FH>)) {`<br>`  # do something with $line`<br>`}` | *Explicit version—similar logic.* |

Note the use of the `defined` operator. This prevents the loop from missing a line if the very last line of a file is the single character "`0`" with no terminating newline—not a likely occurrence, but it can't hurt to be careful.

You can use a similar syntax with a `foreach` loop to read the entire file into memory in a single operation:

```
foreach (<FH>) {                          Read the whole file into
   # do something with $_                 memory, then step through it.
}
```

The all-at-once method uses more memory than the line-at-a-time method, but it is potentially faster. If all you want to do is step through the lines in a short file, it won't likely matter which method you use. All-at-once has its advantages when combined with operations like sorting:

```
print sort <FH>;                          Print a file with its lines sorted
                                          "ASCIIbetically."
```

All-at-once may be appropriate if you need access to more than one line at a time:

■ **Read in a file all at once to manipulate more than one line at a time.**

```
@f = <FH>;                                Read in the whole file and look
foreach ( 0..$#f ) {                      at a "window" of lines.
  if ($f[$_] =~ /\bShazam\b/) {           Looking for Shazam.
    $lo = ($_ > 0) ? $_ - 1 : $_;
    $hi = ($_ < $#f) ? $_ + 1 : $_;
    print map { "$_: $f[$_]" } $lo .. $hi;   Print 3 adjacent lines with line
  }                                          numbers.
}
```

Many of these situations can still be handled with line-at-a-time input, although the code is definitely more complex:

■ **Use a queue to manipulate more than one line at a time.**

```
@f[0..2] = ("\n") x 3;                    Initialize the queue.
for (;;) {
  @f[0..2] = (@f[1, 2], scalar(<FH>));    Queue with a slice assignment.
  last if not defined $f[1];
  if ($f[1] =~ /\bShazam\b/) {            Looking for Shazam.
    print map                            Print 3 adjacent lines with line
      { ($_ + $. - 1) . ": $f[$_]" } 0..2;   numbers, again.
  }
}
```

Maintaining a queue of lines of text with slice assignments makes this slower than the equivalent all-at-once code, but this technique works for arbitrarily large input. The queue could also be implemented with an index variable rather than a slice assignment, which would result in more complex but faster running code.

If your goal is simply to read a file into memory as quickly as possible, you might consider clearing the input separator variable $/ and reading the entire file as a single string. This will read the contents of a file or stream much faster than either of the alternatives above:

```
{
  local $/;                          No input separator.
  $the_file = <FH>;                  Slurp! Entire file in $the_file.
}
```

Finally, the read and sysread operators are useful for quickly scanning a file if line boundaries are of no importance:

■ **Use read or sysread for maximum speed.**

*Compare files by reading blocks from each with* sysread.

```
open FH1, $file1 or die;                Open two files.
open FH2, $file2 or die;
my $chunk = 4096;                       Block size to read.
my ($bytes, $buf1, $buf2, $diff);       Set up buffers, etc.

CHUNK: while ($bytes =
    sysread FH1, $buf1, $chunk) {       Read a chunk from FH1.
  sysread FH2, $buf2, $chunk;           Read a chunk from FH2.
  $diff++, last CHUNK if $buf1 ne $buf2;  Compare chunks.
}
print "$file1 and $file2 differ" if $diff;
```

## Item 12: Use foreach, map and grep as appropriate.

In Perl, there are several different ways of iterating over elements in a list.

There is a strong tendency among Perl programmers to avoid using a for loop and subscripts when iterating through a list. Loops using subscripts tend to be slower than loops that don't, because subscripts take a significant amount of time for Perl to evaluate. In addition, subscripts can be used only on named arrays.

Most programmers use foreach, map, or grep instead. The capabilities of foreach, map, and grep overlap somewhat, but each is designed for a primary purpose. These constructs are easy to abuse—you can write pretty much any kind of loop with any one of them—but doing so can confuse you and anyone else who visits your code in the future. You should use them appropriately.

## Use foreach to iterate read-only over each element of a list

If all you want to do is to cycle over the elements in a list, use foreach:

```
foreach $cost (@cost) {                 Sum the values in @cost.
  $total += $cost;
}

foreach $file (glob '*') {              List all the text files in the
  print "$file\n" if -T $file;          current directory.
}
```

Remember that foreach uses $_ as a control variable by default if none is specified. Also, you can always use the shorter keyword for instead of foreach—Perl knows what you mean.

```
foreach (1 .. 10) {                     Print the first 10 squares.
  print "$_: ", $_ * $_, "\n";
}

for (@lines) {                          Print the first line beginning
  print, last if /^From:/;              with From:.
}
```

## Use map to create a list based on the contents of another list

If you want to create a transformed copy of a list, use map:

```
@sizes = map { -s $_ } @files;          Transform a list of filenames
                                        into a list of sizes.
```

The "transform" expression or block is evaluated in a list context. Sometimes it can be useful to return an empty list or a list of more than one element. Using a match operator inside map can be elegant:

■ Use m// and memory inside map to capture a list of matching substrings.

*Both of the following examples use the match operator m// and parentheses inside* map. *In a list context,* m// *returns a list of the substrings captured in regular expression memory, or the empty list if the match fails.*

```
@stem = map { /(.*)\.txt$/ } @files;    Find all the elements of @files
                                        that end in .txt and return a
                                        list of their "stems."
```

■ **Use `m//` and memory inside `map` to capture a list of matching substrings. (cont'd)**

| | |
|---|---|
| `($from) =`<br>`  map /^From:\s+(.*)$/, @message_lines;` | *Set `$from` to the text to the right of the first (hopefully only?) line starting with `From:`.* |

For efficiency, `$_` is actually an alias for the current element in the iteration. If you modify `$_` within the transform expression of a `map`, you are modifying the list that is being mapped. This is generally considered to be bad style, and, who knows, you may even wind up confusing yourself this way. If you want to modify the contents of a list, use `foreach` (see below).

You should also make sure that `map` is returning a sensible value—don't use `map` as just a control structure:

▼ `map` **should return a sensible value.**

> *This example breaks two of the rules concerning `map`. First, `tr///` modifies `$_` and thus `@elems`. Worse, the return value from `map` is a nonsensical list of values from `tr///`—the number of digits deleted by `tr///` in each element.*

`map { tr/0-9//d } @elems;`                 *PROBABLY WRONG*

▼ `map` **should not modify its arguments.**

> *This returns a sensible value but `tr///` still modifies `@elems`.*

`@digitless = map { tr/0-9//d; $_ } @elems;`    *BAD STYLE*

If you must use `tr///`, `s///` or something similar inside `map`, use a `my` variable to avoid changes to `$_`:

■ **Avoid changes to `$_` by using a `my` variable inside `map`.**

> *In this example, using `tr///` on `my $x` and then returning `$x` leaves `@elems` alone—ugly but functional.*

| | |
|---|---|
| `@digitless = map {`<br>`  (my $x = $_) =~ tr/0-9//d; $x`<br>`} @elems;` | *Strip digits from elements of `@elems`.* |

For more examples using map, see Item 14 and Item 60.

## Use foreach to modify elements of a list

If you actually want to modify the elements in a list, use foreach. As with map (and also grep), the control variable is an alias for the current element in the iteration. Modifying the control variable modifies that element.

```
foreach $num (@nums) {          Multiply all the elements of
  $num *= 2                     @nums by 2.
}

for (@ary) { tr/0-9//d }        Strip digits from elements of
                                @ary.

for (@elems) { s/\d//g }        Slower version using s///.

for ($str1, $str2, $str3) {     Uppercase $str1, $str2, and
  $_ = uc $_;                   $str3.
}
```

## Use grep to select elements in a list

The grep operator has a particular purpose, which is to select or count elements in a list. You wouldn't know this, though, looking at some of the more creative abuses of grep, which usually originate with programmers who feel that a foreach loop isn't quite as cool as a grep. Hopefully, as you try to write Effective Perl, you will stay closer to the straight and narrow.

Here's a conventional use of grep in a list context:

```
print grep /^joseph$/i, @lines;     Print 'joseph' lines, ignoring
                                    case.

print grep                          Probably slightly faster.
  { lc($_) eq 'joseph' } @lines;
```

By the way, the "selection" expression or block argument to grep is evaluated in a scalar context, unlike map's transform expression. This will rarely make a difference, but it's nice to know.

In a scalar context, grep returns a count of the selected elements rather than the elements themselves.

```
$has_false = grep !$_, @array;      Returns count of "false"
                                    elements.

$has_undef =                        Returns count of undef
  grep !defined($_), @array;        elements.
```

## Item 13: Don't misquote.

Perl gives you a plethora of different ways to quote strings.

There are single quotes, where everything is left "as-is" except for escaped backlashes and single quotes:

```
'Isn\'t she "lovely"?'              Isn't she "lovely"?
```

Double quotes, on the other hand, support all kinds of escape sequences. There are the usual \t, \n, \r, etc. from C, as well as octal and hex ASCII escapes like \101 and \x41:

```
"Testing\none\ntwo\nthree"          Testing
                                    one
                                    two
                                    three

"\x50\x65\x72\x6c\x21"              Perl!
```

Double quotes also support the interpolation of the contents of variables and subscript expressions beginning with $ and @. The elements of arrays and slices are interpolated by joining them with the contents of the $" special variable—normally a single space:

```
foreach $key (sort keys %hash) {    Print out the key-value pairs in
  print "$key: $hash{$key}\n";      %hash.
}

@n = 1..3;
print "testing @n\n";               testing 1 2 3

print "testing @{n}sies\n";         testing 1 2 3sies—Use {}
                                    around variable name to keep
                                    it from blending with following
                                    text.
```

There are also escapes (\u, \U, \l, \L, \E) that change the case of characters following them:

```
$v = "very";
print "I am \u$v \U$v\E tired!\n";  I am Very VERY tired!
```

I haven't begun, and I won't attempt, to cover all the nuances of double-quote interpolation in this Item. A full description, with all the gory details, can be found in the perlop man page.

## Alternative quoting: q, qq, and qw

Sometimes it is helpful to be able to use characters other than single or double quotes to enclose strings. So, naturally, Perl allows you to use *any* punctuation character to enclose strings. Just prefix your favorite character with q for a single-quoted string, or qq for a double-quoted string:

```
q*A 'starring' \*role\**              A 'starring' *role*

qq|Don't "quote" me!|                 Don't "quote" me!
```

If you use a matchable delimiter (either (, [, <, or { ), then the end of the string is the corresponding closing delimiter. Perl keeps track of nesting when looking for the closing delimiter:

```
qq<Don't << quote >> me!>             Don't << quote >> me!
```

This is especially handy when dealing with Perl source code in quotes (generally as an argument for eval—see Item 54):

■ Use q{...} and/or qq{...} to quote source code.

```
use Benchmark;                        See Item 37 for more about
$b = 1.234;                           Benchmark.
timethese (10, {
  'sin' => q{                         q{}—code in single quotes.
    for (1..10000) { $a = sin $b }
  },

 'log' => q{                          Another q{}.
    for (1..10000) { $a = log $b }
  }
});
```

Finally, as a shorthand way of creating a list of strings, you can quote with qw ("quote words"). A string inside qw quotes is split on whitespace, returning a list of strings:

```
@ISA = qw(Foo Bar Bletch);            @ISA = ('Foo', 'Bar',
                                      'Bletch');
```

Please don't make the mistake of unintentionally including commas inside qw quotes:

▼ Don't put commas inside qw quotes.

```
@ISA = qw(Foo, Bar, Bletch);          @ISA = ('Foo,', 'Bar,',
                                      'Bletch');—extra commas!
```

### Alternative quoting: here doc strings

Perl's "here doc" or "here document" strings provide yet another way to quote text. Many of you may be familiar with here docs already—Perl's here doc feature is derived from the Unix shell feature of the same name.

A here doc string begins with << followed by an identifier and ends when that identifier appears on a line all by itself somewhere later in the text. The string begins on the line *after* <<. If the identifier is quoted (with single, double, or back quotes), the type of quotes determines the type of string enclosed in the here doc. The default is a double-quoted string:

```
$j = "Joseph"; $h = "Hall";
$m = '$10';
print <<EOT;
Dear $j $h,

You may have just won $m!
EOT
```
*Semicolon after* EOT *is the end of* print—*not part of the string!*

Dear Joseph Hall,

You may have just won $10!

```
print <<'XYZZY';
Dear $j $h,

You may have just won $m!
XYZZY
```
*Single-quoted this time:*

Dear $j $h,

You may have just won $m!

Here docs are useful for quoting long passages of text or source code. I use them frequently when writing CGI scripts.

See Item 58 for more discussion about double-quote interpolation.

## Item 14: Learn the myriad ways of sorting.

### ASCIIbetical sorting

At its most basic, sorting in Perl is simplicity itself. Perl's sort operator takes a list of elements and returns a copy of that list in sorted order:

```
@elements = sort qw(
  hydrogen
  helium
  lithium
);
```
*Yields*
  helium
  hydrogen
  lithium

The sort order is "ASCIIbetical," meaning that the items are sorted by comparing the ASCII values (well, really just the numeric values) of the first, second, third, et cetera characters of each element as necessary.[3] This leads to some interesting results:

```
print join ' ', sort 1 .. 10;        1 10 2 3 4 5 6 7 8 9, since
                                     '10' lt '2'.

print join ' ',                      Dog Fleas has my, since
    sort qw(my Dog has Fleas);       uppercase lt lowercase.
```

Hmm. If ASCIIbetical comparison isn't what you want, you need to write a sort subroutine.

## Comparison (sort) subroutines

A Perl sort subroutine is not an entire sorting algorithm. A better name might be "comparison subroutine."

Sort subroutines are different from ordinary subroutines in that the arguments are passed in via the hard-coded variable names $a and $b rather than as elements of @_.[4] $a and $b are localized for the sort subroutine, as if there were an implicit local($a, $b) at the beginning of the sort operation.

$a and $b get a "bye" from use strict vars—they do not have to be declared explicitly (see Item 36). They belong to the current package, not (necessarily) the main package.

The sort subroutine will be called repeatedly during sorting. Its job is to compare $a and $b and return -1, 0, or 1 depending upon whether $a sorts less than, equal to, or greater than $b. If this reminds you of C's qsort(), well, it should, since Perl typically uses the qsort() built into the C standard library.

Perl's built-in sorting behavior is as though the elements were compared ASCIIbetically with the cmp operator:

```
sub ASCIIbetically { $a cmp $b }     A sort subroutine.
@list = sort ASCIIbetically @list;   Same as @list = sort @list.
```

Here we have used a named subroutine, ASCIIbetically, to specify the sorting order. To change the sorting order, change the way that $a and $b

---

3. The 8-bit aware reader may prefer to say "sorted characterwise" instead of "ASCIIbetically," but neither that nor "characterbetically" rolls off the tongue. I prefer the more colorful term.

4. @_ may be present inside a sort subroutine, but if so it refers to the @_ from the most recently entered subroutine scope—not exactly what you would expect!

are compared. For example, replace the `cmp` operator with `<=>` (see Item 4) to sort numerically:

■ **Sort numerically using the `<=>` (spaceship) operator.**

```
sub numerically { $a <=> $b }          A numerical sort subroutine.
@list = sort numerically
  (16, 1, 8, 2, 4, 32);                (1, 2, 4, 8, 16, 32)
```

A more concise way of using a sort subroutine is to write it as a *sort block*. Just place the body of the subroutine right where the name of the sort subroutine would go:

■ **Write sorts more concisely using sort blocks.**

```
@list = sort { $a <=> $b }             A sort block.
  (16, 1, 8, 2, 4, 32);                (1, 2, 4, 8, 16, 32)
```

Here are some more examples:

```
@list = sort { uc($a) cmp uc($b) }     Sort ignoring case:
   qw(This is a test);                 ('a', 'is', 'test', 'This')

@list = sort { $b cmp $a } @list;      Sort in reverse order—just
                                       switch $a and $b.

@list = sort { -M $a <=> -M $b }       Sort by file mod time—see more
   @files                              efficient version later.
```

*Don't* modify `$a` and `$b`. They are aliased to the original elements, and modifying them will change the original values. Modifying them may also produce an inconsistent sorting order in addition to other unpleasant side effects, and inconsistent sorting orders have a way of producing core dumps or crashes in Perl. Here is an example of just such a bad thing:

▼ **Don't modify `$a` or `$b` inside a sort subroutine.**

```
@list = sort {
  $a =~ tr/A-Z/a-z/;                   Modifies $a—BAD.
  $b =~ tr/A-Z/a-z/;                   Modifies $b—BAD.
  $a cmp $b
} qw(This is a test);
```

Something that comes up from time to time is the need to sort the keys of a hash according to their corresponding values. There is a neat idiom for doing this:

■ **Use $hash{$a} and $hash{$b} to sort hash keys by their corresponding values.**

```
%elems = (B => 5, Be => 4,
  H => 1, He => 2, Li => 3);

@list = sort { $elems{$a} <=> $elems{$b} }
  keys %elems;
```

*This sorts keys by their values, numerically:*
('H', 'He', 'Li', 'Be', 'B')

Finally, you may want to sort on multiple keys. There is a standard idiom using the or operator for this. Here's a slightly contrived example:

■ **Use the or operator to sort on multiple keys.**

```
@first = qw(John Jane Bill Sue Carol);
@last = qw(Smith Smith Jones Jones Smith);

@index = sort {
  $last[$a] cmp $last[$b] or
  $first[$a] cmp $first[$b]
} 0 .. $#first;

for (@index) {
  print "$last[$_], $first[$_]\n";
}
```

*Some data to get us started.*

*Sort by*
 *last name, then*
 *first name.*

Jones, Bill
Jones, Sue
Smith, Carol, *etc.*

Here we are actually sorting a list of indices—a fairly common thing to do. The part I want you to note is the use of the short-circuit Boolean operator or in the sort subroutine. Each time the sort subroutine is called, the part of the expression to the left of the or is evaluated first. If it evaluates to a non-zero "true" value—in this case, meaning that $a doesn't compare equal to $b—then or returns that value and we're done. Otherwise Perl evaluates the comparison on the right-hand side and returns that value.

Note that this wouldn't work if Perl's or operator (or its higher-precedence cousin ||) returned only 1 or 0. It's the fact that or returns the actual value computed on the left- or right-hand side that makes this work.

## Advanced sorting, the mundane ways

Sometimes it takes a significant amount of processing to compare two keys. For example, let's sort on the third field of a password entry:

```
open PASSWD, "/etc/passwd" or die;
@by_uid = sort {
  (split /:/, $a)[2] <=>
  (split /:/, $b)[2]
} <PASSWD>;
```

*The third field contains the numeric user id, so remember to compare with <=>.*

This seems okay at first glance. It does indeed sort the lines in the required order. However, it also performs the relatively complex `split` operation twice each time the sort subroutine is called.

A sort subroutine will typically be called many times for each key. Comparison-based sorting algorithms perform on the order of $n \log n$ comparisons per sort, where $n$ is the number of elements sorted. In order to make your sorts run quickly, you have to make the comparisons run quickly. If your keys require significant transformation before comparison, this means that you will have to find a way to cache the result of the transformation.

In the case above, you could do something like this:

```
open PASSWD, "/etc/passwd" or die;        Read lines into @passwd.
@passwd = <PASSWD>;

%key = map                                 Create a hash—keys are entire
  { $_, (split /:/)[2] } @passwd;          lines from the password file;
                                           values are user ids.

@by_uid = sort {                           Now, sort the keys (lines) by
  $key{$a} <=> $key{$b}                    values (user ids). No expensive
} @passwd;                                 split used here now.
```

Note the use of `map` to return a list that becomes the comparison hash. If you are `map`-averse, you can write it like this instead:

```
for (@passwd) { $key{$_} = (split /:/)[2] }
```

As you look at this, you will realize that the keys of this hash are entire lines from the password file! If this is not to your liking, you can get the same effect by using array indices, but it requires a little more code and is a little harder to read:

```
open PASSWD, "/etc/passwd" or die;
@passwd = <PASSWD>;
@key = map                                 Create an array @key containing
  { (split /:/)[2] } @passwd;              just the keys (user ids).


@by_uid_index = sort {                     Sort indices, using @key array.
  $key[$a] <=> $key[$b]
} 0 .. $#key;

@by_uid = @passwd[@by_uid_index];          Now, rearrange the contents of
                                           @passwd into sorted order.
```

Or just combine the last two statements:

```
@by_uid = @passwd[sort { $key[$a] <=> $key[$b] } 0 .. $#key];
```

Well, this will work, and it's efficient enough, but there are prettier, more Perl-ish ways to present the solution.

## Advanced sorting, the cool ways

Through design, or perhaps trial, or maybe just accident, Perl programmers have come up with some convenient idioms for implementing complex sorting transforms.

One of the things that is less than ideal in the examples above is the need for a separate statement to set up an array or hash of transformed keys. One way of getting around this is something I have nicknamed the "Orcish Maneuver."[5] It uses the little-known ||= operator. Let's revisit the example of sorting filenames by modification date that we saw a little earlier:

■ **Use the Orcish Maneuver to cache key transformations.**

---

*Here's the old way:*

```
@sorted = sort { -M $a <=> -M $b } @files;     Too many uses of -M.
```

*Here it is using the Orcish Maneuver:*

```
@sorted = sort {                        The ||= operator caches the
  ($m{$a} ||= -M $a) <=>                values returned from -M in the
  ($m{$b} ||= -M $b)                    hash %m—as the sort takes
} @files;                               place.
```

---

Wow! What the heck is going on here?

First of all, note that:

```
$m{$a} ||= -M $a
```

has the same semantics as:

```
$m{$a} = $m{$a} || -M $a
```

The first time that the sort subroutine encounters a particular filename $a, $m{$a} has the value undef, which is false, and thus the right-hand side of the ||, -M $a, has to be evaluated. Because this is Perl, not C, the || operator returns the actual result of the right-hand side, not a simple 0 or 1 "true or false" value. This value now gets assigned to $m{$a}. Subsequent tests against the same filename will use the modification time value cached in $m{$a}.

---

5. The "or-cache" ... Arrgh.

The hash %m is a temporary variable and should be empty or undefined when this sort statement is encountered. You may want to wrap this line of code in braces and make %m a my variable, something like:

```
... { my %m; @sorted = sort ... };
```

The most concise all-around sorting technique, though, is the "Schwartzian Transform," named, of course, after Randal Schwartz.[6] A Schwartzian Transform is a sort bracketed by maps.

**Note:** the Schwartzian Transform uses references—if you aren't familiar with them, you may find it helpful to read Item 30 before continuing with this Item.

The best way to show a Schwartzian Transform is to build it up by pieces. Let's take the prior example of the modification time sorting and do it more efficiently. First, let's start with the filenames:

```
@names = <*>;
```

And now, let's turn the names into a same-length list of two-element anonymous lists:

```
@names_and_ages = map { [$_, -M] } @names;
```

Each element is now a reference to a two-element list—a "tuple." The first element of each tuple is the original name (from $_), while the second element is the modification age in days (from -M, implied $_ argument).

In the next step, we sort this list of references using a sort with a sort block:

```
@sorted_names_and_ages = sort {
  $a->[1] <=> $b->[1]
} @names_and_ages;
```

Within the sort block, $a and $b represent elements of the array @names_and_ages. Thus, $a and $b are array references, and $a->[1] represents the second element of a selected tuple, containing the age in days. The net result is that the tuples will be sorted numerically (note the spaceship <=> operator) by ascending ages.

That gets us most of the way there—now all we need is to extract the original names from each tuple. Simple enough, one more map:

```
@sorted_names = map { $_->[0] } @sorted_names_and_ages;
```

And that's it. But that's much too wordy for the seasoned Perl hacker, so here it is all put together as a Schwartzian Transform:

---

6. But not named *by* Randal Schwartz—it's a long story.

■ **Use the Schwartzian Transform for sorts with expensive key transformations.**

```
@sorted_names =
  map { $_->[0] }                          4. Extract original names.
  sort { $a->[1] <=> $b->[1] }             3. Sort [name, key] tuples.
  map { [$_, -M] }                         2. Create [name, key] tuples.
  @files;                                  1. The input data.
```

Read this from bottom to top and you'll see that it does the same thing as the individual statements above—but now all the steps are strung together.

Simple sorts involving a single key and transformation can use the above pattern, changing only the rightmost map and, if necessary, the comparison operator. Here's the password file sorted by the third field using a Schwartzian Transform:

```
open PASSWD, "/etc/passwd" or die;      Open up the file.

@by_uid =
  map { $_->[0] }
  sort { $a->[1] <=> $b->[1] }           Use <=> to compare ids.
  map { [$_, (split /:/)[2]] }           Create [line, uid] tuples.
  <PASSWD>;
```

Note how much more concise this is. We got rid of the hash %key, used to temporarily store the transformed keys. We were also able to eliminate the @passwd array and take the input to the Schwartzian Transform directly from the filehandle. The best part about the Schwartzian Transform, though, is that it tends to be the fastest way to perform complicated sorts like these. Fast *and* concise—now that's a nice combination!

# Regular Expressions

Regular expressions are the most obvious very high-level feature of Perl. A single pattern match in Perl—even a simple one—can perform the work of many lines in a different language. Pattern matches, especially when combined with Perl's handling of strings and lists, provide capabilities that are very difficult to mimic in other programming languages.

The power of regular expressions is one thing. Making use of it is another. Getting the full benefit from regular expressions in Perl requires both experience and understanding. Becoming fluent in regular expressions may seem to be a difficult task, but I commend it to you. Once you have mastered regular expressions in Perl, your programs will be faster, shorter, and easier to write. In other words, more *effective*—which is why you are reading this book, right?

This section discusses many commonly-encountered issues relating to regular expressions. It is not a reference, however. For a complete description of regular expressions and Perl, see the Perl man pages and/or the Camel book. For an illuminating and extremely thorough discussion of regular expressions that reaches far beyond Perl, see Jeffrey Friedl's excellent *Mastering Regular Expressions*, the so-called "Hip Owls book."

## Item 15: Know the precedence of regular expression operators.

The "expression" in "regular expression" is there because regular expressions are constructed and parsed using grammatical rules that are similar to those used for arithmetic expressions. Although regular expressions serve a greatly different purpose, understanding the similarities between them will help you write better regular expressions, and hence better Perl.

Regular expressions in Perl are made up of *atoms*. Atoms are connected by *operators* like repetition, sequence, and alternation. Most regular expression atoms are single-character matches. For example:

| | |
|---|---|
| a | *Matches the letter* a. |
| \$ | *Matches the character* $—*backslash escapes metacharacters.* |
| \n | *Matches newline.* |
| [a-z] | *Matches a lowercase letter.* |
| . | *Matches any character except* \n. |
| \1 | *Matches contents of first memory—arbitrary length.* |

There are also special "zero-width" atoms. For example:

| | |
|---|---|
| \b | *Word boundary—transition from* \w *to* \W. |
| ^ | *Matches start of a string.* |
| \Z | *Matches end of a string or before newline at end.* |

Atoms are modified and/or joined together by regular expression operators. As in arithmetic expressions, there is an order of precedence among these operators:

**Regular expression operator precedence**

| Precedence | Operator | Description |
|---|---|---|
| Highest | (), (?:), etc. | Parentheses and other grouping operators |
| | ?, +, *, {$m$,$n$}, +?, etc. | Repetition |
| | ^abc | Sequence (see below) |
| Lowest | | | Alternation |

Fortunately, there are only four precedence levels—imagine if there were as many as there are for arithmetic expressions! Parentheses and the other grouping operators[1] have the highest precedence.

A *repetition* operator binds tightly to its argument, which is either a single atom or a grouping operator:

| | |
|---|---|
| ab*c | *Matches* ac, abc, abbc, abbbc, *etc.* |
| abc* | *Matches* ab, abc, abcc, abccc, *etc.* |

---

1. A multitude of new grouping operators were introduced in Perl 5.

| | |
|---|---|
| ab(c)* | *Same thing, and memorizes the* c *actually matched.* |
| ab(?:c)* | *Same thing, but doesn't memorize the* c. |
| abc{2,4} | *Matches* abcc, abccc, abcccc. |
| (abc)* | *Matches empty string,* abc, abcabc, *etc.; memorizes* abc. |

Placing two atoms side by side is called *sequence*. Sequence is a kind of operator, even though it is written without punctuation. This is similar to the invisible multiplication operator in a mathematical expression like $y = ax + b$. To illustrate this, let's suppose that sequence were actually represented with the character "•". Then the above examples would look like:

| | |
|---|---|
| a•b*•c | *Matches* ac, abc, abbc, abbbc, *etc.* |
| a•b•c* | *Matches* ab, abc, abcc, abccc, *etc.* |
| a•b•(c)* | *Same thing, and memorizes the* c *actually matched.* |
| a•b•(?:c)* | *Same thing, but doesn't memorize the* c. |
| a•b•c{2,4} | *Matches* abcc, abccc, abcccc. |
| (a•b•c)* | *Matches empty string,* abc, abcabc, *etc.; memorizes* abc. |

The last entry in the precedence chart is *alternation*. Let's continue to use the "•" notation for a moment:

| | |
|---|---|
| e•d\|j•o | *Matches* ed *or* jo. |
| (e•d)\|(j•o) | *Same thing.* |
| e•(d\|j)•o | *Matches* edo *or* ejo. |
| e•d\|j•o{1,3} | *Matches* ed, jo, joo, jooo. |

The zero-width atoms, for example, ∧ and \b, group in the same way as other atoms:

| | |
|---|---|
| ∧e•d\|j•o$ | *Matches* ed *at beginning,* jo *at end.* |
| ∧(e•d\|j•o)$ | *Matches exactly* ed *or* jo. |

It's easy to forget about precedence. Removing excess parentheses is a noble pursuit, especially within regular expressions, but be careful not to remove too many:

```
/^Sender|From:\s+(.*)/;
```
                                                *WRONG—would match:*
                                                X-Not-Really-From: faker
                                                Senderella is misspelled

The pattern was meant to match `Sender:` and `From:` lines in a mail header, but it actually matches something somewhat different. Here it is with some parentheses added to clarify the precedence:

```
/(^Sender)|(From:\s+(.*))/;
```

Adding a pair of parentheses, or perhaps memory-free parentheses (?:…), fixes the problem:

```
/^(Sender|From):\s+(.*)/;
```
                                                $1 *contains* Sender *or* From.
                                                $2 *has the data.*

```
/^(?:Sender|From):\s+(.*)/;
```
                                                $1 *contains the data.*

## Double-quote interpolation

Perl regular expressions are subject to the same kind of interpolation that double-quoted strings are.[2] Interpolated variables and string escapes like \U and \Q are *not* regular expression atoms and are never seen by the regular expression parser. Interpolation takes place in a single pass that occurs before a regular expression is parsed:

```
/te(st)/;          Matches test in $_.
/\Ute(st)/;        Matches TEST.
/\Qte(st)/;        Matches te(st).

$x = 'test';
/$x*/;             Matches tes, test, testt, etc.
/test*/;           Same thing as /$x*/.
```

Double-quote interpolation and the separate regular expression parsing phase combine to produce a number of common "gotchas." For example, here's what can happen if you forget that an interpolated variable is not an atom:

*Read a pattern into $pat and match two consecutive occurrences of it.*

```
chomp($pat = <STDIN>);
```
                                                *For example,* bob.

```
print "matched\n" if /$pat{2}/;
```
                                                *WRONG—*/bob{2}/.

---

2.  Well, more or less. The $ anchor receives special treatment so that it is not always interpreted as a scalar variable prefix.

```
print "matched\n" if /($pat){2}/;        RIGHT—/(bob){2}/.
print "matched\n" if /$pat$pat/;          Brute force way.
```

In this example, if the user types in bob, the first regular expression will match bobb, because the contents of $pat are expanded before the regular expression is interpreted.

All three regular expressions in this example have another potential pitfall. Suppose the user types in the string "hello :-)". This will generate a fatal run-time error. The result of interpolating this string into /($pat){2}/ is /(hello :-)){2}/, which, aside from being nonsense, has unbalanced parentheses.

If you don't want special characters like parentheses, asterisks, periods, and so forth interpreted as regular expression metacharacters, use the quotemeta operator or the quotemeta escape, \Q. Both quotemeta and \Q put a backslash in front of any character that isn't a letter, digit, or underscore:

```
chomp($pat = <STDIN>);            For example, hello :-).
$quoted = quotemeta $pat;          Now hello\ \:\-\).

print "matched\n" if /($quoted){2}/;      "Safe" to match now.
print "matched\n" if /(\Q$pat\E){2}/;     Another approach.
```

As with seemingly everything else pertaining to regular expressions, tiny errors in quoting metacharacters can result in strange bugs:

```
print "matched\n" if /(\Q$pat){2}/;       WRONG—no \E ... means
                                          /hello\ \:\-\)\{2\}/.
```

## Item 16: Use regular expression memory.

Although regular expressions are handy for determining whether a string looks like one thing or another, their greatest utility is in helping parse the contents of strings once a match has been found. To break apart strings with regular expressions, you must use regular expression memory.

### The memory variables: $1, $2, $3, and so on

Most often, parsing with regular expressions involves the use of the regular expression *memory variables* $1, $2, $3, and so on. Memory variables are associated with parentheses inside regular expressions. Each pair of parentheses in a regular expression "memorizes" what its contents matched. For example:

```
$_ = 'http://www.perl.org/index.html';      Memorize hostname and
m#^http://([^/]+)(.*)#;                       path following http://.

print "host = $1\n";                          host = www.perl.org
print "path = $2\n";                          path = /index.html
```

Only *successful* matches affect the memory variables. An unsuccessful match leaves the memory variables alone, even if it appears that part of a match might be succeeding:

*Continued from above:*

```
$_ = 'ftp://ftp.uu.net/pub/';                ftp doesn't match http.
m#^http://([^/]+)(.*)#;                        Same pattern as above.

print "host = $1\n";                           Still www.perl.org.
print "path = $2\n";                           Still /index.html.
```

When a pair of parentheses matches several different places in a string, the corresponding memory variable contains the *last* match:

```
$_ = 'ftp://ftp.uu.net/pub/systems';         Last fragment of the path
m#^ftp://([^/]+)(/[^/]*)+#;                    goes into $2.

print "host = $1\n";                           host = ftp.uu.net
print "fragment = $2\n";                       fragment = /systems
                                               but matched /pub first.
```

In cases involving nested parentheses, *count left parentheses* to determine which memory variable a particular set of parentheses refers to:

```
$_ = 'ftp://ftp.uu.net/pub/systems';         This pattern is similar to
m#^ftp://([^/]+)((/[^/]*)+)#;                  the last one, but also
                                               collects the whole path.

print "host = $1\n";                           host = ftp.uu.net
print "path = $2\n";                           path = /pub/systems
print "fragment = $3\n";                       fragment = /systems
```

The "count left parentheses" rule applies to all regular expressions, even ones involving alternation:

```
$_ = 'ftp://ftp.uu.net/pub';                 Just grab the first
m#^((http)|(ftp)|(file)):#;                    (protocol) portion of a
                                               URL.

print "protocol = $1\n";                       protocol = ftp
print "http = $2\n";                           http =
print "ftp = $3\n";                            ftp = ftp
print "file = $4\n";                           file =
```

The $+ special variable contains the value of the last non-empty memory:

*Continued from above:*

```
print "\$+ = $+\n";                        $+ = ftp
```

The parade of frills continues! Memory variables are automatically localized by each new scope. In a unique twist, the localized variables receive *copies* of the values from the outer scope—this is in contrast to the usual reinitializing of a localized variable:

```
$_ = 'ftp://ftp.uu.net/pub';               Take a URL apart in two steps—
m#^([^:]+)://(.*)#;                         first, split off the protocol.

print "\$1, \$2 = $1, $2\n";                $1, $2 = ftp, ftp.uu.net/pub

{                                           Now, split into host and path.
  print "\$1, \$2 = $1, $2\n";              $1, $2 = ftp, ftp.uu.net/pub
  $2 =~ m#([^/]+)(.*)#;
  print "\$1, \$2 = $1, $2\n";              $1, $2 = ftp.uu.net, /pub
}

print "\$1, \$2 = $1, $2\n";                $1, $2 = ftp, ftp.uu.net/pub
                                            The old $1 and $2 are back.
```

The localizing mechanism used is `local`, not `my` (see Item 23).

## Backreferences

Regular expressions can make use of the contents of memories via *backreferences*. The atoms \1, \2, \3, and so on match the *contents* of the corresponding memories. An obvious (but not necessarily useful) application of backreferences is solving simple word puzzles:

```
/(\w)\1/;                                   Matches doubled word
                                            char—aa, 11, __.

/(\w)\1+/;                                  Two or more—aaa, bb,
                                            222222.

/((\w)\2){2,}/;                             Consecutive pairs—aabb,
                                            22__66 ... remember
                                            "count left parentheses"
                                            rule.

/([aeiou]).*\1.*\1.*\1/;                    Same vowel four times.
/([aeiou])(.*\1){3}/;                       Another way.
/([aeiou]).*?\1.*?\1.*?\1/;                 Non-greedy version
                                            matching first four (see
                                            Item 17).
```

This kind of thing is always good for 10 minutes of fun on a really slow day. Just sit at your Unix box and type things like:

```
% perl -ne 'print if /([aeiou])(.*\1){3}/' /usr/dict/words
```

I get 106 words from this one, including "tarantara." Hmm.

Backreferences are a powerful feature, but you may not find yourself using them all that often. Sometimes they are handy for dealing with delimiters in a simplistic way:

| | |
|---|---|
| `/(['"]).*\1/;` | 'stuff' *or* "stuff", *greedy.* |
| `/(['"]).*?\1/;` | *Non-greedy version (see Item 17).* |
| `/(['"])(\\\1\|.)*?\1/;` | *Handles escapes: \', \".* |

Unfortunately, this approach breaks down quickly—you can't use it to match parentheses (even without worrying about nesting), and there are faster ways to deal with embedded escapes.

## The match variables: $`, $&, $'

In addition to memory variables like $1, $2, and $3, there are three special *match variables* that refer to the match and the string from which it came. $& refers to the portion of the string that the entire pattern matched, $` refers to the portion of the string preceding the match, and $' refers to the portion of the string following the match. As with memory variables, they are set after each successful pattern match.

Match variables can help with certain types of substitutions in which a replacement string has to be computed:

*Go through the contents of* OLD *a line at a time, replacing some one-line HTML comments.*

```
while (<OLD>) {
  while (/<!--\s*(.*?)\s*-->/g) {        Extract info from
    $_ = $` . new_html($1) . $'          comment and check it out.
      if ok_to_replace($1);              Replace comment.
  }
  print NEW $_;
}
```

Some people complain that using match variables makes Perl programs run slower. This is true. There is some extra work involved in maintaining the values of the match variables, and once any of the match variables appears in a program, Perl maintains them for *every* regular expression match in the program. If you are concerned about speed, you may want to rewrite code that uses match variables. You can generally rephrase such code as substitutions that use memory variables. In the case above, you could do the obvious (but incorrect):

```
while (<OLD>) {
  while (/<!--\s*(.*?)\s*-->/) {
    s/<!--\s*(.*)\s*-->/new_html($1)/e
      if ok_to_replace($1);
  }
  print NEW $_;
}
```
*Use substitution rather than match variables for replacement. However, /g won't work; thus this is broken for lines that contain more than one comment.*

Or, a correct but slightly more involved alternative:

```
while (<OLD>) {
  s{(<!--\s*(.*?)\s*-->)}{
    ok_to_replace($2) ?
      new_html($2) : $1;
  }eg;
  print NEW $_;
}
```
*Use s///eg for replacement (looks better using braces as delimiters).*

In most cases, though, I would recommend that you write whatever makes your code clearer, including using match variables when appropriate. Worry about speed after everything works and you've made your deadline (see Item 22).

The localizing behavior of match variables is the same as that of memory variables.

## Memory in substitutions

Memory and match variables are often used in substitutions. Uses of $1, $2, $&, and so on within the replacement string of a substitution refer to the memories from the match part, not an earlier statement (hopefully, this is obvious):

```
s/(\S+)\s+(\S+)/$2 $1/;
```
*Swap two words.*

```
%ent = (
  '&' => 'amp', '<' => 'lt',
  '>' => 'gt'
);
$html =~ s/([&<>])/&$ent{$1};/g;
```
*Here is an approach to HTML entity escaping.*

a&b *becomes* a&amp;b

```
$newsgroup =~ s/(\w)\w*/$1/g;
```
comp.sys.unix *becomes* c.s.u.

Some substitutions using memory variables can be accomplished without them if you look at what to throw away, rather than what to keep.

```
s/^\s*(.*)/$1/;
```
*Eliminate leading whitespace, hard way.*

```
s/^\s+//;
```
*Much better!*

```
$_ = "FOO=bar BLETCH=baz";
s/(FOO=\S+)|\w+=\S+/$1/g;
```
*Throw away assignments except FOO=.*

```
s/(this|that)|(\w)/$1\U$2/g;
```
*Uppercase all words except this and that.*

You can use the /e (eval) option to help solve some tricky problems:

```
s/(\S+\.txt)\b/-e $1 ? $1 :
   "<$1 not found>"/ge;
```
*Replace all the nonexistent foo.txt.*

Substitutions using /e can sometimes be more legibly written using matching delimiters and possibly the /x option (see Item 21):

```
s{
   (\S+\.txt)\b   # ending in .txt?
}{
   -e $1 ? $1 : "<$1 not found>"
}gex;
```
*Same as above, written with /x option to ignore whitespace (including comments) in pattern.*

## Matching in a list context

In a list context, the match operator m// returns a list of values corresponding to the contents of the memory variables. If the match is unsuccessful, the match operator returns an empty list. This doesn't change the behavior of the match variables: $1, $2, $3, and so on are still set as usual.

Matching in a list context is one of the most useful features of the match operator. It allows you to scan and split apart a string in a single step:

```
($name, $value) = /^([^:\s]*):\s+(.*)/;
```
*Parse an RFC822-like header line.*

```
($bs, $subject) =
   /^subject:\s+(re:\s*)?(.*)/i;
```
*Get the subject, minus leading re:.*

```
$subject =
   (/^subject:\s+(re:\s*)?(.*)/i)[1];
```
*Or, instead of a list assignment, a literal slice.*

```
($mode, $fn) = /begin\s+(\d+)\s+(\S+)/i
```
*Parse a uuencoded file's begin line.*

Using a match inside a `map` is even more succinct. This is one of my favorite ultra-high-level constructs:

```
($date) =
  map { /^Date:\s+(.*)/ } @msg_hdr;
```
*Find the date of a message in not very much Perl.*

```
@protos =
  map { /^(\w+)\s+stream\s+tcp/ } <>;
print "protocols: @protos\n";
```
*Produce a list of the named tcp stream protocols by parsing `inetd.conf` or something similar.*

Note that it turns out to be extremely handy that a failed match returns an empty list.

A match with the `/g` option in a list context returns *all* the memories for each successful match:

```
print "fred quit door" =~ m/(..)\b/g;
```
*Prints `editor` — last two characters of each word.*

## Memory-free parentheses

Parentheses in Perl regular expressions serve two different purposes: grouping and memory. Although this is usually convenient, or at least irrelevant, it can get in the way at times. Here's an example we just saw:

```
($bs, $subject) =
  /^subject:\s+(re:\s*)?(.*)/i;
```
*Get the subject, minus leading `re:`.*

We need the first set of parentheses for grouping (so the ? will work right), but they get in the way memory-wise. What we would like to have is the ability to group without memory. Perl 5 introduced a feature for this specific purpose. *Memory-free parentheses* (?:...) group like parentheses, but they don't create backreferences or memory variables:

```
($subject) =
  /^subject:\s+(?:re:\s*)?(.*)/i;
```
*Get the subject, no bs.*

Memory-free parentheses are also handy in the match-inside-map construct (see above), and for avoiding delimiter retention mode in `split` (see Item 19). In some cases they also may be noticeably faster than ordinary parentheses (see Item 22). On the other hand, memory-free parentheses are a pretty severe impediment to readability and probably are best avoided unless needed.

### Tokenizing with regular expressions

Tokenizing or "lexing" a string—dividing it up into lexical elements like whitespace, numbers, identifiers, operators, and so on—offers an interesting application for regular expression memory.

If you have written or tried to write computer language parsers in Perl, you may have discovered that the task can seem downright hard at times. Perl seems to be missing some features that would make things easier. The problem is that when you are tokenizing a string, what you want is to find out *which* of several possible patterns matches the *beginning* of a string (or at a particular point in its middle). On the other hand, what Perl is good at is finding out *where* in a string a *single* pattern matches. The two don't map onto one another very well.

Let's take the example of parsing simple arithmetic expressions containing numbers, parentheses, and the operators +, -, *, and /. (Let's ignore whitespace, which we could have substituted or `tr`-ed out beforehand.) One way to do this might be:

```
while ($_) {                                    Tokenize contents of $_
  if (/^(\d+)/) {                               into array @tok.
    push @tok, 'num', $1;
  } elsif (/^([+\-\/*()])/) {
    push @tok, 'punct', $1;
  } elsif (/^([\d\D])/) {
    die "invalid char $1 in input";
  }
  $_ = substr($_, length $1);                   Chop off what we
}                                               recognized and go back
                                                for more.
```

This turns out to be moderately efficient, even if it looks ugly. However, a tokenizer like this one will slow down considerably when fed long strings because of the `substr` operation at the end. You might think of keeping track of the current starting position in a variable named `$pos` and then doing something like:

```
if (substr($_, $pos) =~ /^(\d+)/) {
```

However, this do-it-yourself technique probably won't be much faster and may be slower on short strings.

One approach that works reasonably well, and that is not affected unduly by the length of the text to be lexed, relies on the behavior of the match operator's /g option in a scalar context—we'll call this a "scalar m//g match." Each time a scalar m//g match is executed, the regular expression engine starts looking for a match at the current "match position," generally after the end of the preceding match—analogous to the $pos variable mentioned above. In fact, the current match position can be accessed (and changed) through Perl's pos operator. Applying a scalar m//g match allows you to use a single regular expression, and it frees you from having to keep track of the current position explicitly:

```
while (/
  (\d+) |   # number
  ([+\-\/*()]) |  # punctuation
  ([\d\D])  # something else
/xg) {
  if ($1 ne "") {
    push @tok, 'num', $1;
  } elsif ($2 ne "") {
    push @tok, 'punct', $2;
  } else {
    die "invalid char $3 in input";
  }
}
```

*Use a match with the /g option. The /x option is also used to improve readability (see Item 21).*

*Examine $1, $2, $3 to see what was matched.*

The most recent versions of Perl support a /c option for matches, which modifies the way scalar m//g operates. Normally, when a scalar m//g match *fails*, the match position is reset, and the next scalar m//g will start matching at the beginning of the target string. The /c option causes the match position to be *retained* following an unsuccessful match. This, combined with the \G anchor, which forces a match beginning at the last match position, allows you to write more straightforward tokenizers:

```
{
  if (/\G(\d+)/gc) {
    push @tok, 'num', $1;
  } elsif (/\G([+\-\/*()])/gc) {
    push @tok, 'punct', $1;
  } elsif (/\G([\d\D])/gc) {
    die "invalid char $1 in input";
  } else {
    last;
  }
  redo;
}
```

*A naked block for looping.*
*Is it a number?*

*Is it punctuation?*

*It's something else.*

*Out of string?*
*We're done.*

*Otherwise, loop.*

Although it isn't possible to write a single regular expression that matches nested delimiters, with scalar m//gc you can come fairly close:.

■ **Find nested delimiters using scalar m//gc.**

*Here is an approach to matching nested braces. {qw({ 1 } -1)} is an anonymous hash ref—it could have been written less succinctly as {('{' => 1, '}' => -1)}.*

```
$_ = " Here are { nested {} { braces } }!";
```
*Input goes into $_.*

■ **Find nested delimiters using scalar m//gc. (cont'd)**

```
{                                                    $c counts braces.
  my $c;
  while (/([{}])/gc) {                               Find braces
    last unless ($c += {qw({ 1 } -1)}->{$1}) > 0     and count them
  };                                                 until count is 0.
}
print substr substr($_, 0, pos()), index($_, "{");   Print found string.
```

## Item 17: Avoid greed when parsimony is best.

One of the stickier problems you may encounter in dealing with regular expressions is *greed*.

Greed isn't about money, at least where regular expressions are concerned. It's the term used to describe the matching behavior of most regular expression engines, Perl's included. A general rule[3] is that a Perl regular expression will return the *longest* match it can find, at the *first* position in a string at which it can find a match of any length. Repetition operators like * and + "gobble up" characters in the string until matching more characters causes the match to fail:

```
$_ = "Greetings, planet Earth!\n";        Some data to match.

/\w+/;                                     Matches Greetings.
/\w*/;                                     Matches Greetings.

/n[et]*/;                                  Matches n in Greetings.
/n[et]+/;                                  Matches net in planet.

/G.*t/;                                    Matches Greetings,
                                           planet Eart.
```

This is normally a desirable behavior. But not always. Be especially careful when using greedy regular expressions to match delimited patterns like quoted strings and C comments:

▼ **Don't use greedy regular expressions with delimiters.**

*These examples illustrate incorrect patterns for matching text enclosed by delimiters—in this case single-quoted strings and C comments.*

```
$_ = "This 'test' isn't successful?";      Hoping to match 'test'.

($str) = /('.*')/;                         Matches 'test' isn.
```

---

3. But not strictly accurate, as you will see.

▼ **Don't use greedy regular expressions with delimiters. (cont'd)**

```
$_ = "/* temp */ x = 10; /* too much? */";     Hoping to match /* temp */.
s#(/\*.*\*/)##;                                 OOPS—erases the whole string!
```

In these examples, Perl keeps matching beyond what appears to be the end of the pattern. But the match operator hasn't run amok: `'`, `/`, and `*` are all matched by `.`, and the match ends at the last occurrence of `'`, or `*/`. We can fix the single-quoted string example by excluding single quotes from the characters allowed inside the string:

```
$_ = "This 'test' isn't successful?";
($str) = /('[^']*')/;                           Matches 'test' now.
```

Straightening out the regular expression for C comments is more troublesome. I will bet confidently that when you write your first regular expression that you *believe* matches C comments, it will not work. Here is one of many possibilities—it seems reasonable at first:

```
s#/\*([^*]|\*[^/])*\*/##g;                      ALMOST works.
```

Do you see the problem with it? It fails on the following input:

```
/***/
```

The reason is that there is no way for it to match an asterisk inside the comment that isn't followed by exactly one other character, thus an odd number of asterisks fails to match. It has other problems, too, but this one is enough. The real answer looks like this:[4]

```
s#/\*[^*]*\*+([^/*][^*]*\*+)*/##g;              CORRECT
```

You are not likely to understand the how and why of this without recourse to a diagram of the underlying state machine:

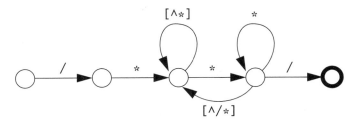

4. As long as it isn't necessary to deal with things like comments embedded in strings, anyway.

And if you haven't suffered through a class in discrete math or compiler construction, this may not help you either. In fact, a good many people will go through their lives using regular expressions like the above without knowing why they work. This isn't necessarily bad; it's just not ideal.

Now, if it's this hard to construct a regular expression for something as simple as C comments, imagine what it could be like to try to write one for something more complex, like HTML comments, or strings with character escapes. Pretty scary.

Fortunately, Perl 5 has *non-greedy* repetition operators. This is a powerful and enormously helpful new feature that allows you to write simple regular expressions for cases that previously required complex or even impossibly difficult regular expressions.

You can make any repetition operator (*, +, {*m*,*n*}) non-greedy by following it with a question mark. The operator will now match the *shortest* string that results in a pattern match, rather than the longest. This makes the examples above trivially simple:

■ **Do use non-greedy regular expressions with delimiters.**

*These examples illustrate patterns that correctly match text enclosed by delimiters.*

```
$_ = "This 'test' isn't successful?";
($str) = /('.*?')/;                              Matches 'test'.

$_ = "/* temp */ x = 10; /* too much? */";
s#(/\*.*?\*/)##;                                 Deletes /* temp */.
```

You can now attempt more ambitious things, like a double-quoted string with character escapes (let's support \", \\, and \123):

```
$_ = 'a "double-q \"string\042"';
($str) = /("(\\["\\]|\\\d{1,3}|.)*?")/;
print $str;                                      "double-q \"string\042"
```

The only problem with non-greedy matching is that it can be slower than greedy matching. Don't use non-greedy operators unnecessarily. But *do* use non-greedy operators to avoid having to write complex regular expressions that might or might not be correct.

## Procedural regular expressions versus deterministic finite automatons (DFAs)

Perl and most other tools with robust pattern-matching capabilities that include features like backreferences use what I call a *procedural* approach to regular expression pattern matching. When Perl encounters a regular expression in a program, it compiles it into a treelike structure and saves it away. When that regular expression is used to match a string, Perl looks for the match by "executing" the compiled regular expression. Consider a simple regular expression and target string:

```
$_ = 'testing';
/t(e|es)./;
print "matched: $&\n";                    matched: tes
```

If Perl could talk, it might describe the matching process something like this:

"OK, start at first character position. Looking for a t. Got one.

"Now, an alternation, first one is e. Looking for e. Got one.

"OK, the alternation matched. Next thing is a dot. Need one char to match the dot. Got an s.

"Anything else? Nope. Guess we're done."

If you have no background experience with tools like *lex* or *flex*, or if this is the only kind of regular expression you have ever known, you probably don't see anything unusual with this interpretation of this regular expression. On the other hand, if you are familiar with *flex*, you might be thinking, "Hmm, why didn't that match test instead?"

Well, you *could* get it to match test by rewriting it:

```
$_ = 'testing';
/t(es|e)./;
print "matched: $&\n";                    matched: test
```

This illustrates the difference—outwardly, at least—between procedural regular expressions and state machine or DFA regular expressions.[5] Tools like *flex* go far beyond parsing regular expressions. They go through an involved process that generates a deterministic state machine from the regular expression, rendering it into what is basically a table of numbers. If you use *flex* on the regular expression above, it will generate an internal state machine that looks something like this:

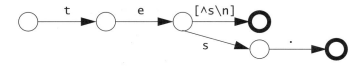

---

5. The Hip Owls book uses the term "NFA regular expressions" to refer to what I call "procedural" matching.

The bold circles represent "accepting states" in which a complete match has been found. This view of the regular expression is somewhat different from the one that Perl has. For one thing, this DFA would have matched `test`, not `tes`, from the string `testing`. For another, the process of creating a DFA from a regular expression discards the syntactic structure of the original regular expression. In general, DFA-based tools always find the longest match for a regular expression, regardless of the order of alternations or grouping of repetition operators. On the other hand, as you can see, the arrangement of the parts of a Perl regular expression *is* significant. The flexibility to change what a pattern matches by rearranging its parts helps make Perl regular expressions particularly powerful and expressive.

If you are more familiar with the DFA view of regular expressions than the procedural view, you should take some time to think about procedural regular expressions. Experiment with them. You can do things with procedural regular expressions that are very difficult or impossible to do with DFA regular expressions, especially if you make use of Perl's non-greedy repetition operators.

The down side to procedural regular expressions is that they generally run slower than DFA regular expressions. But they are not *that* much slower, and they do compile into an internal represention significantly faster.

## Item 18:  Remember that whitespace is not a word boundary.

You will frequently use the set of whitespace characters, \s, the set of word characters, \w, and the word boundary anchor, \b, in your Perl regular expressions. Yet you should be careful when you use them *together*. Consider the following pattern match:

```
@who = `who`;                                  donna   pts/3  Oct  1 18:33
$_ = pop @who;
($user, $tty) = /(\w+)\s+(\w+)/;               It looks innocuous at first.
```

This works fine on input like "`joebloe ttyp0…`". However, it will not match at all on strings like "`webmaster-1 ttyp1…`" and will return a strange result on "`joebloe pts/10…`". This match probably should have been written:

```
($user, $tty) = /(\S+)\s+(\S+)/;               BETTER—\S next to \s.
```

There is probably something wrong in your regular expression if you have \w adjacent to \s, or \W adjacent to \S. At the least, you should examine such regular expressions *very* carefully.

Another thing to watch out for is a "word" that contains punctuation characters. Suppose you want to search for a whole word in a text string:

```
print "word to search for: ";
$word = <STDIN>;                          Hmm—are word
print "found\n" if                        boundaries what you
    $text =~ /\b\Q$word\E\b/;              want?
```

This works fine for input like hacker and even Perl5-Porter, but fails for words like goin', or any word that does not begin and end with a \w character. It also will consider isn a matchable word if $text contains isn't. The reason is that \b matches transitions between \w and \W characters—not transitions between \s and \S characters. If you want to support searching for words delimited by whitespace, you will have to write something like this instead:

```
print "word to search for: ";
$word = <STDIN>;
print "found\n" if                        BETTER—use whitespace
    $text =~ /(^|\s)\Q$word\E($|\s)/;      as a delimiter.
```

The word boundary anchor, \b, and its inverse, \B, are zero-width patterns. Even though they are not the only zero-width patterns (^, \A, etc. are others), they are the hardest to understand. If you are not sure what \b and \B will match in your string, try substituting for them:

```
$text = "What's a \"word\" boundary?";
($btext = $text) =~ s/\b/:/g;             Insert colon at word
($Btext = $text) =~ s/\B/:/g;             boundaries and not-word
print "$btext\n$Btext\n";                 boundaries.

% tryme
:What:':s: :a: ":word:" :boundary:?
W:h:a:t's a :"w:o:r:d": b:o:u:n:d:a:r:y?:
```

The results at the ends of the string should be especially interesting to you. Note that if the last (or first) character in a string is not a \w character, there is no word boundary at the end of the string. Note also that there are not-word boundaries between consecutive \W characters (like space and double quote) as well as consecutive \w characters.

## Matching at the end of line: $, \Z, /s, /m

Of course, $ matches at the end of a line—or does it? Officially, it matches at the end of the string being matched, *or* just before a final newline occurring at the end of the string. This feature makes it easy to match newline-terminated data:

```
print "some text\n" =~ /(.*)$/;
```
           *Prints* `"some text"`, *as if newline wasn't there.*

```
print "some text" =~ /(.*)$/;
```
           *Same thing.*

The /s (single-line—sort of) option changes the meaning of . (period) so that it matches any character instead of any character but newline. This is useful if you want to capture newlines inside a string:

```
print "2\nlines\n" =~ /(.*)/;
```
           `2` *(Period won't match newline.)*

```
print "2\nlines\n" =~ /(.*)/s;
```
           `2\nlines\n`

However, /s *does not* change the meaning of $:

```
$_ = "some text\n";
s/.$/<end>/s;
```
           *Yields* `some tex<end>\n`. *(Replaces the character before* `\n`.)

To force $ to really match the end of the string, you need to be more insistent. One way to do this is to use the (?!...) regular expression operator:

```
$_ = "some text\n";
s/.$(?!\n)/<end>/s;
```
           *Now yields* `some text<end>`.

Here, (?!\n) ensures that there are no newlines after the $.[6]

Ordinarily, $ only matches before the end of the string or a trailing newline. However, the /m (multi-line) option modifies the operation of $ so that it can also match before intermediate newlines. The /m option also modifies ^ so that it will match a position immediately following a newline in the middle of the string:

```
$_ = "2\nlines";
s/^/<start>/mg;
```
           `<start>2\n<start>lines`

```
$_ = "2\nlines";
s/$/<end>/mg;
```
           `2<end>\nlines<end>`

---

6. In earlier versions of Perl you may have to surround the $ with memory-free parentheses—(?:$) instead of $—since the regular expression parser recognizes $( as a special variable. This behavior was recently changed so that $ preceding ( is now recognized as an anchor, not part of a variable—as has long been the case with $ preceding ).

```
%scores =                              %scores = (
  <<'EOF' =~ /^(.*?):\s*(.*)/mg;         'fred' => 205,
fred: 205                                'barney' => 195,
barney: 195                              'dino' => 30
dino: 30                               ); (See Item 13 for more
EOF                                    about here-doc strings.)
```

The \A and \Z anchors retain the original meanings of ^ and $, respectively, whether or not the /m option is used:

```
$_ = "2\nlines";
s/\A/<start>/mg;                       <start>2\nlines

$_ = "2\nlines";
s/\Z/<end>/mg;                         2\nlines<end>
```

## Item 19: Use split for clarity, unpack for efficiency.

The elegance of list assignments in Perl is infectious, especially when combined with pattern matches. As you start using both features, you may find yourself writing code like:

```
($a, $b, $c) =                         Get first 3 fields of $_.
  /^(\S+)\s+(\S+)\s+(\S+)/;
```

Of course, this is a natural application for split:

```
($a, $b, $c) = split /\s+/, $_;        Get first 3 fields of $_.

($a, $b, $c) = split;                  Splits $_ on whitespace by
                                       default.
```

The two approaches take about the same amount of time to run, but the code using split is simpler.

You can use pattern matches for more complex chores:

```
($a) =                                 Get 5th field of $_
  /[^:]*:[^:]*:[^:]*:[^:]*:([^:])/;    (delimited by colons).

($a) = /(?:[^:]*:){4}([^:])/;          Another way to do it.
```

Using split, we have the alternative:

```
($a) = (split /:/)[4];                 Get 5th field of $_
                                       (delimited by colons).
```

If you go to the trouble to benchmark these examples, you may find that the version using a pattern match runs significantly faster than the version using `split`. This wouldn't be a problem, except that the pattern match is significantly harder to read and understand. This is a general rule—pattern matches tend to be faster, and `split` tends to be simpler and easier to read. In cases like this, you have a decision to make. Do you use the faster code, or do you use the code that is easier to understand? I think the choice is obvious. If you must have speed, use a pattern match. But in general, readability comes first. If speed is not the most important issue, use `split` whenever the problem fits it.

List slices work effectively in combination with `split`:

```
$_ = "/my/file/path";                      Get whatever follows the
$basename = (split /\//, $_)[-1];          last /, or the whole thing.
```

You can use `split` several times to divide a string into successively smaller pieces. For example, suppose that you have a line from a Unix `passwd` file whose fifth field (the "GCOS" field) contains something like `"Joseph N. Hall, 555-2345, Room 888"`, and you would like to pick out just the last name:

```
($gcos) = (split /:/)[4];                  Fifth field in $gcos.
($name) = (split /,/, $gcos);              Stuff before , in $name.
($last) = (split / /, $name)[-1];          Last name in $last.
```

There are some situations where `split` can yield elegant solutions. Consider one of our favorite problems, matching and removing C comments from a string. You could use `split` to chop such a string up into a list of comment delimiters and whatever appears between them, then process the result to toss out the comments:

■ Use `split` to process strings containing multi-character delimiters.

*The following code will print $_ with C comments removed. It deals with double-quoted strings that possibly contain comment delimiters. The memory parentheses in the* `split` *pattern cause the delimiters, as well as the parts between them, to be returned.*

```
for (split m!("(:?\\\W|.)*?"|/\*|\*/)!) {   Split on strings and delimiters.
  if ($in_comment) {
    $in_comment = 0 if $_ eq "*/"           Look for */ if in a comment.
  } else {
    if ($_ eq "/*") {                       Look for /* if not in a comment.
      $in_comment = 1;
      print " ";                            Comments become a space.
    } else {
      print;                                If not in a comment, print.
    }
  }
}
```

## Handling columns with `unpack`

From time to time, you may encounter input that is organized in columns. Although you can use pattern matches to divide data up by columns, the unpack operator (see Item 53) provides a much more natural and efficient mechanism.

Let's take some output from a typical `ps` command line (a few columns have been lopped off the right so the output will fit here):

```
% ps l
  F   UID   PID  PPID CP PRI NI   SZ  RSS    WCHAN S TT
  8   100  7363  7352  0  48 20 1916 1492 write3ve S pts/3
  8   100 14227  7363  0  58 20  868  704 write3ve S pts/3
  8   998 28693  3327  0  58 20 3068 1724          T pts/2
```

Here, a `split` on whitespace would be ineffective, because the fields are determined on a column basis, not on a whitespace basis. Note that the WCHAN field doesn't even exist for the last line. This is a good time to trundle out the unpack operator.

■ Use unpack to process column-delimited data.

---

*The following example extracts a few fields from the output of the `ps` command and prints them.*

```
chomp (@ps = `ps l`);                      Collect some output.

shift @ps;                                 Toss first line.
for (@ps) {
  ($uid, $pid, $sz, $tt) =                 Unpack data and print it.
    unpack '@3 A5 @8 A6 @30 A5 @52 A5', $_;
  print "$uid $pid $sz $tt\n";
}
```

---

Note that the @ specifier does not return a value. It moves to an absolute position in the string being unpacked. In the example above, "@8 A6" means six characters starting at position 8.

You may find it aggravating to have to manually count out columns for the unpack format. The following program may help you get the right numbers with less effort:

*Put a "picture" of the input in $_, and this program will generate a format.*

```
$_ =
'    aaaaabbbbbb                 ccccc              ddddd';
```

```
while (/(\w)\1+/g) {
    print '@' . length($`) . ' A' . length($&) . ' ';
}
print "\n";
```

You could also experiment interactively with the debugger (see Item 39) to find the correct column numbers.

## Item 20: Avoid using regular expressions for simple string operations.

Regular expressions are wonderful, but they are not the most efficient way to perform all string operations. Although regular expressions can be used to perform string operations like extracting substrings and translating characters, they are better suited for more complex operations. Simple string operations in Perl should be handled by special-purpose operators like index, rindex, substr, and tr///.

Bear in mind that all regular expression matches, even simple ones, have to manipulate memory variables. If all you need is a comparison or a substring, manipulating memory variables is a waste of time. For this reason, if no other, you should prefer special-purpose string operators to regular expression matches whenever possible.

### Compare strings with string comparison operators

If you have two strings to compare for equality, use string comparison operators, not regular expressions:

```
do_it() if $answer eq 'yes';
```
*Fastest way to compare strings for equality.*

The string comparison operators are at least twice as fast as regular expression matches:

```
do_it() if $answer =~ /^yes$/;
```
*Slower.*

```
do_it() if $answer =~ /yes/;
```
*Even slower, and probably wrong, without anchors; e.g. on "my eyes hurt".*

A few more complex comparisons are also faster if you avoid regular expressions:

```
do_it() if lc($answer) eq 'yes';
```
*Faster.*

```
do_it() if $answer =~ /^yes$/i;
```
*Slower.*

## Find substrings with `index` and `rindex`

The `index` operator locates an occurrence of a shorter string in a longer string. The `rindex` operator locates the rightmost occurrence, still counting character positions from the left:

```
$_ = "It's a Perl Perl Perl Perl World.";

$left = index $_, 'Perl';                    7
$right = rindex $_, 'Perl';                  22
```

The `index` operator is very fast—it uses a Boyer-Moore algorithm for its searches. Perl will also compile `index`-like regular expressions into Boyer-Moore searches. You could write:

*Continued from above:*

```
/Perl/;                          Slow, with a gratuitous
$left = length $';               use of $'.
```

or, avoiding the use of `$'` (see Item 16 and Item 21):

```
$perl = 'Perl';                          Yes, the pos operator does
/$perl/og;                               have uses. This is still
$left = pos($_) - length($perl);         slow, though.
```

However, the overhead associated with using a regular expression match makes `index` several times faster than `m//` for short strings.

## Extract and modify substrings with `substr`

The `substr` operator extracts a portion of a string, given a starting position and (optional) length:

```
$str = "It's a Perl World.";

print substr($str, 7, 4), "\n";          Perl
print substr($str, 7), "\n";             Perl World
```

The `substr` operator is much faster than a regular expression written to do the same thing (also see Item 19):

*Continued from above:*

```
print ($str =~ /^.{7}(.{4})/), "\n";     Perl — but yuck!
```

The nifty thing about `substr` is that you can make replacements with it by using it on the *left side* of an expression. The text referred to by `substr` is replaced by the string value of the right-hand side:

*Continued from above:*

```
substr($str, 7, 4) = "Small";
```
It's a Small World.

You can combine `index` and `substr` to perform s///-like substitutions, but in this case s/// is usually faster:

```
$str = "It's a Perl World.";

substr($str, index($str, 'Perl'), 4) =
    "Mad Mad Mad Mad";
```
It's a Mad Mad Mad Mad World.

```
$str =~ s/Perl/Mad Mad Mad Mad/;
```
*Less noisy, and probably faster.*

You can also do other lvalue-ish things with a `substr`, such as binding it to substitutions or tr///:

```
$str = "It's a Perl World.";

substr($str, index($str, 'Perl'), 4)
    =~ tr/a-z/A-Z/;
```
It's a PERL World.

## Transliterate characters with tr///

Although it is possible to perform character-level substitutions with regular expressions, the tr/// operator provides a much more efficient mechanism:

■ **Use tr///, not regular expressions, to transliterate characters.**

```
$_ = "secret message";

tr/n-za-m/a-z/;
```
*frperg zrffntr—string "rot13" encoded.*

```
@h{'n'..'z','a'..'m'} = ('a'..'z');
s/([a-z])/$h{$1}/g;
```
*Over 20 times slower, not counting initializing the hash!*

The tr/// operator has other uses as well. It is the fastest way to count characters in a string, and it can be used to remove duplicated characters:

```
$digits = tr/0-9//;
```
*Count digits in $_, fast.*

```
tr/ \n\r\t\f/ /s;
```
*Repeated whitespace becomes single space.*

```
$_ = "Totally\r\nDOS\r\n";
tr/\r//d;
```
*Convert DOS text file to Unix.*

## Item 21:  Make regular expressions readable.

Regular expressions are often messy and confusing. There's no denying it—it's true.

One reason that regular expressions are confusing is that they have a very compact and visually distracting appearance. They are a "little language" unto themselves. However, this little language isn't made up of words like `foreach` and `while`. Instead, it uses atoms and operators like `\w`, `[a-z]` and `+`.

Another reason is that what regular expressions do can be confusing in and of itself. Ordinary programming chores generally translate more or less directly into code. You might think "count from 1 to 10" and write `for $i (1..10) { print "$i\n" }`. But a regular expression that accomplishes a particular task may not look a whole lot like a series of straightforward instructions. You might think "find me a single-quoted string" and wind up with something like `/'(?:\\'|.)*?'/`.

It's a good idea to try to make regular expressions more readable, especially if you intend to share your programs with others, or if you plan to work on them some more yourself at a later date. Of course, trying to keep regular expressions *simple* is a start, but there are a couple of Perl features you can use that will help you make even complex regular expressions more understandable.

### Use /x to add whitespace to regular expressions

Normally, whitespace encountered in a regular expression is significant:

| | |
|---|---|
| `($a, $b, $c) = /^(\w+) (\w+) (\w+)/;` | *Find three words separated by one space, at start of $_.* |
| `$_ = "Testing`<br>`one`<br>`two";` | *$_ contains embedded newlines (same as if we had used \n).* |
| `s/`<br>`/<lf>/g;` | *Replace newlines with <lf>* |
| `print "$_\n";` | *Testing<lf>one<lf>two* |

The /x flag, which can be applied to both pattern matches and substitutions, causes the regular expression parser to ignore whitespace (so long as it isn't preceded by a backslash, or isn't inside a character class), including comments:

```
($str) = /( ' (?: \\' | . )*? ' )/x;
```
*Find a single-quoted string, including escaped quotes.*

This can be especially helpful when a regular expression includes a complex alternation:

```
($str) = / (
  " (?:
    \\\W | # special char
    \\x[0-9a-fA-F][0-9a-fA-F] | # hex
    \\[0-3]?[0-7]?[0-7] | # octal
    [^"\\] # ordinary char
  )* "
) /x;
```
*Find a double-quoted string, including hex and octal escapes.*

## Break complex regular expressions into pieces

As you saw in Item 15, regular expressions are subject to double-quote interpolation. You can use this feature to write regular expressions that are built up with variables. In some cases, this may make them easier to read:

```
$num = '[0-9]+';
$word = '[a-zA-Z_]+';
$space = '[ ]+';

$_ = "Testing 1 2 3";
@split = /($num | $word | $space)/gxo;
print join(":", @split), "\n";
```
*Create some "subpatterns."*

*Some sample data.*
*Match into an array.*
Testing: :1: :2: :3

The pattern this example creates is /([0-9]+ | [a-zA-Z_]+ | [ ]+)/gxo. We used the /o ("compile once") flag, because there is no need for Perl to compile this regular expression more than once.

Notice that there weren't any backslashes in the example. It's hard to avoid using backslashes in more complex patterns. However, because of the way Perl handles backslashes and character escapes in strings (and regular expressions), backslashes must be doubled to work properly:

```
$num = '\\d+';
$word = '\\w+';
$space = '\\ +';

$_ = "Testing 1 2 3";
@split = /($num | $word | $space)/gxo;
print join(":", @split), "\n";
```
*'\\d+' becomes the string '\d+', etc.*

*Some sample data.*
*Match into an array.*
Testing: :1: :2: :3

The pattern this example creates is /(\d+ | \w+ | \ +)/gxo.

If we want a literal backslash in a regular expression, it has to be back-slashed (e.g., /\\/ matches a single backslash). Because backslashes in variables have to be doubled, this can result in some ugly looking strings—'\\\\' to match a backslash and '\\\\\\w' to match a back-slash followed by a \w character. This is not going to make our regular expressions more readable in any obvious way, so when dealing with sub-patterns containing backslashes, it's wise to make up some strings in vari-ables to hide this ugliness. Let's rewrite the double-quoted string example from above, this time using some variables:[7]

```
$back = '\\\\';                              Pattern for backslash.

$spec_ch = "$back\\W";                       Escaped char like \", \$.
$hex_ch = "${back}x[0-9a-fA-F]{2}";          Hex escape: \xab.
$oct_ch = "${back}[0-3]?[0-7]?[0-7]";        Oct escape: \123.
$char = "[^\"$back]";                        Ordinary char.

($str) = /(                                  Here's the actual pattern
  " (                                        match.
    $spec_ch | $hex_ch | $oct_ch | $char
  )* "
)/xo;
```

If you are curious as to exactly what a regular expression built up in this manner looks like, print it out. Here's one way:

*Continued from above:*

```
print <<EOT;                                 Just wrap everything in a
/(                                           double-quoted here-doc
  " (                                        string.
    $spec_ch | $hex_ch | $oct_ch | $char
  )* "
)/xo;
EOT
```

*This will print:*

```
/(
  " (
    \\\W | \\x[0-9a-fA-F]{2} | \\[0-3]?[0-7]?[0-7] | [^"\\]
  )* "
)/xo;
```

---

7. If something like "${back}[0-3][0-7]{2}" worries you, feel free to write it as $back . "[0-3][0-7]{2}".

This is a fairly straightforward example of using variables to construct regular expressions. See the Hip Owls book for a much more complex example—a regular expression that can parse an RFC822 address.

## Item 22:  Make regular expressions efficient.

Although Perl's regular expression engine contains many optimizations for efficiency, it's possible—and easy at times—to write matches and substitutions that run much slower than they should.

Efficiency may not always be your primary objective. In fact, efficiency should *rarely* be a primary objective in software development. Generally, a programmer's first priority should be to develop adequate, robust solutions to problems. It doesn't hurt, though, to keep efficiency in mind.

Let's look at a few common issues for regular expressions in Perl. The list below is by no means exhaustive, but it's a start, and it should get you headed in the right direction.

### Compile once with /o

The regular expressions for most pattern matches and substitutions are compiled into Perl's internal form only once—at compile time, along with the rest of the surrounding statements:

*The pattern /\bmagic_word\b/ is compiled only once, since it remains constant. The compiled form is then used over and over again at run time.*

```
foreach (@big_long_list) {              Count occurrences of
  $count += /\bmagic_word\b/;           magic_word in
}                                       @big_long_list.
```

When a pattern contains interpolated variables, however, Perl recompiles it *every time it is used*:

*The pattern /\b$magic\b/ is recompiled every time it is used in a match, since it contains an interpolated variable.*

```
print "give me the magic word: ";      Count occurrences of the
chomp($magic = <STDIN>);               magic word in
foreach (@big_long_list) {             @big_long_list.
  $count += /\b$magic\b/;
}
```

The reason for this behavior is that the variables making up the pattern might have changed since the last time the pattern was compiled, and thus the pattern itself might be different. Perl makes this assumption to be safe, but such recompilation is often unnecessary. In many cases, like the

/\b$magic\b/ example above, variables are used to construct a pattern that will remain the same throughout the execution of the program containing it. To recompile such a pattern each time it is used in a match is grossly wasteful. This problem arises often, and naturally there is a feature in Perl to help you solve it. Perl's /o ("compile once") flag causes a regular expression containing variables to be compiled *only once*—the first time it is encountered at run time:

■ **Use /o to compile patterns only once.**

*The pattern /\b$magic\b/o is compiled on the first iteration of the* foreach *loop, using whatever the value of* $magic *is at that time. The pattern is never compiled again, even if the value of* $magic *changes.*

```
print "give me the magic word: ";
chomp($magic = <STDIN>);
foreach (@big_long_list) {
  $count += /\b$magic\b/o;
}
```
*Count occurrences of the magic word in* @big_long_list—*note added /o.*

The /o flag also works for substitutions. Note that the replacement string in the substitution continues to work as it normally does—it can vary from match to match:

```
print "give me the magic word: ";
chomp($magic = <STDIN>);
foreach (@big_long_list) {
  s/\b$magic\b/rand_word()/eo;
}
```
*Replace occurrences of* $magic *with something returned by* rand_word(). *See also examples at end of Item 29.*

## Don't use match variables

I mentioned in Item 16 that the match variables ($`, $&, and $') impose a speed penalty on your Perl programs. Whenever a Perl program uses one of the match variables, Perl has to keep track of the values of the match variables for *every single pattern match in the program*.

▼ **Don't use match variables ($`, $&, $') if speed is important.**

*Using a match variable anywhere in your program activates a feature that makes copies of the match ($&), before-match ($`) and after-match ($') strings for every single match in the program.*

```
$_ = "match variable";
/.*/;
print "Gratuitous use of a $&\n";
```
*Uh-oh: We activated the match variable feature.*

▼ **Don't use match variables ($`, $&, $') if speed is important. (cont'd)**

```
while (<>) {                          This now runs slower because
  push @merlyn, $_ if /\bmerlyn\b/;   of the use of $& above!
}
```

Perl isn't smart enough to know which pattern(s) the match variables might be referring to, so Perl sets up the values of the match variables every time it does a pattern match. This results in a lot of extra copying and unnecessary shuffling around of bytes.

Fortunately, the penalty isn't that severe. In most cases (particularly if some I/O is involved, as above), your program will run only slightly slower, if at all. In test cases designed to spot the penalty, the extra time consumed can range from a few percent to 30 to 40 percent. Jeffrey Friedl reports a contrived test case in which the run time with a match variable present was 700 times longer, but it is unlikely you will face a situation like this.

## Avoid unnecessary alternation

Alternation in regular expressions is generally slow. Because of the way the regular expression engine in Perl works, each time an alternative in a regular expression fails to match, the engine has to "backtrack" (see the next subheading) in the string and try the next alternative:

*The pattern match below finds a word boundary, then tries to match* george. *If that fails, it backs up to the boundary and tries to match* jane. *If that fails, it tries* judy, *then* elroy. *If a match is found, it looks for another word boundary.*

```
while (<>) {
  print if
    /\b(george|jane|judy|elroy)\b/;
}
```

There are some instances in which alternation is completely unnecessary. In these cases, it is usually vastly slower than the correct alternative. The classic mistake is using alternation instead of a character class:

▼ **Don't use alternation (a|b|c) instead of a character class ([abc]).**

*Using an alternation instead of a character class can impose a tremendous speed penalty on a pattern match.*

```
while (<>) {                                Look for Perl variable-name-
  push @var, m'((?:\$|@|%|&)\w+)'g;         like things. Single quote
}                                           delimiters turn off variable
                                            interpolation inside pattern.
```

▼ **Don't use alternation (a|b|c) instead of a character class ([abc]). (cont'd)**

```
while (<>) {
  push @var, m'([$@%&]\w+)'g;
}
```
*Look for Perl variable-name-like things. This is about four times faster than the version using alternation.*

## Avoid unnecessary backtracking

Perl's procedural regular expression engine (see Item 17) works by stepping through a compiled version of a pattern, in effect using it as if it were a little program trying to match pieces of text:

- When you write a sequence, you are creating instructions that mean "try to match this, followed by that, followed by . . ."

- When you write an alternation, you are creating instructions that mean "try to match this first; if that doesn't work, back up and try to match that; if that doesn't work . . ." and so on.

- When you use a repetition operator like + or *, you are instructing the engine to "try to find as many of these in a row as you can."

Consider the pattern `/\b(\w*t|\w*d)\b/`, which looks for words ending in either t or d. Each time you use this pattern, the engine will look for a word boundary. It will then do the first alternation, looking for as many word characters in a row as possible. Then it looks for a t. Hmm—it won't find one, because it already read all the word characters. So it will have to back up a character. If that character is a t, that's great—now it can look for a word boundary, and then it's all done. Otherwise, if there was no match, the engine keeps backing up and trying to find a t. If it runs all the way back to the initial word boundary, then the engine tries the second half of the alternation, looking for a d at the end.

You can see that this is a very complicated process. Well, the regular expression engine is meant to do complicated work, but this particular pattern makes that work much more complicated than it has to be.

An obvious shortcoming is that if the engine starts out at the beginning of a word that ends in d, it has to go all the way to the end and back searching fruitlessly for a t before it even starts looking for a d. We can definitely fix this. Let's get rid of the alternation:

```
/\b\w*[td]\b/
```

This is an improvement. Now, the engine will scan the length of the word only once, regardless of whether it ends in t, d, or something else.

We still haven't addressed the general backtracking issue. Notice that there is no need for the regular expression engine to continue backtracking more than a single character back from the end of a word. If that character isn't a t or d, there's no point in continuing, because even if we did find one earlier in the string it wouldn't be at the end of the word.

There's no way to force Perl to change this backtracking behavior (at least not so far as I know), but you can approach the problem in a slightly different manner. Ask yourself: "If I were looking for words ending in t or d, what would I be looking for?" More than likely, you'd be looking at the ends of words. You'd be looking for something like:

```
/[td]\b/
```

Now, this is interesting. This little regular expression does everything that the other two do, even though it may not be obvious at first. But think about it. To the left of the t or d there will be zero or more \w characters. We don't care what sort of \w characters they are; so, tautologically if you will, once we have a t or d to the left of a word boundary, we have a word ending in t or d.

Naturally, this little regular expression runs much faster than either of the two above—about twice as fast, more or less. Obviously there's not much backtracking, because the expression matches only a single character!

## Use memory-free parentheses

If you are using parentheses for grouping alone, you won't need a copy of what the parentheses matched. You can save the time required to make the copy by using Perl's memory-free parentheses:

■ **Use memory-free parentheses (?:…) to speed up pattern matches.**

| | |
|---|---|
| *There's no point in memorizing the contents of the inner parentheses in this pattern, so if you want to save a little time, use memory-free parentheses.* | |
| `($host) = m/(\w+(\.\w+)*)/;` | *Find hostname-like thing (`foo.bar.com`) and put it into `$host`.* |
| `($host) = m/(\w+(?:\.\w+)*)/;` | *Same thing, but no memory for the inner parens.* |

The time saved isn't generally all that great, and memory-free parentheses don't exactly improve readability. But sometimes, every little bit of speed helps!

See Item 16 for more about memory-free parentheses.

## Benchmark your regular expressions

As with many other things in Perl, one of the best ways to determine how to make a pattern match run quickly is to write several alternative implementations and benchmark them.

Let's use the `Benchmark` module (see Item 37) to see how much of a difference those memory-free parentheses above really make:

■ Time your regular expressions with `Benchmark`.

```
use Benchmark;                              Read some data. (I used 1,000
@data = <>;                                 lines of an HTTP access log.)

my $host;
timethese (100,
 { mem => q{                                The test code goes in an eval
  for (@data) {                             string (see Item 54).
   ($host) = m/(\w+(\.\w+)+)/; }
  },

 memfree => q{                              Some more test code.
  for (@data) {
   ($host) = m/(\w+(?:\.\w+)+)/; }
  }
 }
);
```

The results:

```
Benchmark: timing 100 iterations of mem, memfree...
       mem: 12 secs (12.23 usr  0.00 sys = 12.23 cpu)
   memfree: 11 secs (10.64 usr  0.00 sys = 10.64 cpu)
```

Not bad: it takes about 15 percent longer to run the version without the memory-free parentheses.

# Subroutines

## Item 23: Understand the difference between my and local.

The difference between my and local is one of the more subtle and difficult aspects of Perl. It is subtle because the occasions when you can observe functional differences between my and local are somewhat infrequent. It is difficult because the differences in behavior that do result can be unexpected and very hard to understand.

People sometimes state the difference between my and local as something like "my variables only affect the subroutine they're declared in, while local variables affect all the subroutines called from that subroutine." *But this is wrong*, because my has nothing to do with subroutines, local has nothing to do with subroutines, and of course the difference between them has nothing to do with subroutines. It may look that way, but the truth—as you will see—is something else entirely. Nevertheless, I am treating local and my in this section because their use in subroutines is extremely important.

### Global variables

In Perl, all variables, subroutines, and other entities that can be named have *package scope* (or just "global scope") by default. That is, they exist in the symbol table of some package. Braces, subroutines, and/or files alone do not create local variables.[1] (For more about packages and symbol tables, see Item 42 and Item 57.)

In most cases, global names are placed in the appropriate package symbol table during the compilation phase. Names that cannot be seen at compile

---

1. Certain constructs like foreach and map do automatically localize iteration variables. Seems like for every rule, there's a quasi-exception.

time are inserted during execution. Let's run a program named `tryme` to see:[2]

*Print out the contents of the main symbol table (%main::, a.k.a. %::).*

```
print join " ", keys %::;          Created at compile time.
$compile_time;

                                   Soft ref (see Item 30),
${"run_time"};                     created at run time.

% tryme
ARGV 0 FileHandle:: @ stdin STDIN " stdout STDOUT $ stderr
STDERR _<perlmain.c compile_time DynaLoader::  _<tryme ENV
main:: INC DB:: _ /
```

Notice, in this example, that the identifier `compile_time` is present in the symbol table before the variable `$compile_time` is actually reached during execution. If you were unsure of Perl's compiler-like nature before, an example like this should confirm it to you.

You've probably been told since almost the beginning of your programming career (or hobby, or however you prefer to describe it) that global variables are *bad*. Good programs shouldn't use a lot of global variables, the saying goes, because global variables create hidden interfaces, make code difficult to read and modify, and even make it hard for compilers to optimize your code.

You may or may not agree completely with this. However, I'm sure that if you have written programs longer than a few hundred lines, especially as part of a team effort, you'll agree with it at least partially. You should see the need for a mechanism to support *local variables* in Perl. Of course, Perl does support local variables, and in fact is more generous in its support than most languages. Most languages give you only a single mechanism for creating local variables. Perl gives you two.

## Lexical (compile-time) scoping with `my`

Perl's `my` operator creates variables with *lexical* scope. A variable created with `my` exists from the point of declaration through the end of the enclosing scope. An *enclosing scope* is a pair of braces, a file, or an `eval` string (see Item 54). The scope is lexical in that it is determined solely by an inspection of the program text during compilation. Another way of saying

---

2. You can also use the debugger for this (see Item 39), but these examples were easier for me to illustrate in the text with short programs.

this is that the scope of a my variable can be determined by simply looking at the source code. For example:

```
$a = 3.1416;
{
  my $a = 2.7183;
  print $a; # 2.7183;                ◄─────  Scope of my $a
}
print $a; # 3.1416;
```

Here, the variable $a in use outside the braces is the global $a. The variable $a inside the braces is the lexical $a, which is local to those braces. Now, if this seems amazingly obvious and mundane to you, well, it should. This is the way that most commonly used programming languages handle scopes. But this is Perl, and you shouldn't be surprised to hear that there are a few wrinkles. In fact, there are more than a few wrinkles. Let's look at some of them.

First, let's revisit our inspection of the symbol table. Here's a program similar to the one at the beginning of this Item but with things reordered a bit. This time we'll use my:

```
my $compile_time;            This is a my variable.
$compile_time;               Use it.
print join " ", keys (%::);
```

This time, when we run it, we get:

```
% tryme
ARGV 0 FileHandle:: @ stdin STDIN " stdout STDOUT $ stderr
STDERR _<perlmain.c DynaLoader::  _<tryme ENV main:: INC DB:: _
/
```

Hmm. Where did compile_time go? Let's look at something else:

```
$compile_time;               This isn't a my variable.
my $compile_time;            But this is.
print join " ", keys (%::);
```

When we run this example, we get:

```
% tryme
ARGV 0 FileHandle:: @ stdin STDIN " stdout STDOUT $  stderr
STDERR _<perlmain.c compile_time DynaLoader::  _<tryme ENV
main:: INC DB:: _ /
```

Now, compile_time is back.

What these examples demonstrate is that my variables do not "live" in the package symbol tables. In the example with my $compile_time first, there is only one variable named $compile_time in the file, and it never gets into the package symbol table. In the other example, there are two separate variables named $compile_time: the global one in the symbol table, and my $compile_time, which is not in a symbol table.[3]

You can always access the value of package globals via qualified names. Qualified names (those containing ::) always refer to a variable in a symbol table. For example:

```
{
  my $a = 3.1416;
  $main::a = 2.7183;
  print "(in) a = $a\n";                    (in) a = 3.1416
  print "(in) main::a = $main::a\n";        (in) main::a = 2.7183
  print "(in) ::a = $::a\n";                (in) ::a = 2.7183
}
print "(out) a = $a\n";                     (out) a = 2.7183
```

Symbol tables are also used for a variety of other things including soft references and typeglobs. Because my variables are not in a symbol table, you can't get at them using either technique. Here's a demonstration involving soft references:

```
my $a = 3.1416;
${'a'} = 2.7183;
print "my a = $a\n";                        my a = 3.1416
print "{a} = ${'a'}\n";                     {a} = 2.7183
```

Typeglobs work the same way. In fact, as this example demonstrates, typeglobs, soft references, and qualified variable names never refer to lexical (my) variables:

```
$a = 2.7183;
my $a = 3.1416;
*alias = *a;
print "my a = $a\n";                        my a = 3.1416
print "alias = $alias\n";                   alias = 2.7183
print "{a} = ${'a'}\n";                     {a} = 2.7183
print "::a = $::a\n";                        ::a = 2.7183
```

Notice that the *alias typeglob refers to the global *a, even though the typeglob assignment comes after my $a. It makes no difference where the assignment comes—a typeglob always refers to an entry in the symbol

---

3. Actually, it's in a compile-time symbol table, but that symbol table is not accessible at run time.

table, and my variables aren't going to be there. The rest of the wrinkles have to wait until we have begun discussing local variables.

## Run-time scoping with local

Perl's other scoping mechanism is local. local has been around a lot longer than my. In fact, my was introduced only in Perl 5. What, you may wonder, is so wrong with local that Larry Wall felt it worthwhile to add an entirely different scoping mechanism to supplant it? To answer this question, let's just look at how local works. At some point you will start to see the virtues of my.

local is a *run-time* scoping mechanism.[4] Unlike my, which basically creates new variables in a private symbol table during compilation, local has a run-time effect: It *saves* the values of its arguments on a run-time stack, then *restores* them when the thread of execution leaves the containing scope. At first glance, local and my appear to do very similar things. Here's an example similar to the one in the box on page 89, with the my replaced by local:

```
$a = 3.1416;                          Here's a simple local
{                                     example.
  local $a = 2.7183;
  print "$a\n";                       2.7183
}
print "$a\n";                         3.1416
```

Although this looks like the example with my, and although it produces the same output, something very different is going on in the innards of Perl.

In the case of my, as you have seen, Perl creates a separate variable that cannot be accessed by name at run time. In other words, it never appears in a package symbol table. During the execution of the inner block, the global $a on the outside continues to exist, with its value of 3.1416, in the symbol table.

In the case of local, however, Perl saves the current contents of $a on a run-time stack. The contents of $a are then *replaced* by the new value. When the program exits the enclosing block, the values saved by local are restored. There is only one variable named $a in existence throughout the entire example. To better illustrate this, let's use a soft reference to take a peek into the symbol table:

---

4. You may hear local called "dynamic scoping" elsewhere, but I believe "run-time scoping" is more accurate and understandable.

```
$a = $b = 3.1416;
{
  local $a = 2.7183;
  my $b = 2.7183;
  print "IN: local a = $a, my b = $b\n";
  print "IN: {a} = ${'a'}, {b} = ${'b'}\n";
}
print "OUT: local a = $a, my b = $b\n";
```

Running this produces:

```
% tryme
IN: local a = 2.7183, my b = 2.7183
IN: {a} = 2.7183, {b} = 3.1416
OUT: local a = 3.1416, my b = 3.1416
```

How interesting. The trick of using the soft reference to look at the global $a that worked with my seems to have no effect with local. This is as it should be. my *creates a different variable*, while local *temporarily saves the value of the existing one*. Because local is a run-time, not a compile-time mechanism, the changes that local makes to global variables can be observed outside the lexical scope containing the local operator. The most notorious example of this is the nested subroutine call:

```
$a = 3.1416;
sub print_a { print "a = $a\n" }
sub localize_a {
  print "entering localize_a\n";
  local $a = 2.7183;
  print_a();
  print "leaving localize_a\n";
}
print_a();
localize_a();
print_a();
```

Running this yields:

```
% tryme
a = 3.1416
entering localize_a
a = 2.7183
leaving localize_a
a = 3.1416
```

This is the oft-cited example that leads to the description of local as having something to do with subroutine calls, which, as I stated earlier, it does not.

## When to use my; when to use local

In general, you should use my rather than local if you have a choice. One reason for this is that my is faster than local. It takes some time to save a value on the stack:

```
use Benchmark;
timethese (10, {
  'local' => q{for (1..10000) {local $a = $_; $a *= 2;} },
  'my' => q{for (1..10000) { my $a = $_; $a *= 2;} },
} );
```

```
% tryme
Benchmark: timing 10 iterations of local, my...
    local:  5 secs ( 5.04 usr  0.00 sys =  5.04 cpu)
       my:  3 secs ( 3.11 usr  0.00 sys =  3.11 cpu)
```

Another reason to use my is that it's easier to understand and doesn't create the strange "non-local" side effects that local does.

Yet another reason to use my is that the lexical variables it creates form the basis for closures in Perl (see Item 29).

However, one compelling reason to use local, or at least to be familiar with it, is that there is a lot of Perl 4 code out there that uses it. Replacing local with my isn't as easy as a search and replace with a text editor—you will have to examine each use of local individually to see whether it takes advantage of one of the "features" of local. It is probably best to leave code that uses local alone as long as it is performing well. Also, some things *have* to be done with local.

Special variables—any $-punctuation variable or other variable that Perl handles specially—can only be localized with local. It is an error to attempt to localize a special variable with my:

```
sub response {
  local $_ = <STDIN>;                   my $_ would be a
  /^y/i ? "yes" : "no: $_";             compile-time error.
}
```

local can be used in a number of other situations in which my can't. You can use it on a variable in another package:

```
package foo;
$a = 3.1416;
{
  package main;                         In main package now.
  local $foo::a = 2.7183;
```

```
   package foo;                          Back to foo package.
   print "foo::a = $a\n";                foo::a = 2.7183
}
print "foo::a = $a\n";                   foo::a = 3.1416
```

You can also use local on *elements* of arrays and hashes. Yes, strange but true. You can even use local on a slice:

```
@a = qw(Jolly Green Giant);
{
   local(@a[0, 1]) = qw(Grumbly Purple);
   print "@a\n";                         Grumbly Purple Giant
}
print "@a\n";                            Jolly Green Giant
```

You can also use local on typeglobs (see Item 57). In theory, local could be made to work on almost any value, but there are limitations in the current implementation. For example, as of this writing you cannot use local on a dereferenced value like $$a.

### local **and** my **as list operators**

One way in which local and my are the same is syntax. Both local and my can be applied to single scalars, arrays, and hashes:

```
local $scalar;
my @array;
local %hash;
```

You can initialize a variable while localizing it:

```
local $scalar = 3.1416;
my @array = qw(Mary had a little lamb);
local %hash = (
   H => 1, He => 2, Li => 3
);
```

If you use parentheses around the argument(s) to my and local, the argument(s) become a list, and assignments are now evaluated in a list context:

```
local($foo, $bar, $bletch) = @a          First 3 elements from @a.
```

Watch out for the usual list assignment "gotchas":

```
local $foo, $bar, $bletch = @a;
```
*WRONG—don't forget the parens!* $bletch *gets size of* @a; *only* $foo *is localized.*

```
my (@a, @b) = @c;
```
*WRONG—localizes* @a *and* @b *but only* @a *gets values.*

```
my ($a) = <STDIN>;
```
*WRONG—reads all of standard input.*

## Item 24:  Avoid using @_ directly—unless you have to.

Unlike many programming languages, Perl has no built-in support for named or "formal" parameters. The arguments to a subroutine are always passed in via the argument list variable @_. It is up to the author of the subroutine to give the arguments names and check them for consistency. In general, you should always start off a subroutine by copying its arguments and giving them names. The preferred method is to use my:

*This subroutine will remove digits from a string.*

```
sub digits_gone {
  my $str = shift;
  $str =~ tr/0-9//d;
  $str;
}
```
*Default arg for* shift *in sub is* @_ *(see Item 8).*

*Return translated string.*

The idiomatic way to read arguments passed to a subroutine is to use shift to get them one at a time or a list assignment to read them all:

*This subroutine counts different types of chars in a string.*
*Usage:* char_count $str, $chars1, $chars2, ...

```
sub char_count {
  my $str = shift;
  my @chars = @_;
  my @counts;
  for (@chars) {
    $_ =~ s/\\/\\\\/g;
    $_ =~ s#/#\\/#g;
    push @counts,
        eval "\$str =~ tr/$_//";
  }
  @counts;
}
```
*Get first arg.*
*Get rest into* @chars.

*Handle special chars.*

*Count chars with* tr///
*(see Item 20).*

*Return list of counts.*

Another reason to copy and name subroutine arguments is that the elements of @_ are actually aliases for the values that were passed in. Modifying an element of @_ modifies the corresponding subroutine argument—a sort of "call by reference" semantics. Subroutines can modify their arguments, but attempts to do so can fail if the arguments are read-only:

```
sub txt_file_size {                          POOR style. We try to
  $_[0] .= '.txt' unless /\.\w+$/;           automatically append
  -s $_[0];                                  '.txt' to extension-less
}                                            files, but this is goofy.
```

If we try to call this subroutine as txt_file_size "test", it fails with an error message as it tries to modify the read-only value "test". Also, if we call it with a modifiable argument, say txt_file_size $myfile, it may append '.txt' to the argument, which is likely not what we want.

But sometimes this aliasing "feature" turns out to be genuinely useful. For example:

*This subroutine will normalize some values "in place."*

```
sub normalize_in_place {
  my $max = 0;
  for (@_) {                                 Find maximum
    $max = abs($_) if abs($_) > $max;        magnitude of args.
  }
  return unless $max;
  for (@_) { $_ /= $max }                    Normalize args. Note that
  return;                                    $_ is an "alias of an
}                                            alias"—works fine!

($x, $y, $z) = 1..3;
normalize_in_place $x, $y, $z;
printf "%.2g %.2g %.2g\n",                   0.33 0.67 1
  $x, $y, $z;
```

If you are trying to optimize for speed, it may be faster for you to use @_ without copying it, because copying values takes a significant amount of time. If you do so, remember that array subscripting tends to be slow, so try to use constructs like foreach, grep, and map that allow you to iterate over an array without having to subscript its elements repeatedly. The best approach, of course, would be to write two or more different versions and Benchmark them (see Item 37).

Even though subroutine arguments are passed as aliases, any array arguments is flattened into a list. You can modify the elements of an array argument, but not the array itself:

*Throw out the "bad" element—NOT!*

```
sub no_bad {
  for $i (0..$#_) {
    if ($_[$i] =~ /^bad$/) {
      splice @_, $i, 1;
      print "in no_bad: @_\n";
      return;
    }
  }
  return;
}

@a = qw(ok better fine great bad good);
no_bad @a;
print "after no_bad: @a\n";
```

*You can rearrange the contents of @_ all you want, but it won't affect the original arguments.*

*When we run this program, we get:*

```
% tryme
in no_bad: ok better fine great good
after no_bad: ok better fine great bad good
```

Finally, on a slightly different topic, subroutines that are called with no arguments usually have an empty @_ of their own. However, if a subroutine is called with an ampersand and no parentheses, it inherits the current @_:

```
sub inner {
  print "\@_ = @_\n";
}

sub outer {
  &inner;
}

outer 1..3;
```

*&inner with no parens is the only syntax that "works."*

`@_ = 1 2 3`

## Item 25: Use wantarray to write subroutines returning lists.

You probably already know that subroutines can return either scalar or list values. Perhaps you have written both kinds of subroutine. You also probably understand the significance of scalar and list context in Perl. In an idle moment, you may have even wondered how something like the following worked:

*Create a sorted list of text files in a directory.*

```
sub sorted_text_files {
  local *DIRH;                          Localize the dirhandle.
  my $dir = shift;
  opendir DIRH, $dir or die "eh?: $!";
  @files = grep { -T }                  It's not relevant to
      map { "$dir/$_" } readdir DIRH;   wantarray, but note that
  sort @files;                          we have to add the dir
}                                       prefix to make this work.
```

If you write something like:

```
print join " ", sorted_text_files "/etc";
```

then you get the expected list of files. Because it's what you expect, you probably don't see anything magical about it. However, things are different if you instead write:

```
print join " ", scalar(sorted_text_files "/etc");
```

In this case, you get *no output*.

Maybe what's going will become more apparent if you change the last line, sort @files, to read @files = sort @files. Now, instead of nothing at all, you get a number. Hmm.

What you are seeing is the result of the way that Perl evaluates the return value of a subroutine. The context—list or scalar—of the return value of a subroutine is determined by *the context in which the subroutine is called*. The context is noted when the subroutine is called, and that context is applied to whatever expression winds up as the return value.[5] If you need to know what the calling context is, you can use the wantarray operator, which returns true if the subroutine call appeared in a list context. Let's say that you want to modify the sorted_text_files subroutine so that it returns a join-ed list of filenames if evaluated in a scalar context. You could rewrite it like this:

*Create a sorted list of text files in a directory (improved version).*

```
sub sorted_text_files {
  local *DIRH;                          Localize the dirhandle.
  my $dir = shift;
  opendir DIRH, $dir or die "eh?: $!";
```

---

5. You probably shouldn't think too hard about how Perl's "last expression evaluated" return mechanism works, especially in conjunction with the calling context. Some things, like why we have bilateral symmetry, or whether you should inhale or exhale on your golf backswing, are better left to the philosophers. But as I said earlier, you *do* get the source code.

```
        @files = grep { -T }
            map { "$dir/$_" } readdir DIRH;
        if (wantarray) {                         List or scalar context?
          sort @files;                           List: return a list.
        } else {
          join " ", sort @files;                 Scalar: return a string.
        }
    }
```

The wantarray operator is also occasionally useful for answering questions. When I was writing the Idiomatic Perl section and wanted to find out whether grep's block argument was evaluated in a scalar or list context, I wrote something like the following:

```
sub how { print wantarray ? "arrayish" : "scalarish" }
grep { how() } 1;
```

If you run this, it produces the output:

```
scalarish
```

—which pretty much settles the question.

## Item 26:  Pass references instead of copies.

Two disadvantages of the "plain old" method of subroutine argument passing are that (1) even though you can modify its elements, you can't modify an array or hash argument itself, and (2) copying an array or hash into @_ takes time. Both of these disadvantages can be overcome with references (see Item 30).

Passing arrays and hashes by reference is straightforward:

*Print out the contents of an array, with each element prefixed by an index.*

```
sub print_em {
  my $array_ref = shift;                  Argument is an array ref.
  my $i;
  foreach (@$array_ref) {                 Loop through elements in
    print ++$i, ": $_\n";                 the array and print them.
  }
  return;
}
```

*Find all the elements in a hash that aren't in an array.*

```
sub minus {                               Arguments are a hash ref
  my %hash = %{shift()};                  and an array ref. Make a
  my $array_ref = shift;                  copy of the hash.
```

```
    foreach (@$array_ref) {              Loop through the array
      delete $hash{$_};                  and delete hash elements.
    }
    \%hash;                              Return ref to the hash we
  }                                      just created.

  %h = (
    H => 1, He => 2, Li => 3, Be => 4
  );
  $h_r = minus \%h, [qw(He Li)];
  print join " ", %$h_r;                 H 1 Be 4
```

The second example also *returns* a reference to a hash. It would be considerably less efficient to return %hash itself. Returning "just" the hash
variable actually results in %hash being unwound into a list of key-value
pairs, which are then used to construct an entirely new hash. This is
*much* less efficient than returning a reference to the hash that already
exists—and which will otherwise be destroyed when the subroutine exits.
Think of it as recycling.

In the days before references, programmers sometimes resorted to passing typeglobs (see Item 57) when it was necessary to pass an array or hash
by reference. Here's an example of using typeglobs to construct a subroutine that takes two arrays by reference (using Perl 5 syntax):

> *Take two arguments the old-fashioned (and inefficient) way. Note that the
> arguments are passed as typeglobs (*a, *b), not references (\@a, \@b).*

```
  sub two_arrays {
    local *a1 = shift;                   Create a private a1 and
    local *a2 = shift;                   a2.
    print "a1[1] is $a1[1]\n";
    print "a2[1] is $a2[1]\n";
  }
  @a = 1..3;                             When run, prints:
  @b = 4..6;                             a1[1] is 2
  two_arrays *a, *b;                     a2[1] is 5
```

There is no reason to write code like this any more, but if you deal with a
lot of legacy code, you may run into something like it.

## Using local * on reference arguments

Subroutines that take arguments by reference for speed sometimes lose
some of their speed advantage as they continually dereference those arguments. The syntax also becomes distracting and hard to follow. Here's a
subroutine that takes two arrays and returns a list made up of the largest
elements from the arrays compared pairwise:

*Return maximum elements from two arrays, comparing pairwise.*

```
sub max_v {
  my ($a, $b) = @_;                        Args are array refs.
  my $n = @$a > @$b ? @$a : @$b;           $n has count of elements.
  my @result;
  for (my $i = 0; $i < $n; $i++) {
    push @result, $$a[$i] > $$b[$i] ?      Compare pairs from @$a
      $$a[$i] : $$b[$i];                   and @$b.
  }
  @result;
}
```

Those doubled dollar signs aren't very pretty, are they? One way to get around this problem is to alias variables to the arrays. Assigning a reference to a typeglob has the effect of creating an aliased variable of the type appropriate to the reference:

*Return maximum elements from two arrays, comparing pairwise (improved version).*

```
sub max_v_local {                          Alias the two array ref
  local (*a, *b) = @_;                     arguments.
  my $n = @a > @b ? @a : @b;
  my @result;
  for (my $i = 0; $i < $n; $i++) {         Now we can write @a and
    push @result, $a[$i] > $b[$i] ?        @b instead. @a and @b are
      $a[$i] : $b[$i];                     local to this subroutine.
  }
  @result;
}
```

This subroutine is somewhat easier to read once you get past the somewhat strange-looking first assignment. It will probably execute faster than the first version. When I tested this example, I saw about a 10 percent speed increase—not enormous, but significant.

## Passing filehandles

Passing filehandles and dirhandles is a somewhat awkward matter in Perl. In the years B.R. (before references), programmers had to use typeglobs to pass filehandles and dirhandles. Once references were introduced, the FileHandle and DirHandle modules improved the situation somewhat. It also became possible to pass references to typeglobs, which is more efficient than passing "bare" typeglobs. The recently introduced IO module and the so-called *FOO{BAR} (typeglob subscript) syntax have added still

more options. Let's look at all of them in brief. The filehandle typeglob
looks like this (Perl 5 syntax again):

```
sub fh_by_typeglob {
  local *FH = shift;
  print FH "your message here\n";
}

open FILE, ">temp.txt" or die $!;
fh_by_typeglob *FILE;
```

This trusty old mechanism is still in widespread use, because it is well
known and it is *relatively* efficient—an extra symbol table lookup or two
is insignificant if most of what's going on is I/O, and it *does* take time to
load a module like FileHandle.

The FileHandle module creates objects that can be treated like ordinary
scalars:

```
use FileHandle;
sub fh_by_FileHandle {
  my $fh = shift;
  print $fh "your message here\n";
}

$file = new FileHandle "temp.txt", "w";
die "couldn't open: $!" unless $file;
fh_by_FileHandle $file;
```

The syntax for passing typeglobs by reference shouldn't look all that surprising—but notice that you don't have to dereference a globref to use it as
a filehandle:

```
sub fh_by_globref {
  my $fh = shift;
  print $fh "your message here\n";        Typeglob ref is OK in the
}                                           filehandle slot.

open FILE, ">temp.txt" or die $!;
fh_by_globref \*FILE;
```

Recent versions of Perl now include the IO classes, which are intended to
eventually replace FileHandle, DirHandle, and other earlier I/O classes.
IO::File works very much like FileHandle:

```
use IO::File;
sub fh_by_IOFile {
  my $fh = shift;
```

```
    print $fh "your message here\n";
  }

  $file = new IO::File "temp.txt", "w";
  die "couldn't open: $!" unless $file;
  fh_by_IOFile $file;
```

And, finally, recent versions of Perl have a new kind of reference—the *ioref*. An ioref is a reference to a structure internal to Perl that describes a filehandle and/or dirhandle. You can create an ioref with the *FOO{BAR} syntax and then use it like a filehandle or an object from IO::File :

```
  sub fh_by_ioref {
    my $fh = shift;
    print $fh "your message here\n";              Ioref OK in filehandle slot.
  }

  open FILE, ">temp.txt" or die $!;               Create an ioref from a
  fh_by_ioref *FILE{IO};                          filehandle.
```

By now you're probably wondering which of these methods you should use. Unfortunately, this is one of those cases where I can't offer you any firm guidance. I will make a few suggestions, though:

- IO::File is the wave of the future—use it if your version of Perl supports it and you don't have a specific reason to avoid it.

- Creating an ioref from a plain old filehandle using the *FOO{BAR} syntax is probably the most efficient method available in recent versions of Perl.

- Lots of people are familiar with passing filehandles via typeglobs, and it's not particularly *in*efficient.

The situation for dirhandles is similar. You can use the DirHandle module, iorefs (e.g., $ioref = *DIRH{IO}), or a dirhandle typeglob. You can also use the newer IO::Dir class. Which one you choose will depend on the circumstances—there are no hard and fast rules. However, there will not be too many occasions when you will actually *want* to pass dirhandles to subroutines. Usually, the pathname is more appropriate, because you can't (not yet, anyway) use a dirhandle in place of a directory pathname:

● **Recursing through a directory tree**

*This subroutine counts all the normal files and directories in a directory tree.*

```
sub count_recurse {
  local *DIRH;                                    local not required, but cleaner.
```

● **Recursing through a directory tree (cont'd)**

```
my ($file_ct_ref, $dir_ct_ref,          Args are refs to scalar counts,
    $dir_name) = @_;                      directory name.
$$dir_ct_ref++;                          Count this directory.

opendir DIRH, $dir_name or               Read directory.
  die "couldn't open $dir_name: $!";
my @dir = readdir DIRH;
closedir DIRH;                           Close DIRH before recursing!

for $file (@dir) {                       Loop through filenames and
  next if $file eq '.' or $file eq '..'; test them.
  if (-f "$dir_name/$file") {
    $$file_ct_ref++;                     Count a file.
    next;
  };                                     -d _ would be considerably
  next unless -d "$dir_name/$file";      more efficient (see Item 56).
  next if -l "$dir_name/$file";          Skip symlinks.
  count_recurse($file_ct_ref,           Then recurse.
      $dir_ct_ref, "$dir_name/$file");
  }
}

$file_ct = $dir_ct = 0;                  Demo it on ".".
count_recurse \$file_ct, \$dir_ct, ".";
print "$file_ct files, $dir_ct dirs\n";
```

Looks like a lot of work, doesn't it? If you are trying to traverse a directory tree, you may not need to go to all this trouble—check out the File::Find module first.

## Item 27: Use hashes to pass named parameters.

Although Perl provides no method of automatically naming parameters in the subroutine to which they are passed (in other words, no "formal parameters"[6]—see Item 23), there are a variety of ways that you can *call* functions with an argument list that provides both names and values. All of these mechanisms require that the subroutine being called do some extra work while processing the argument list. In other words, this feature isn't built into Perl either. However, this is a blessing in disguise. Different implementations of named parameters are appropriate at different times. Perl makes it easy to write and use almost any implementation you want.

A simple approach to named parameters looks like this:

---

6. Not yet, anyway. An extension of the prototyping mechanism (see Item 28) to allow formal parameters is contemplated but not implemented as of this writing.

■ **Parse named parameters with a hash.**

---

*This illustrates a simple method of using named parameters in a Perl subroutine.*

---

```
sub uses_named_params {
my %param = (
    foo => 'val1',                      Here are some defaults for
    bar => 'val2',                      parameters foo and bar.
    @_                                  Then overlay input args on
  );                                    defaults.

  # now, use $param{foo}, $param{bar}, etc.
}
```

You would call it in this way:

```
uses_named_params(bar => 'myval1', bletch => 'myval2');
```

That wasn't very many lines of code, was it? And they were all fairly simple. This is a natural application for hashes. You may want to allow people to call a subroutine with either "positional" parameters *or* named parameters. The simplest thing to do in this case is to prefix parameter names with a minus sign. Check the first argument to see if it begins with a minus. If it does, process the arguments as named parameters. Here's one straightforward approach:

```
sub uses_minus_params {
  my @defaults = (                      Param names now begin
    -foo => 'val1',                     with a minus.
    -bar => 'val2',
  );

  if ($_[0] =~ /^-/) {                  Read in params as a
    push @defaults, @_;                 hash if first arg starts
  } else {                              with '-'.
    my $n = 1;
    while (@_) {                        Or give positional
      $defaults[$n] = shift;            params names.
      $n += 2;
    }
  }

  my %param = @defaults;                Create param hash.

  # now, use $param{-foo}, $param{-bar}
}
```

You can call this subroutine with either named or positional parameters:

```
uses_minus_params(-foo => 'myval1', -xtra =>'myval2');
uses_minus_params('myval1', 'myval2');
```

**Note:** Stay away from single-character parameter names, for example, -e and -x. In addition to being overly terse, those are *file test operators* (see Item 56).

If you use this method for processing named parameters, you refer to the arguments inside your subroutine by using a hash whose keys are prefixed with minus signs, for example, $param{-foo}, $param{-bar}. Using identifiers preceded by minus signs as arguments or keys may look a little funny to you at first ("Is that really Perl?"), but Perl actually treats barewords preceded by minus signs as though they were strings beginning with minus signs. This is generally convenient, but this approach does have a couple of drawbacks. First, if you want to use the positional argument style and need to pass a negative first argument, you have to supply it as a string with leading whitespace or do something else equally ungainly. Second, although an identifier with a leading minus sign gets a little special treatment from Perl, the identifier isn't always *forcibly* treated as a string, as it would be to the left of => or alone inside braces.[7] Thus, you may have to quote a parameter like -print, lest it turn into -1 (while also printing the value of $_).

There are plenty of applications where these issues don't present a problem, but there are some where where one or both do. In this case, you may want to resort to yet another technique, which is to pass named parameters in an anonymous hash:

```
sub uses_anon_hash_params {
  my @defaults = (              Plain old param names
    foo => 'val1',              again.
    bar => 'val2',
  );

  my %param;
  if (ref $_[0] eq 'HASH') {    If argument is a hash
    %param = (@defaults, %{shift()});    ref, overlay it on defaults.
  } else {
    my $n = 1;                  Otherwise, give
    while (@_) {                positional params
      $defaults[$n] = shift;    names.
      $n += 2;
    }
```

---

7. More recent versions of Perl quote barewords appearing to the left of => even when prefixed by minus signs, so -print => 'foo' now works as expected.

```
                %param = @defaults;                        Then construct a hash.
            }
            # use $param{foo}, $param{bar}
        }
```

The syntax for using named and positional parameters now looks like:

```
    uses_anon_hash_params( {foo => 3, test => 10} );
    uses_anon_hash_params(-123, 345);
```

Or even:

```
    uses_anon_hash_params {foo => 3, test => 10};
```

This is a pretty complicated piece of boilerplate to have at the beginning of a subroutine. If you have several subroutines that accept named parameters, you will probably want to create a subroutine that does most of the work. Here is a subroutine that implements the anonymous hash technique:

■ **Process parameters in an anonymous hash with a subroutine.**

*This subroutine pre-processes named or positional arguments and returns the result as a hash reference.*

```
sub do_params {                                The arguments are a reference
  my $arg = shift;                             to an argument list and a
  my @defaults = @{shift()};                   reference to an array (not hash)
  my %param;                                   of param names and default
                                               values in positional order.

  if (ref $$arg[0] eq 'HASH') {                Overlay named parameters.
    %param = (@defaults, %{$$arg[0]});
  } else {
    my $n = 1;                                 Or name positional
    my @arg = @$arg;                           parameters.
    while (@arg) {
      $defaults[$n] = shift @arg;
      $n += 2;
    }
    %param = @defaults;
  }
  \%param;                                      Return a reference to a hash of
}                                               params.
```

And here's how you might use it:

```
sub uses_anon_hash_params {
  my $param =
    do_params(
      \@_,
      [foo => 'val1', bar => 'val2']
    );

  for (keys %$param) {
    print "$_: $$param{$_}\n";
  }
}
```
*First, call* do_params *with a reference to the arg list and an array of defaults.* do_params *returns a reference to a hash.*

*Now, use* $$param{foo}, $$param{bar}, *etc.*

Each of the techniques illustrated here has its own advantages and drawbacks. Use the technique that best suits your application, or, if none is quite right, adapt one as necessary.

## Item 28: Use prototypes to get special argument parsing.

Perl has supported subroutine *prototypes* for some time. Perl prototypes are not named, typed formal parameters along the lines of those in ISO C,[8] but are rather a mechanism that allows programmers to write subroutines whose arguments are treated like those of built-in operators.

As an example, consider implementing a pop2 function that removes and returns two elements from the end of an array. Suppose you want to be able to use it like the built-in pop:

```
@a = 1..10;
$item = pop @a;
($item1, $item2) = pop2 @a;
```
*Here's how we* pop.
*How we'd like to* pop2.

Normally, if you wanted to implement something like pop2, you would use references (see Item 26):

```
sub pop2_ref { splice @{$_[0]}, -2, 2 }
```

But this has to be called with a reference to an array, not the name of the array:

```
@a = 1..10;
($item1, $item2) = pop2_ref \@a;
```

You have to use prototypes in order to write a function that gets the special treatment of its argument list that a built-in operator like pop does. A prototype appears at the beginning of a subroutine declaration or definition:

```
sub pop2 (\@) { splice @{$_[0]}, -2, 2 }
```

---

8. Not yet, anyway.

Prototypes are made up of prototype atoms. Prototype atoms are characters, possibly preceded by a backslash, indicating the type of argument(s) to be accepted by a subroutine. In this example, the \@ atom indicates that the subroutine pop2 is to take a single named array argument. A backslashed atom, like \$ or \@, causes Perl to pass a reference to the corresponding argument, so in this case the array argument to pop2 will be passed as a reference, not as a list of values.

**Prototype atoms**

| Kind | Syntax | Description |
|------|--------|-------------|
| Name | \$, \@, \%, \&, \* | Returns reference to variable name or argument beginning with $, @, %, etc. |
| Scalar | $ | Forces scalar context. |
| List | @, % | Gobbles the rest of the arguments; forces list context. |
| Block | & | Code ref; sub keyword optional if first argument. |
| Glob | * | Create a typeglob ref. |
| Optional | ; | Separate required args from optional args. |

Prototypes also invoke argument type and number checking where appropriate. For example, if you try to invoke pop2 on a non-array value:

```
pop2 %hash
```

the result is a compile-time error:

```
Type of arg 1 to main::pop2 must be array (not associative
array deref)
```

Let's look at a couple of examples. First, how about a subroutine that takes two array arguments and "blends" them into a single list—one element from the first array, then one from the second, then another from the first, and so on:

```
sub blend (\@\@) {
  local (*a, *b) = @_;                    Faster than lots of derefs.
  my $n = $#a > $#b ? $#a : $#b;
  my @res;
```

```
    for my $i (0..$n) {              Could have been map {
      push @res, $a[$i], $b[$i];     $a[$_], $b[$_] } 0..$n,
    }                                but for and push are
    @res;                            faster.
}
```

Here's how you would use it:

```
blend @a, @b;
blend @{[1..10]}, @{[11..20]};
```

Along the same lines, how about a subroutine that will iterate through the elements of a list like foreach, but *n* at a time:

```
sub for_n (&$@) {                First argument is a code
  my ($sub, $n, @list) = @_;     ref (anonymous
  my $i;                         subroutine).
  while ($i <= $#list) {
    &$sub(@list[$i .. ($i + $n - 1)]);   Pass $n elements at a
    $i += $n;                            time to the subroutine.
  }
}
```

Some sample usage:

```
@a = 1..10;                            Loop through @a, two
for_n { print "$_[0], $_[1]\n" } 2, @a;   elements at a time.
```

Prototypes are intended mostly for the use of module writers, but you may find ordinary uses for them as well. For example, prototypes make an excellent parameter-checking mechanism for functions that take a fixed number of scalar arguments.

You should be careful when using atoms like \@ and \% in code that you are going to share with the world, because other programmers may not expect subroutines to take arguments by reference without an explicit backslash. But this shouldn't be a problem, since you always document your code, right?

## Item 29:  Use subroutines to create other subroutines.

It's easy to get a Perl subroutine to "return" another subroutine. Just create and return a *code ref*—a reference to another subroutine (see Item 30). There are two mechanisms for creating code refs: the reference operator \ and the anonymous subroutine constructor sub {...}:

```
sub named { print "Named!\n" }
```

```
sub code_ref1 {
  \&named;                                    Return a reference to
}                                             &named.

sub code_ref2 {                               Return a reference to an
  sub { print "Anonymous!\n" };               anonymous subroutine.
}
```

The simplest and (I think) most aesthetically pleasing way to call a subroutine from a code ref is via the dereferencing arrow ->:[9]

```
$func1 = code_ref1;                           $func1 and $func2 contain
$func2 = code_ref2;                           code refs.

$func1->();                                   Named!
$func2->();                                   Anonymous!

&$func1();                                    Alternative syntax for the
&$func2();                                    above.
```

Of course, the example above doesn't do anything particularly useful. It shows how to return and call code refs, sure, but it's just a useless extra level of indirection. This isn't a productive way to code unless we can return subroutines whose functionality is *computed* at run time.

## Creating closures

An interesting thing happens when an anonymous subroutine uses a my variable defined in an enclosing scope. Each time the enclosing scope is entered, the subroutine gets a different copy of the my variable. An anonymous subroutine that refers to a my variable from an enclosing scope is called a *closure*. Or, stated another way, a closure is an anonymous subroutine that has access to private variables of its own that are otherwise inaccessible.

Closures are a tricky subject, best approached with some examples. First, let's look at a very simple use of closures:

```
for (0..2) {
  my $time = time;                            A new $time each time.

  push @stamp, sub { $time };                 Each new anonymous
  sleep 2;                                     subroutine has its very
}                                              own $time.
```

---

9. This feature was added fairly recently. If your version of Perl doesn't support it, use the alternative syntax.

```
for (0..2) {                        Prints:
  print "stamp->($_): ",           stamp->(0): 877051119
    $stamp[$_]->(), "\n";          stamp->(1): 877051121
}                                   stamp->(2): 877051123
```

The first loop generates three code refs, each of which is a reference to a separate copy of sub { $time }. Each of those copies has its own copy of $time, created when my $time was encountered at the top of the loop. Each copy of $time can be accessed by the copy of sub { $time } that it is bound to, even (or especially) later in the execution of the program when the my variable has gone out of scope.

Generally, subroutines are used to generate closures:

```
sub make_counter {                  Create and return a
  my $i = 0;                        closure. Each copy of the
  sub { $i++ };                     subroutine has its own
}                                   counter $i.

$count1 = make_counter;
$count2 = make_counter;             Prints:
print "count1 is ", $count1->(), "\n";    count1 is 0
print "count1 is ", $count1->(), "\n";    count1 is 1
print "count2 is ", $count2->(), "\n";    count2 is 0
print "count2 is ", $count2->(), "\n";    count2 is 1
```

Each time make_counter is called, it returns a reference to a new copy of sub { $i++ }, with its own private copy of $i. When one of those copies is called later, it still has access to its copy of $i—even though the call comes from outside the scope that originally defined the my variable.

Perl closures have uses that parallel those of object-oriented constructs (see Item 49). Whereas object-oriented programming is all about data with associated functions, closures are all about functions with associated data. Two or more closures can even share a common set of variables, allowing a programming style that starts to look very object-oriented indeed:

■ **Closures can share a set of variables.**

*This example illustrates how closures can share variables. The subroutine make_iter creates closures that can be used to traverse an array several elements at a time.*

```
sub make_iter {                     The subroutine make_iter
  my $aref = shift;                 takes an array ref and returns
  die "make_iter requires array ref"    a hash ref containing pairs of
    unless ref($aref) eq 'ARRAY';   names and code refs.
  my $i;                            $i and $aref are shared.
```

■ **Closures can share a set of variables. (cont'd)**

```
    {
      'next' => sub {
        my $n = shift;
        if ($n + $i > @$aref) {
          $n = @$aref - $i;
        }
        my @result = @$aref[$i .. $i+$n-1];
        $i += $n;
        @result;
      },

      'position' => sub {
        if (@_) {
          my $new = shift;
          $i = $new if
              $new >= 0 and $new <= $#$aref;
          return;
        } else {
          $i;
        }
      }
    }
  }
}

@a = (1..10);

($next_a, $posn_a) =
  @{make_iter \@a}{'next', 'position'};

$posn_a->(2);
while ((@b) = $next_a->(3)) {
  print join(", ", @b), "\n";
}
print "posn now: ", $posn_a->(), "\n";
```

*The* next *subroutine takes a numeric argument and returns that many values from the array pointed to by* $aref. *It also increments the* $i *counter.*

*There is some range-checking.*

*If supplied an argument, the* position *subroutine sets the current iterating position* $i *within the* $aref *array.*

*If not supplied an argument,* position *returns the current iterating position.*

*Code refs are returned in an anonymous hash so callers don't get them mixed up.*

*Here's our sample array.*

*Assign returned code refs to* $next_a *and* $posn_a.

*Start at index 2.*
3, 4, 5
6, 7, 8
9, 10
posn now: 10

While the subroutines generated in the next example aren't, strictly speaking, closures, the following illustrates the use of eval to create code refs whose bodies are read from a file:

```
sub make_binary {
  eval "sub { $_[0] }";
}
while (<DATA>) {
  my ($name, $code) =
    split /\s+/, $_, 2;
  $op{$name} = make_binary $code;
}
```

*Subroutine to create a code ref with string* eval *(see Item 54).*
*Read subroutine bodies from* <DATA> *and create code refs out of them.*

```
for (sort keys %op) {
  print "2 $_ 3 = ",
    $op{$_}->(2, 3), "\n";
}
__DATA__
add $_[0] + $_[1]
sub $_[0] - $_[1]
mul $_[0] * $_[1]
div $_[0] / $_[1]
max $_[0] > $_[1] ? $_[0] : $_[1]
```

*Call each of the*
*subroutines for arguments*
*(2, 3).*
*When run, prints:*
2 add 3 = 5
2 div 3 = 0.6666666667
2 max 3 = 3
2 mul 3 = 6
2 sub 3 = -1
*(Note sorted order.)*

## Creating subroutines for pattern matching

It's not uncommon to need to perform one or more pattern matches that are specified at run time. For example, you might be writing a Perl program to sort through your mail or news. Such a program would likely read in a "kill file" of patterns to match against the headers. You can specify matches at run time by interpolating variables into regular expressions, but such regular expressions will be repeatedly compiled (see Item 22), at a considerable cost in speed. The /o option provides a means for compiling a pattern match containing interpolated variables only once. However, if you have *several* such matches to deal with, you are faced with a bit of a sticky wicket.

Using closures in combination with eval allows you to generate subroutines that have particular regular expressions "locked in" with the same flexibility (and efficiency!) as if the expressions were specified at compile time. Here's how it's done:

■ **Create pattern matching subroutines with closures and string eval.**

```
sub make_grep {
  my $pat = shift;
  eval 'sub { grep /$pat/o, @_ }';
}

$find_us =
  make_grep q/(?i)\b(joseph|randal)\b/;


@found = &$find_us(<STDIN>);
```

*The subroutine "factory." The*
*pattern is passed in as the first*
*(only) parameter as a string.*

*Create a code ref in $find_us*
*that looks for joseph or randal,*
*case ignored.*

*Find all matching lines from*
STDIN.

The key to this construct is the use of string eval in make_grep. Using /o inside string eval still means "compile once," but "once" now means once per eval, not once per program execution. It almost seems like cheating.

If you want plain old pattern matching instead of grep-ing, that's easy enough:

```
sub make_match {
  my $pat = shift;
  eval 'sub { $_[0] =~ /$pat/o; }'
}
```
*A similar subroutine that creates just a pattern match.*

```
$is_big =
  make_match q/\b(big|large|huge)\b/;
```
*Create a subroutine looking for* big, large *or* huge.

```
if ($is_big->($_)) { ... }
```
*Use it.*

# References

At their heart, Perl references are a simple and extraordinarily useful feature, but their simplicity is obscured by a difficult syntax. In this section we will look at an overview of references, then consider some of their more useful applications.

## Item 30: Understand references and reference syntax.

A reference is a scalar value. It can be stored in a scalar variable, or as an element of an array or hash, as is done with numbers and strings. You can think of a reference as a pointer to some other object in Perl. References can point to any kind of object, including other scalars (even references), arrays, hashes, subroutines, and typeglobs.

Aside from a general pointer-like behavior, however, references do not have very much in common with pointers in C or C++. You can only create references to existing objects; you cannot modify them afterward to do something like point to the next element of an array. You can convert references into strings or numbers, but you cannot convert a string or number back into a reference. Although a reference is treated syntactically like any other scalar value, a reference "knows" to what type of object it points. Finally, each reference to a Perl object increments that object's reference count, preventing the object from being scavenged by Perl's garbage collector.

### Creating references

References can be created in several different ways. The simplest is to use the reference operator \ on a variable:

```
$a = 3.1416;
$scalar_ref = \$a;                          A reference to $a.
```

The effect of the reference operator is to create a reference pointing at the value of its argument:

The reference operator works on any kind of variable:

```
$array_ref = \@a;                   Works on arrays,
$hash_ref = \%a;                    hashes,
$sub_ref = \&a;                     subroutines, and even
$glob_ref = \*a;                    typeglobs.
```

It also works on array and hash elements, and values:

```
$array_el_ref = \$a[0];             Create refs to array and
$hash_el_ref = \$a{'hello'};        hash elements.

$one_ref = \1;                      $one_ref is read-only.
$mode_ref = \oct('0755');           So is $mode_ref.
```

The reference operator works in a very strange way on a list of values, returning a list of references rather than a reference to a list. It decides *what* to return references to by using a seemingly arbitrary heuristic:

*These make a certain amount of sense.*

```
sub val { return 1..3 };            The ref operator returns
$ref1 = \(&val);                    the type of reference.
print ref $ref1, "\n";              CODE
$ref2 = \(val());
print ref $ref2, " $$ref2\n";       SCALAR 3
($ref3) = \(val());
print ref $ref3, " $$ref3\n";       SCALAR 1
```

*But these are a little weird.*

```
$ref4 = \(1..3);
print ref $ref4, " @$ref4\n";       ARRAY 1 2 3
$ref5 = \(1, 2, 3);
print ref $ref5, " $$ref5\n";       SCALAR 3
$ref6 = \(1, 2..3);
print ref $ref6, " @$ref6\n";       ARRAY 2 3
```

You can understand why I recommend that you avoid using the reference operator in front of lists.

The anonymous array constructor [...], which looks like an ordinary list except that the contents are enclosed by brackets rather than parentheses, creates an unnamed array in memory and returns a reference to it. The anonymous array constructor is the customary method of creating a reference to a list of items:

```
$a_ref = [1..3];
print ref $a_ref, " @$a_ref\n";          ARRAY 1 2 3
```

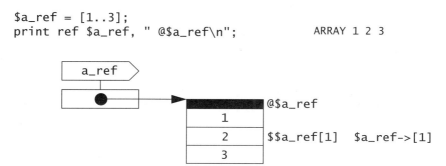

The anonymous hash constructor {...}, which uses braces rather than brackets, works similarly:

```
$h_ref = {};                      Empty anonymous hash.
$h_ref->{'joe'} = 'bloe';         Add an element.
$h_ref->{'john'} = 'public';      Add another.
```

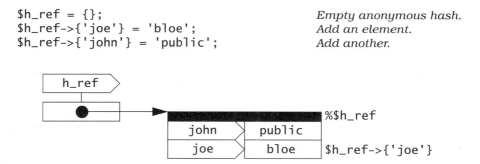

There are many uses for both anonymous arrays and anonymous hashes. See Items 32 and 33 for more examples.

A sub definition without a name returns a reference to an anonymous subroutine. References to subroutines are also called *code refs*:

```
$greetings =                          $greetings is a code ref.
   sub { print "hello, world!\n" };
$greetings->();                       Hello, world.
&$greetings();                        Hello, world.

$SIG{INT} =                           Using an anonymous sub
   sub { print "not yet--i'm busy\n" };   as a signal handler.
```

References to anonymous subroutines are very useful. They are somewhat like function pointers in C. On the other hand, since anonymous subroutines are created dynamically, not statically, they have peculiar properties that are more like something from LISP (see Item 29).

There isn't often much need to construct a reference to an anonymous scalar value, but you can do something like the following if need be:

```
undef $s_ref;
$$s_ref = 2.718;
print ref $s_ref, " $$s_ref\n";              SCALAR 2.718
```

This works through "auto-vivification," discussed later in this Item.

Finally, and somewhat mysteriously, you can create references to an undocumented LVALUE type (not exactly the meaning of "lvalue" I give in the Introduction):

```
$a = "Testing 1 2 3";
$lvref = \substr($a, 0, 7);                  $lvref is an LVALUE ref.
$$lvref = "Pelham";                          Like assigning to substr!
print "a = $a\n";                            Pelham 1 2 3
```

## Using references

Using the value that a reference points to is called *dereferencing*. There are several different forms of dereferencing syntax. The "canonical" form of dereferencing syntax is to use a block returning a reference in a place where you could otherwise use a variable or subroutine identifier. Whereas using an identifier would give you the value of the variable with that name, using a block that returns a reference gives you the value to which the reference points:

*Canonical syntax for scalar references.*

```
$a = 1;                                      $a is an ordinary scalar.
$s_ref = \$a;                                $s_ref is a reference to
                                             the value of $a.
print "${$s_ref}\n";                         Prints 1.
${$s_ref} += 1;                              Works just like a variable.
```

*Canonical syntax for array references.*

```
@a = 1..5;                                   $a_ref is a reference to
$a_ref = \@a;                                the value of @a.
print "@a\n";                                Prints 1 2 3 4 5.
print "@{$a_ref}\n";                         Also prints 1 2 3 4 5.
push @{$a_ref}, 6..10;                       Adds elements to @a.
```

The code inside the block can be arbitrarily complex, so long as the result of the last expression evaluated yields a reference:

```
$ref1 = [1..5];
$ref2 = [6..10];
$val = ${
    if ($hi) {$ref2} else {$ref1}
}[2];
print "$val\n";
```
*Returns 3rd element of some array, depending on $hi.*
*Either* 3 *or* 8.

If the reference value is contained in a scalar variable, you can dispense with the braces and just use the name of the scalar variable, with the leading $, instead. You can use more than one $ if it's a reference to a reference:

*Scalar variable syntax for references.*

```
$a = 'testing';
$s_ref = \$a;
$s_ref_ref = \$s_ref;
print "$$s_ref $$$s_ref_ref\n";
```
`testing testing`

```
$h_ref = {
    'F' => 9, 'Cl' => 17, 'Br' => 35
};
```
*Initialize $h_ref with an anonymous hash.*

```
print "Elements are ", join ' ',
    sort(keys %$h_ref), "\n";
print "F's number: $$h_ref{'F'}\n";
```
`Elements are Br Cl F`

`F's number: 9`

Expressions like $$h_ref{'F'}, or the even more awkward equivalent ${$h_ref}{'F'}, occur frequently. There is a more visually appealing "arrow" syntax that you can use to write subscripts for array and hash references:

```
${$h_ref}{'F'}
$$h_ref{'F'}
$h_ref->{'F'}
```
*Canonical syntax.*
*Scalar variable syntax.*
*Arrow syntax.*

The arrow syntax also works on code refs:

```
sub { print sort @_ }->(4,2,5,3,1);
```
*Prints* 12345.

You can cascade arrows. Furthermore, if the left and right sides of an arrow are both subscripts, you can omit the arrow:

```
$student->[1] = {
    'first' => 'joe', 'last' => 'bloe'
};
print "$student->[1]->{'first'}\n";
print "$student->[1]{'first'}\n";
```
*This is a ref to an array of refs to hashes.*

`joe`
`joe`—*same thing.*

The data structure in this example looks something like this:

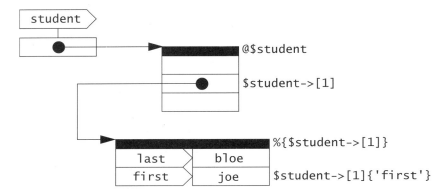

Be careful about leaving out too many arrows or braces. For example, if you omit the first arrow, you get an array of hash references, which is different:

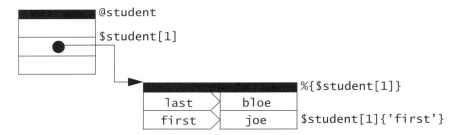

There are more examples of complex data structures built from references in the other items in this section.

Finally, as noted earlier, all references, no matter what their type, are handled like ordinary scalars—they have no special "type" that distinguishes them syntactically from other scalars.[1] However, a reference value contains information about the type of object to which it points. You can get to this information with the ref operator:

```
$s_ref = \1;
print ref $s_ref, "\n";          SCALAR
$c_ref = sub { 'code!' };
print ref $c_ref, "\n";          CODE
```

The ref operator works differently on blessed objects (see Item 49).

1. Mostly, anyway. Don't use a reference as a hash *key*. Hash keys are always converted to strings—which are no longer references. If you must use references as hash keys, use the Tie::RefHash module.

## Auto-vivification

If you use a scalar lvalue with an undefined value as if it were a reference to another object, Perl will automatically create an object of the appropriate type for you and make that scalar a reference to that object. This is called *auto-vivification*. For example, the following code creates an array of four elements and makes $ref a reference to it:

```
undef $ref;                          $ref is now empty.
$ref->[3] = 'four';                  $ref springs into being!
```

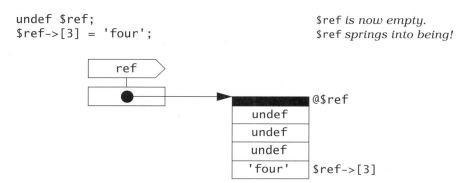

A longer example of auto-vivification is discussed in Item 31.

## Soft references

If you dereference a string value, Perl will return the value of the variable with the name given in the string. The variable will be created if necessary. This is called a *soft reference*.

```
$str = 'pi';
${$str} = 3.1416;
print "pi = $pi\n";                  pi = 3.1416

${'e' . 'e'} = 2.7183;
print "ee = $ee\n";                  ee = 2.7183
```

Such a variable name does not have to be a legal identifier:

```
${' '} = 'space';                    The space variable.
${ } = 'space';                      ILLEGAL now; used to be
                                     same as ${' '}.
${'  '} = 'two space';               The space space variable.
${"\0"} = 'null';                    The null variable.
```

Note that soft references have nothing to do with reference counts (see Item 34). Only ordinary "hard" references increment reference counts. Turning on strict refs disables soft references (see Item 36)—this is often a good idea.

## Item 31:  Create lists of lists with references.

Before the introduction of references, Perl had no support for complex data types. Programmers had to resort to tricks in cases in which they needed to maintain structures like lists of lists. One common means was using strings together with split and join:

*Factorize numbers, very inefficiently.*

```
@factor = ('') x 20;
for ($i = 2; $i < 20; $i++) {
  for ($j = 2; $j < $i; $j++) {
    if ($i % $j == 0) {
      $factor[$i] .= "$j ";          Build up strings like
    }                                 "2 3 4 6".
  }
}

for ($i = 2; $i < 20; $i++) {        12: 2 3 4 6
  print("$i: $factor[$i]\n");        13:
}                                     etc.
```

References give you a way to create lists of lists and other nested structure—one that is *much* more efficient and elegant than repeatedly disassembling and reassembling strings.

Here, for example, are some lists of lists:

```
@a = ( [1, 2], [3, 4] );           An array of refs to arrays.
print $a[1][0];                     Prints 3.

$a = [ [1, 2], [3, 4] ];           A ref to an array of refs to
                                    arrays.
print $a->[1][0];                   Also prints 3.
```

Note that the type of parentheses/brackets you use must match the type of structure you are creating (see Item 32).

You can also create these structures dynamically. Here is the factorization example rewritten to use references:

*Still algorithmically awful, but at least it uses references.*

```
for ($i = 2; $i < 20; $i++) {
  for ($j = 2; $j < $i; $j++) {
    if ($i % $j == 0) {
      push @{$factor[$i]}, $j;      Build up arrays instead of
    }                               strings.
  }
}
```

```
for ($i = 2; $i < 20; $i++) {
  print("$i: @{$factor[$i] || []}\n");
}
```

*Writing || [] inside the array reference avoids warnings under -w.*

In this example, @factor is an array of references to arrays. We do not have to initialize it at all, because it is created automatically by auto-vivification (see Item 30) as we try to add elements to it.

Let's look at this more closely. Assume that @factor is undefined to start with. The very first time we encounter the statement containing the push operator will be when $i is 4 and $j is 2. Perl first tries to access $factor[4]. It's not there, so as usual, Perl creates an array of the requisite size and fills it with undef values. Now, @factor is defined:

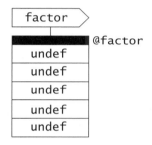

Perl now tries to push the value 2 onto the list @{$factor[4]}. The syntax suggests that $factor[4] should be a reference to an array, and so Perl auto-vivifies an empty anonymous array and puts a reference to it in $factor[4]:

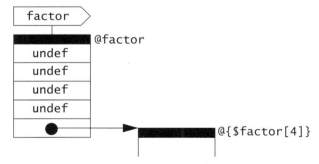

Finally, Perl pushes the value 2 onto the newly created list.

The principles demonstrated in this example can be used to create other structures, like multidimensional arrays and hashes of hashes:

```
$d3[2][2][2] = 5;
$d3[2]->[2]->[2] = 5;
${${$d3[2]}[2]}[2] = 5;
```

*3-d array on the fly.*
*Same, explicit arrows.*
*Ugly canonical syntax.*

| | |
|---|---|
| ```$d3->[2][2][2] = 5;```<br>```${${$d3->[2]}[2]}[2] = 5;```<br>```${${${$d3}[2]}[2]}[2] = 5;``` | *Similar, but starting with a ref. Pretty ugly without the arrows, eh?* |
| ```$course{'CS'}{'101'} =```<br>  ```'Intro to Programming';``` | *A hash of hashes starting with %course.* |

For more ways to create and manipulate nested structures, see Item 35.

## Item 32: Don't confuse anonymous arrays with list literals.

The anonymous array constructor [...] looks very much like the parentheses that surround list literals. They both seem to serve the same purpose—building lists. However, anonymous array constructors differ from list literals in important ways.

### An anonymous array constructor returns a reference, not a list

The purpose of an anonymous array constructor is to allow you to create a reference to an array object without having to create a named array:

| | |
|---|---|
| ```{ my @arr = 0..9; $aref = \@arr }``` | *If you didn't have [...], you might try this.* |
| ```print $$aref[4];``` | *Prints 4.* |
| ```$aref = do { \(my @arr = 0..9) };```<br>```$aref = [0..9];``` | *Or perhaps this.*<br>*But you do have [...]!* |

You can assign the array references created by anonymous array constructors to array variables, but the result is probably not what you want. Be careful to use array variables with lists, and use scalar variables with anonymous array constructors:

▼ Don't confuse (...) and [...].

```
@files = [ glob '*.c' ];              Meant to use parentheses,
                                      perhaps?
print "@files\n";                     Something like ARRAY(0xa4600).

@two_d_array = [                      The outside should be
  [1..3], [4..6], [7..9]             parentheses, not brackets.
];

for $row (@two_d_array) {              Yields the enigmatic:
  print join(',', @$row), "\n";       ARRAY(0xa45d0),ARRAY(0xa4654),
}                                      ARRAY(0xa4558).
```

It's easy to make a similar mistake with hashes and the anonymous hash constructor:

```
%vars = {
    pi => 3.1416,
    ee => 2.7183
}
```
*Whoops—should have used parentheses instead of braces, or $vars instead of %vars.*

## An anonymous array constructor creates a list context, but parentheses don't

List and scalar contexts are created by operators and subroutines. The anonymous array constructor is an operator. Parentheses *aren't*. Just putting parentheses around something will not change a scalar context into a list context.

You can see this for yourself:

*Parentheses do not a list context make.*

```
sub arrayish {
    print "arrayish\n" if wantarray
}

$foo = arrayish();
$foo = (arrayish());
$foo = (arrayish(), ());

$foo = [ arrayish() ];
($foo) = arrayish();
```
*Will print* arrayish *if used in a list context.*

*Nope.*
*Not yet.*
*Dang, it's stubborn.*

arrayish
arrayish

This is part but not all of the problem that results if you mistakenly assign a would-be list literal instead of an anonymous array constructor to a scalar variable. The other part of the problem is that when you dereference the scalar variable, Perl will take whatever weird value wound up in the scalar and dereference it—perhaps interpreting it as a soft reference. Of course, what you are going to get is total nonsense anyway, but these two effects can combine to make the debugging process difficult by treating you to some very strange behaviors up front. For example:

```
$file_list_ref = ( glob '*.c' );

print "@$file_list_ref\n";
print "$file_list_ref\n";
```
*Meant to use [...] instead of parens, probably.*
*Prints nothing?*
*Prints* foo.c *or something.*

With all this in mind, a clever reader should be able to figure out what's going on here:[2]

```
$aref = (1..10);
print $$aref;                          Prints nothing?
print $aref;                           Also prints nothing?
```

## Item 33: Build C-style structs with anonymous hashes.

People often ask me whether Perl has "real data structures, like C." I am forced to answer the same way that I answer questions about lists of lists:

"Well, yes . . . and no."

You already know that there are only a few data types in Perl: scalars, arrays, hashes, subroutines, plus a few odds and ends like filehandles. Structures, like those used in C or Pascal, are not among those types. So in one sense, Perl doesn't have structures. But, on the other hand, hashes provide a very similar effect:

```
$student{'last'} = 'Smith';
$student{'first'} = 'John';
$student{'bday'} = '01/08/72';
```

When referring to an element of a hash, you can omit the quote marks around the key so long as it is a valid Perl identifier:

```
$student{last} = 'Smith';
```

This looks somewhat like an element of a structure, doesn't it? Your first reaction to this might be something like, "Eww, that's using a string to look up a member of a structure! That's horribly inefficient! A real structure would use some kind of numeric offset computed by the compiler." However, this is wishful thinking where Perl is concerned, and you shouldn't let it bother you at all.[3] Perl is an interpreted language. Accessing variables and elements of arrays and hashes is relatively slow no matter what. The time required to look up an element of a hash is of little consequence in the grand scheme of things.

---

2. Stumped? The .. operator does not return a list in a scalar context. Instead, it returns a boolean value, which in this case will be false—an empty string, to be exact. So $aref gets the empty string, and $$aref is a soft reference to the "empty string" variable, ${''}.
3. Perl may eventually optimize certain cases like $foo->{bar} into array accesses, but in most cases this would not provide a dramatic increase in speed.

"Structures" made out of hashes can be passed into subroutines and put to use there:

```
sub student_name {
  my %student = @_;
  "$student{first} $student{last}";
}
print student_name(%student);
```

Now, this may look useful, but it is not particularly efficient. When you pass a hash as an argument, what you are actually doing is unrolling the hash into a list of elements, then reading those elements back into an entirely new hash inside the subroutine. There are also some syntactic limitations. You can't easily pass two hashes this way:

```
sub roommates {
  my %roomie1 = @_;
  my %roomie2 = ????          OOPS—roomie1 ate all the
                              args.
```

So, although hashes are the right general idea, they aren't perfect. What works better is using references to hashes and, in particular, using anonymous hash constructors to create them:

```
$student = {
  last => 'Smith',
  first => 'John',
  bday => '01/08/72'
};
```

You also can create an empty structure and fill it in one piece at a time. Using the arrow syntax to access the members of your "structures" makes things look even more like C or C++:

```
$student = {};
$student->{last} = 'Smith';           Quotes aren't required
$student->{first} = 'John';           around identifiers inside
$student->{bday} = '01/08/72';        braces.
```

Because you are manipulating scalars, not hashes, passing them into subroutines is more efficient, and passing more than one at a time is no problem:

```
sub roommates {
  my ($roomie1, $roomie2) = @_;
  # clever code left as exercise ...
}
roommates($student1, $student2);
```

This technique is the basis for the way that objects are constructed in most Perl classes. For more about object-oriented Perl, see Item 49. For more ways to use anonymous hashes, see Item 27.

## Item 34: Be careful with circular data structures.

Perl uses a reference counting approach[4] to memory management. Each time an object (scalar, array, hash, etc.) acquires a name or a new reference, Perl increments that object's reference count. Whenever an object loses a name or a reference, Perl decrements its reference count. Once an object's reference count reaches zero, Perl deletes the object and reclaims the storage used by it.

Reference counting fails when objects point to one another in a circular or self-referential fashion. A simple $a = \$a will create a cycle, but let's consider the following more interesting example:

```perl
package circular;
sub New {
  shift;                          Ignore package name.
  bless { name => shift };
}

sub DESTROY {
  my $self = shift;
  print "$self->{name}: nuked\n";
}

package main;
{
  my $a = New circular 'a';
  my $b = New circular 'b';

  $a->{next} = $b;
  $b->{next} = $a;
}
print "the end\n";
```

The block inside the main package creates two objects belonging to the class circular, each one containing a reference to the other. The situation looks like this just before the end of the block:

---

4. It is possible that in the future Perl will employ some other sort of memory management strategy, in which case this Item may no longer be relevant. Reference counting is fast and efficient, however, and it may be a while before a compelling replacement comes along.

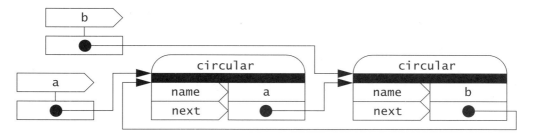

Each object has a reference count of two: one due to the reference from $a/$b and the other due to the reference from the other object. The lexical variables $a and $b go out of scope once the block exits, and then we have the following situation:

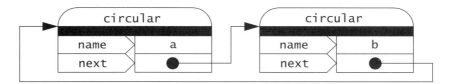

Hmm. We can no longer get at these objects, because neither has a name and we have no external references to either of them. They are just taking up space. Unfortunately, there's nothing Perl can do to help us, because both objects still have a reference count of one. These objects will continue to hang around until the entire program exits. Eventually, these objects *will* be formally destroyed. At the very end of a thread of execution, Perl makes a pass with a "mark-sweep" garbage collector. This final pass will destroy all of the objects created by the interpreter, accessible or otherwise. If you run the example above, you will see the final pass in action:

```
% tryme
the end
b: nuked
a: nuked
```

As you might expect, the objects are destroyed *after* the interpreter executes the last statement in the normal flow of the program.

This final pass is important. Perl can be used as an embedded language. If the interpreter were used repeatedly within the same process to execute code like the above, it would leak memory if there were not a sure-fire means of destroying all the objects created during that thread. There is no way to clean up this mess once you get into it, but you can prevent it by the careful application of brute force. You have to implement a technique for

explicitly breaking the circular references. One solution that would work
in the case above is the following:

```perl
package main;
{
  my $a = New circular 'a';
  my $b = New circular 'b';
  $a->{next} = $b;
  $b->{next} = $a;
  $head = $a;                              A link into the data.
}
undef $head->{next};                       Break the cycle.
undef $head;                               Have to get this one too.
```

Here we save a link into the circular data structure into the variable `$head`.
Because there is only a single cycle in the structure, breaking a single link
is enough to allow Perl to reclaim all the objects in it. If this doesn't seem
thorough enough, you can handle them all yourself:

```perl
while ($head) {                           Explicitly traverse and
  $next = $head->{next};                  clean up.
  undef $head->{next};
  $head = $next;
}
undef $head;                              Every last one.
```

Here we traverse the structure and explicitly destroy every one of the troublesome references. Note that what we are doing is destroying *references*
to the objects we want to delete so that their reference count goes to zero.
There is no way to explicitly destroy an object in Perl regardless of its reference count—if there were, it could be a horrendous source of bugs and
crashes.

Another approach is to do the work in two passes, in a fashion somewhat
like a mark-sweep collector. First, we acquire a list or "catalog" of the references that need to be destroyed:

```perl
$ptr = $head;                            Construct a list of
do {                                     references (to references)
  push @refs, \$head->{next};            in @refs.
  $head = $head->{next};
} while ($ptr != $head);
$ptr = $head = undef;                    Don't leave any lying
                                         around.
```

This loop traverses the self-referential structure and collects a list of references to all the references that need to be destroyed. The next pass just
traverses the list and destroys them:

```
foreach (@refs) {
  print "preemptive strike on $$_\n";
  undef $$_;
}
```

A two-pass approach is extravagant in the case of a simple circular list such as this one, but in the case of a graphlike structure containing many cycles, it may be the only alternative.

## Item 35: Use map and grep to manipulate complex data structures.

Sometimes it's useful to take a "slice" out of a multidimensional array or hash, or to select slices that have certain characteristics. Conversely, you may need to assemble a collection of lists into a 2-D array, or perhaps assemble a collection of 2-D arrays into a 3-D array. Perl's map and grep operators are a perfect choice for chores like these.

### Slicing with map

Let's begin with a program that reads a file containing 3-D coordinates into memory:

● Reading a file of 3-D coordinates into memory

*This program will read a file of 3-D coordinates into memory. Each line of the file will contain the x, y, and z coordinates of a single point, separated by whitespace. For example:*

```
# point data
1 2 3
4 5 6
9 8 7
```

```
open POINTS, "points" or
  die "couldn't read points data: $!\n";
while (<POINTS>) {
  next if /^\s*#.*$/;
  push @xyz, [ split ];
}

foreach $pt (@xyz) {
  print "point ", $i++,
    ": x = $pt->[0], y = $pt->[1], ",
    "z = $pt->[2]\n";
}
```

*Skip comments, then split a line into 3 values, put 'em in an anonymous array, and append it to @xyz.*

*Prints:*
*point 1: x = 1, y = 2, z = 3*
*point 2: x = 4, y = 5, z = 6*
*point 3: x = 9, y = 8, z = 7*

The point data is read into a structure that looks like the following:

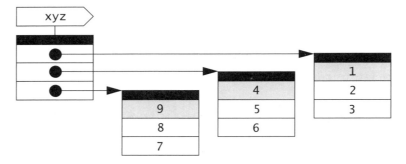

Now, let's suppose you would like to have just the *x* (0th) element from each point, as indicated by the shading in the figure. You could write a loop using an explicit index, or perhaps use a `foreach` loop:

```
for ($i = 0; $i < @xyz; $i++) {
  push @x, $xyz[$i][0];
}
```
*Here's a `for` loop with an explicit index.*

```
foreach (@xyz) {
  push @x, $_->[0];
}
```
*The same general idea, with a `foreach` loop.*

But, really, this is a natural application for `map`:

■ **Use `map` to take slices of complex data structures.**

```
@x = map { $_->[0] } @xyz;
```
*Select the 0th element from each anonymous array in @xyz.*

### Nesting with `map`

On the other hand, suppose that you are starting out with parallel arrays @x, @y, and @z containing vectors of points:

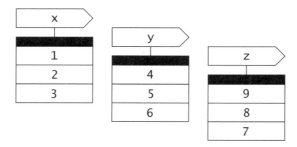

You now would like to assemble them into a single 3-D structure like the one shown earlier. Once again, you could use some sort of explicit looping structure:

```
for ($i = 0; $i < @x; $i++) {          Turn @x, @y, and @z into @xyz, the
   $xyz[$i][0] = $x[$i];               slow and tedious way.
   $xyz[$i][1] = $y[$i];
   $xyz[$i][2] = $z[$i];
}
```

However, `map` provides a much more elegant alternative:

■ **Use [...] inside `map` to create more deeply nested structures.**

```
@xyz = map                             Turn @x, @y, and @z into @xyz,
   { [ $x[$_], $y[$_], $z[$_] ] } 0 .. $#x;   the Perl-ish way.
```

No doubt you can envision a host of variations on the slicing and nesting themes. For example, switching the *x* (0th) and *y* (1st) coordinates:

```
@yxz = map {                           Swap x and y coordinates.
   [ $_->[1], $_->[0], $_->[2] ]
} @xyz;

@yxz = map                             It's prettier using a slice.
   { [ @$_[1, 0, 2] ] } @xyz;
```

Or, perhaps, creating a new list containing the magnitudes of the points:

```
@mag = map { sqrt(                     Compute magnitude of each
   $_->[0] * $_->[0] +                 point in @xyz and put results into
   $_->[1] * $_->[1] +                 a list.
   $_->[2] * $_->[2]
) } @xyz;
```

The Schwartzian Transform (see Item 14) is an application that uses both slicing and nesting operations with `map`:

```
@sorted_by_mtime =
   map { $_->[0] }                     . . . then slice.
   sort { $a->[1] <=> $b->[1] }
   map { [ $_, -M $_ ] }               First, nest . . .
   @files;
```

## Selecting with grep

Suppose that you would like to filter @xyz so that it contains only points whose *y* coordinate is greater than its *x* coordinate.

You could write a loop (how did you guess I was going to say that?):

```
foreach $pt (@xyz) {          Select points with y > x, using a
  if ($pt->[1] > $pt->[0]) {  foreach loop.
    push @y_gt_x, $pt;
  }
}
```

But this time, we have a task that is perfectly suited to grep:

■ **Use grep to select elements from nested structures.**

```
@y_gt_x = grep { $_->[1] > $_->[0] } @xyz;   Select points with y > x.
```

Of course, you can combine map and grep—for example, to gather up the $x$ coordinates of the points with $y$ greater than $x$:

```
@x = map { $_->[0] }                 Select x coordinates for points
  grep { $_->[1] > $_->[0] } @xyz;   with y > x.

@x = map {                           Select x coordinates for points
  $_->[1] > $_->[0] ?                with y > x, another way.
    ($_->[0]) :
    ()
} @xyz;
```

# Debugging

Although Perl is a great language for writing one-liners, it is also well-suited for writing larger programs. Perl programs several hundred lines long are common, and many people have written useful programs several thousand lines long. Greater length generally means greater complexity, and with complexity comes bugs. Debugging Perl programs is somewhat different than debugging programs written in fully compiled languages. Let's look at some of those differences:

- **Perl has a shorter compile-link-run cycle.** Actually it's more like "Run." You do not have to explicitly compile a Perl program before running it. Perl programs *are* compiled, but they are not compiled into machine code,[1] nor is there an explicit link phase.[2] A Perl program is parsed and translated into a structure of opcodes by Perl during its compile phase. The compile phase is immediately followed by a run phase during which the opcodes are actually interpreted.

  One consequence of this shorter cycle is that it is easier to make small changes to Perl programs than to programs written in a fully compiled language like C or C++. For example, you can abort your program, sprinkle a few `print` statements throughout a section of code that you are suspicious of, run the program again, and repeat this cycle as quickly as you can edit your program's source. You don't have to wait for your program to compile and link each time.

- **Perl programs are used in weird environments.** Perl programs are frequently used in environments other than the command line—CGI programming, TCP/IP clients and/or servers, `cron` jobs, and e-mail processing, to name a few. Perl is a great glue language—it's the "duct

---

1. There is a Perl compiler in testing as of this writing, but it does not compile Perl to native machine language.
2. Perl modules written in C or C++ can be dynamically loaded, but this occurs as the Perl program begins executing.

tape of the Internet."[3] You can write these kinds of programs in C or C++, of course, but they are generally much easier to write in Perl.

Debugging programs that don't use standard input and/or standard output, or that run in unusual environments, can be challenging. You can and should test such programs from the command line, but of course programs that work well on the command line always seem to head south when they are actually used in situ.

■ **There's More Than One Way to Do It (TMTOWTDI).** Perl offers you a wide choice of stylistic options. You can write Perl programs that spawn a lot of subprocesses, in the vein of shell scripts, or you can write programs that do the same thing without spawning any. You can write hundreds of lines of Perl without initializing or declaring a single variable, or you can enable static and run-time checks (see Item 36) that require you to declare and initialize *all* variables. You can take advantage of Perl's object-oriented programming features, or not. You can create hierarchical data structures using references (see Item 30), or you can achieve the same effect the old-fashioned way with parallel arrays and a few tricks. You can even write code in C or C++ and hook it up to Perl (see Item 47).

The style of programming you choose will affect your style of debugging. If you let subprocesses do a lot of your work for you, the Perl debugger may not help you as much as when you write everything in Perl. Of course, you also may have less to debug. If you don't bother to turn on warnings, you may write more succinct code, but may have to rely more on finely honed debugging skills.

The art of debugging Perl is as broad and deep as Perl itself. There is no "right" way to debug Perl.

## Item 36:  Enable static and/or run-time checks.

Perl provides for both static and run-time checks for a variety of things. Perl is normally a wide open Big Sky language, seemingly best suited for cowboys who can find their own way, but when you turn on warnings and `strict` pragmas it becomes a much more civilized tool. It can be downright dogmatic at times.

Of the checks that appear below, I especially recommend use `strict` (which includes `strict vars`, `strict subs` and `strict refs`) for general

---

3.  Apparently coined by Hassan Schroeder, a Java webmaster at Sun Microsystems, in *Web Developer* (Vol. 2, No.1, Spring 1996): "God knows, Perl was the duct tape of the Internet." I think Perl still *is* the duct tape of the Internet.

use. Any program that is going to grow to more than 20 lines will probably benefit from use strict.

-w is also a generally useful tool, but it has some annoying limitations at present. I discuss it in more detail below.

One general principle about using the checks that follow: If you plan to use them at all in a program, start using them *from the very beginning*. Retro-fitting use strict and -w to a program can be very difficult, whereas developing from scratch with them turned on is easy.

### Static checks—strict vars and strict subs

Misspellings are an all-too-common source of errors in Perl programs:

```
@temp = <FH>;                          Read lines into @temp.
# ... some intervening code ...
while (@tmp) {                         OOPS—meant to use @temp.
}
```

It's easy to misspell a variable name in a language that does not require you to declare variables before they are used. If you are a cut-and-paste programmer (I confess that this is my most common technique of code reuse), such mistakes are inevitable. Fortunately, you can use the strict vars pragma to catch and prevent such errors. A Perl program that uses strict vars either must declare all of its variables via my or use vars, or use an explicit package name with them:

■ **use strict vars to require declarations.**

| | |
|---|---|
| use strict vars; | *Now have to declare variables.* |
| $x, $y, $z; | *ERROR at compile time.* |
| use strict 'vars'; | vars *is really a string (see below).* |
| my $x;<br>use vars qw($y);<br>$x, $y, $::z; | *Declare $x with* my.<br>*Declare $y with* use vars.<br>*Use explicit main package.* |

The identifier vars following use strict is really a string argument to the strict module's import method (see Item 42). In some cases you may need to quote it—for example, use strict 'vars' or use strict qw(vars)—to avoid warnings or errors; or, if you prefer, you can quote it all the time.

You can turn off `strict vars` for a portion of a program with `no strict vars`:

```
use strict vars;

{
  no strict vars;                    strict vars off for this block.
  $pi = 3.1416;                      $pi OK.
}

print "pi = $::pi\n";                But $pi must be declared or
                                     have explicit package here.
```

There are some cases in which you must declare variables with `use vars` (or `use subs`) rather than `my`:

```
use strict vars;
use vars qw($global1);

BEGIN {
  $global1 = 3.1416;                 my $global2 exists only within
  my $global2 = 2.7183;              this BEGIN block.
}

print "global1 = $global1\n";        OK—declared.
print "global2 = $global2\n";        ERROR—$global2 undeclared.
```

At present, some variables with special uses, like $a and $b, are ignored by `strict vars`. This behavior may change in the future, so don't rely on it.

When identifiers have no other interpretation, Perl treats them as strings (this is sometimes called *poetry mode*[4]). Such "barewords" are another potential source of errors:

```
for ($i = 0; $i < 10; $i++) {
  print $a[i];                       OOPS—meant to say $a[$i].
}
```

In this example, the subscript i, which should have been $i, is interpreted as the string "i", which then appears to be the number 0—thus the contents of $a[0] are printed ten times. Using `strict subs` turns off poetry mode and generates errors for inappropriately used identifiers:

```
use strict subs;                     Or use strict 'subs' — subs is
                                     actually a bareword, which is
                                     what we're trying to avoid.
```

---

4. *Poetry mode?* What's that, you say? Look up "poetry" in *Programming Perl*.

```
for ($i = 0; $i < 10; $i++) {
  print $a[i];                     ERROR—Bareword "i" not
}                                  allowed.
```

The `strict subs` pragma gets along with the sanctioned forms of bareword quoting—alone inside hash key braces, or to the left of an arrow:

```
use strict subs;
$a{name} = 'ok';                   Bareword as hash key is OK.
$a{-name} = 'ok';                  Also OK.
%h = (last => 'Smith',            Bareword left of => is OK.
  first => 'Jon');
```

Both `strict vars` and `strict subs` are easy to get along with. They rarely, if ever, break idiomatic Perl code. All you have to do is declare your variables.

## Dynamic checks—`strict refs`

The `strict refs` pragma disables soft references (see Item 30). Soft references aren't often a source of bugs, but they are a somewhat obscure feature that can be accidently misused. Problems with soft references are usually due to a lack of understanding of the way that ordinary references work. For example, if you are trying to write a data structure to a file and read it back in again, you might misguidedly write the following:

▼ **Avoid unintentionally using soft references.**

---

*The root of the problem in this example is that you can't read references from a file, nor convert string or numeric types to references in general (see Item 30). It manifests itself in a strange way.*

```
$a = { H => 1, He => 2, Li => 3, Be => 4 };   $a is a hash ref.
open SAVE, ">save";
print SAVE $a, "\n";                This writes something like
close SAVE;                         'HASH(0x9d450)' to the file.

open SAVE, "save";
chop($a = <SAVE>);                  Sets $a = 'HASH(0x9d450)'.
print keys %$a;                     Nothing? Of course—no hash
                                    there.
```

---

In this example, what gets written to the file `save` is the single line:

```
HASH(0x9d450)
```

Obviously, the data in the anonymous hash isn't there, so there's no hope of ever getting it back. You will see this quickly once you look at the contents of save. But what you may not understand is why the program "works" without producing an error.

What is happening is that the variable $a is being assigned the string 'HASH(0x9d450)'. When the last line attempts to use $a as a reference to a hash, Perl treats the string as the *name of a variable*. In other words:

```
print keys %{'HASH(0x9d450)'};
```

This is not what you want at all. If you turn on `strict refs`, Perl will catch it at run time:

```
Can't use string ("HASH(0x9d450)") as a HASH ref while "strict
refs" in use at tryme line 12, <SAVE> chunk 1.
```

By the way, an easy way to handle a "persistent" data structure problem like this is to use the `Data::Dumper` module (see Item 37):

■ Use **Data::Dumper** to save and restore data structures.

```
use Data::Dumper;
$a = { H => 1, He => 2, Li => 3, Be => 4 };    Some sample data.
open SAVE, ">save";
print SAVE Data::Dumper->Dump([$a], ['a']);    Dump hash ref with name 'a'.
close SAVE;

$a = undef;                                     Nothing up my sleeve. . . .
do "save";                                      Read and execute file "save".
print keys %$a;                                 "HLiHeBe" or similar.
```

The combination of `strict vars`, `strict subs`, and `strict refs` is available in one convenient unit as `use strict`. I recommend `use strict` for all programs of significant length. Remember that you can temporarily turn off strict-ness that gets in your way by putting `no strict` (or `no strict vars`, `no strict subs`, etc.) in a block:

*Here's a program that prompts for a variable name and dumps its contents to standard output:*

```
use strict;
print "variable name: ";          Prompt for the name.
chop(my $var = <STDIN>);          Read it into $var.
{
  no strict 'refs';               Because $var is a string, $$var
  print "$var = $$var\n";         is a symbolic reference, and we
}                                 have to turn off strict refs.
```

### Dynamic checks—warnings with `-w`

Perl has a warnings feature that can be enabled from the command line with the -w flag:

```
% perl -w myscript
```

or from inside a script by appending the -w flag to the #! line:

```
#!/usr/local/bin/perl -w
```

Turning on warnings enables a *large* number of run-time checks. These cover a vast spectrum of possibilities, from `Possible attempt to put comments in qw() list` to `umask: argument is missing initial 0` to `Misplaced _ in number`.

Most often, though, -w will complain about uses of uninitialized values:

```
#!/usr/local/bin/perl -w
print "$a\n";
```

```
% tryme
Use of uninitialized value at tryme line 2.
```

Code that you wouldn't necessarily expect to produce warnings sometimes does:

```
@a = (1,2);
print "@a[0..2]\n";                        -w complains here.
```

In earlier versions of Perl, -w was very (or excessively) aggressive in reporting uses of uninitialized values. The following produce unitialized value warnings in Perl 5.003:

```
$sum += 1;                                 Warning if $sum uninitialized.

for $word (split) {                        More annoyingly, for every new
  $count{$word} += 1;                      word.
}
```

More recent versions of Perl have a kinder, gentler -w that produces many fewer gratuitous warnings. Neither of the above cases produces a warning under Perl 5.004 (assuming that $sum, $word, etc. have been declared).

You can turn off warnings for a section of code by changing the value of the $^W variable. It is a good idea to make this change `local`:

```
{
  local $^W = 0;                           Warnings off till end of block.
  print "a = $a\n";                        No complaints if $a not yet
}                                          initialized.
```

The biggest drawbacks of the current warnings system in Perl are that (1) *individual* warnings cannot be turned on and off, and (2) there are no lexically scoped warnings (this is the same scoping issue that distinguishes my and local—see Item 23). These are the "annoying limitations" I referred to above. Both of these issues likely will be addressed in future releases of Perl.

I recommend that programmers new to the Perl language, regardless of their experience in other languages, use -w at least long enough that the results are no longer surprising. You should also use -w in combination with use strict when developing code for important applications or for public distribution. Of course, if you are an "all warnings, all the time" sort of programmer, just turn it on and keep it on.

Run-time warnings impose a small speed penalty on programs. In addition, it is not a good idea to present unexpected or spurious warning messages to users. Thus, in general, -w warnings should be used only during development. Warnings should be *turned off* for code that is released to the world, much as assert() tests shouldn't be compiled into final versions of C programs.

The use strict pragma is lightweight and can be left in released code with no ill effects.

## Tracking dangerous data—taint checking

Perl programs that are running setuid (that is, with different real and effective user or group ids) are subject to *taint checking*. You can also enable taint checking explicitly with the -T command line option.

Taint checking is a run-time feature that tracks the flow of data inside a Perl program. Data that is derived from user input or the outside world in general (command line arguments, environment variables, file or streams input) is marked as *tainted*. Perl will not allow tainted data to be used in ways that are insecure—for example, as input to a shell command line. To give you an idea of how taint checking works, let's consider the following simple program:

```
print "enter pattern: ";
chop($pat = <STDIN>);
print `grep $pat *`;
```

If you run this with taint checking enabled, you will see the following message:

```
Insecure dependency in `` while running with -T switch
```

Perl is telling us that the contents of the backticks are insecure. This is because the data in the variable $pat was taken directly from standard input. It is a bad idea to send user input directly to the shell—suppose the user types in:

```
enter pattern: ; rm *
```

To untaint the contents of $pat, we must process the input with a regular expression match and assign $pat the value of one of the memory variables ($1, $2, etc.). This is the only way to untaint data in Perl. Here is one possible fix:

```
print "enter pattern: ";              Prompt for pattern.
chop($pat_in = <STDIN>);              Read it.
$pat_in =~ tr/\0-\037\177-\377//d;    Remove unprintables.
$pat_in =~ s/(['\\])/\$1/g;           Escape quote, backslash.

$pat_in =~ /(.*)/;                    Here's where we untaint by
$pat = $1;                            using pattern memory.

print `grep '$pat' *`;                We've made this safer now—
                                      note the addition of single
                                      quotes to grep's argument.
```

The statements that do the actual untainting are the two lines:

```
$pat_in =~ /(.*)/;
$pat = $1;
```

Note that we could have skipped the `tr///` and `s///` steps above it and still untainted the contents of $pat, without making any changes to them. Yes, even taint checking lets you shoot yourself in the foot. Some tainting problems admit prettier solutions than this one, but the real purpose behind the required untainting step is to force you to at least look at each possible source of tainted input and then deal with it in some way. It's up to you to make sure it's the right way.

Back to our example—if you run it as it now stands, you get a different error message:

```
Insecure $ENV{PATH} while running with -T switch
```

Perl is telling us that our PATH environment variable is insecure. To make our PATH secure, we must set it to a known quantity. Once we set it, Perl also checks to make sure that each of the directories listed in it is writeable only by its owner and/or group.

To fix the program, add the line

```
$ENV{PATH} = "/bin:/usr/bin";
```

somewhere near the top.

Taint checking is valuable for CGI programming applications, especially when CGI scripts must run setuid as a user with more privileges than the user nobody. A conservative way to start off a CGI script is:

■ **Use taint checks and other safety/debugging features in CGI scripts.**

```
#!/usr/local/bin/perl -Tw        Taint checks and warnings on.
use strict;                      Code cleanly.
$ENV{PATH} = "/bin:/usr/bin";    Straight and narrow PATH.
$| = 1;                          Unbuffer STDOUT.
```

Because of taint checking, Perl scripts actually can be more secure than programs written in C.

## Item 37: Use debugging and profiling modules.

In addition to the use strict pragmas mentioned above, there are a variety of modules that are especially helpful in debugging and tuning software. Some of these modules are shipped with the basic distribution of Perl. Others you'll have to get from the CPAN.

### Get verbose messages with diagnostics

Do you think that Perl's warnings and error messages tend to be a little obscure? If so, try using the diagnostics pragma module. The diagnostics module produces verbose output for warnings and errors:

```
use diagnostics;        Turn on blabbermouth mode.
$^W = 1;                Turn on warnings.

print $not_defined;     Uninitialized var warning.
print 1/$not_defined;   Division by zero error.
```

```
% tryme
Use of uninitialized value at tryme line 7 (#1)
    (W) An undefined value was used as if it were already
defined.  It was interpreted as a "" or a 0, but maybe it was a
mistake.  To suppress this warning assign an initial value to
your variables.

Use of uninitialized value at tryme line 8 (#1)

Illegal division by zero at tryme line 8 (#2)
    (F) You tried to divide a number by 0.  Either something
was wrong in your logic, or you need to put a conditional in to
guard against meaningless input.
```

```
Uncaught exception from user code:
        Illegal division by zero at tryme line 8.
```

There you go! More than you ever wanted to know.

Because diagnostics reports errors in a way that is more useful to developers than to end users, it probably should not be turned on in released code, and particularly not in modules.

## Benchmark with Benchmark

Benchmark is an easy-to-use module that allows you to compare the relative speed of pieces of Perl code. As an example, let's use Benchmark to compare the relative speeds of several methods of iterating over an array:

```
use Benchmark;
@a = (1..10000);

timethese (100, {
  for => q{
    my $i;
    my $n = @a;
    for ($i = 0; $i < $n; $i++) { $a[$i]++ }
  },

  foreach => q{
    foreach $a (@a) { $a++ }
  },
} )

% tryme
Benchmark: timing 100 iterations of for, foreach...
      for: 27 secs (27.18 usr  0.00 sys = 27.18 cpu)
  foreach: 11 secs (10.54 usr  0.00 sys = 10.54 cpu)
```

I'm sold on the foreach loop. How about you?

Note the use of q{...} single-quoted strings in the example above. This style of quoting is especially appropriate for strings containing Perl code.

## Dump data with Data::Dumper

Data::Dumper is a versatile module that allows you to dump the contents of one or more variables or data structures as a text stream. This in itself is handy, but the text stream written by Data::Dumper is actually Perl and can be eval-ed to reconstruct the original data.

Data::Dumper readily handles simple constructs:

```
use Data::Dumper;
$a = { H => 1, He => 2, Li => 3, Be => 4 };
print Dumper $a;

% tryme
$VAR1 = {
          H => 1,
          Li => 3,
          He => 2,
          Be => 4
        };
```

You can associate names with data by calling the Dump method:

```
use Data::Dumper;
$a = { H => 1, He => 2, Li => 3, Be => 4 };
$b = { B => 5, C => 6, N => 7, O => 8 };
print Data::Dumper->Dump([$a, $b], [qw(a b)]);

$a = {
       H => 1,
       Li => 3,
       He => 2,
       Be => 4
     };
$b = {
       B => 5,
       C => 6,
       N => 7,
       O => 8
     };
```

Data::Dumper can also handle self-referential structures:

```
use Data::Dumper;
$c = { name => "C" };
$b = { name => "B", next => $c };
$a = { name => "A", next => $b };
$c->{next} = $a;
print Data::Dumper->Dump([$a, $b, $c], [qw(a b c)]);

% tryme
$a = {
       name => 'A',
       next => {
                 name => 'B',
                 next => {
                           name => 'C',
                           next => $a
                         }
```

```
              }
        };
    $b = $a->{next};
    $c = $a->{next}{next};
```

Data::Dumper has many other capabilities and a lengthy man page that describes them. Be sure to check it out.

### Dump in detail with Devel::Peek

If the output from Data::Dumper isn't giving you the kind of detail you want, Devel::Peek should satisfy your curiosity. Devel::Peek dumps the contents of variables or data structures in a low-level format that is most appropriate for developers working on Perl XSUBs (see Item 47) and programs that call Perl.

Here's Devel::Peek operating on a simple scalar:

```
use Devel::Peek qw(Dump);
$a = 1234;
Dump $a;
```

```
% tryme
SV = IV(0xa6460)
  REFCNT = 1
  FLAGS = (IOK,pIOK)
  IV = 1234
```

Decoded, this gobbledygook says that the value is an SV (scalar value) of the IV (integer value) type, with a reference count of one, and a valid (IOK) integer value of 1234. Suppose that we also use $a as a string:

```
use Devel::Peek qw(Dump);
$a = 1234;
"$a";
Dump $a;
```

```
% tryme
SV = PVIV(0xa5108)
  REFCNT = 1
  FLAGS = (IOK,POK,pIOK,pPOK)
  IV = 1234
  PV = 0xff528 "1234"
  CUR = 4
  LEN = 11
```

Now, $a has both integer (IV) and string (PV) values. As a final example, consider a "magic" variable like $!:

```
use Devel::Peek qw(Dump);
open F, "bogus-file";
Dump $!;
$a = $!;
Dump $a;
```

This gives us:

```
SV = PVMG(0xa5ec8)
  REFCNT = 1
  FLAGS = (GMG,SMG)
  IV = 0
  NV = 0
  PV = 0
  MAGIC = 0xa5188
SV = PVMG(0xa5d48)
  REFCNT = 1
  FLAGS = (NOK,POK,pNOK,pPOK)
  IV = 0
  NV = 2
  PV = 0xb6148 "No such file or directory"
  CUR = 25
  LEN = 26
```

The first variable dumped is $!, which uses a larger "magic" structure. Magic variables can get their values via functions—the MAGIC field shows the value of the function pointer.

The second variable is $a, which you will notice contains both string (PV) and floating-point (NV) values. Both were set when $a was assigned the value of $!. Note also that although $a also winds up with the larger PVMG structure, it isn't itself magic, because none of the magic flags are set.

## Profile with Devel::DProf

To profile a Perl program as it runs, use Devel::DProf.

Assuming that DProf is installed on your system, you apply it to your program by using the -d option on the command line:

```
% perl -d:DProf my_script
```

When the script has completed running, a file named tmon.out, containing raw profiling data, will be left in the current directory. The dprofpp program (installed as part of the DProf distribution) can be used to analyze this data.

Here is some sample profiling output from dprofpp:

```
% dprofpp
Total Elapsed Time =  103.31 Seconds
```

```
     User+System Time =    70.35 Seconds
   Exclusive Times
   %Time Seconds    #Calls sec/call Name
    55.9   39.39       376   0.1048 News::NNTPClient::fetch
    10.2    7.190       62   0.1160 main::decode_uu
     3.92   2.760       70   0.0394 main::save_data
     3.71   2.610       13   0.2008 MIME::Base64::decode_base64
     1.35   0.950      379   0.0025 News::NNTPClient::response
     1.01   0.710      378   0.0019 News::NNTPClient::cmd
     0.87   0.610       13   0.0469 main::decode_mime_multi
     0.44   0.310      378   0.0008 News::NNTPClient::command
     0.34   0.240      379   0.0006 News::NNTPClient::returnval
     0.27   0.190      259   0.0007 News::NNTPClient::head
     0.23   0.160      516   0.0003 main::CODE(0xa6a78)
     0.21   0.150      516   0.0003 main::CODE(0x130ac0)
     0.21   0.150      516   0.0003 main::CODE(0x1f748c)
     0.20   0.140      129   0.0011 main::skip_article
     0.20   0.140      379   0.0004 News::NNTPClient::okprint
```

The `dprofpp` program can produce many other types of output—take a look at the man page for more information.

## Item 38: Learn to use a debugging version of Perl.

You don't actually need a debugging version of Perl to debug Perl programs. However, it's fun to have one to play with, and it's also instructive to build one so that you can see how to install more than one copy of Perl on your system. You *will* need a debugging version of Perl if you plan to write XS modules (see Item 47) or call Perl from another program.

### Building a debugging version of Perl

If the -D command line option on your installed version of Perl doesn't work, you need to build a debugging version of Perl for your private use. If the -D option *does* work, you may want to ask your system administrator why Perl was installed that way, because debugging support slows Perl down somewhat.

To build a debugging version of Perl, you first need to acquire and unpack a copy of the Perl distribution that you want to install. This could be either an official "released" version or a recent development version. Both should be available through the CPAN. Configure it by running ./Configure in the top level directory of the source. You will need to provide answers that are slightly different than usual to some of the questions:

- Decide where you are going to install the Perl tree, then respond appropriately to the question:

```
Installation prefix to use? (~name ok) [/usr/local]
```

For example, if you want the Perl tree installed in /home/joseph/perl, respond with /home/joseph/perl here.

You should *not* install the debugging version of Perl in the same location as your regular copy, because the regular copy would then be overwritten. Install the debugging version in a completely separate location so that *none* of the debugging Perl tree overlaps the existing tree.

■ The next question to watch for is:

```
What optimizer/debugger flag should be used? [-0]
```

You want to *disable* compiler optimization and *enable* debugging symbols. In most cases, this means responding to this question with the single flag -g; however, the answer will depend on the C compiler that you are using. Do not mix -O with -g—source code debuggers do not generally work well with optimized code.

■ Then you will see something like:

```
Any additional cc flags? [-DDEBUGGING -I/usr/local/include]
```

Be sure to answer this question with -DDEBUGGING—this option enables Perl's -D command line option. (Configure normally suggests -DDEBUGGING if you specified the -g compiler flag.) It should appear by default if you answered the optimizer flag question with -g. You should probably also add -DDEBUGGING_MSTATS, which turns on memory usage statistics gathering if you are using Perl's built-in malloc(). If Configure suggests other flags here, leave them in.

■ If you have enabled -DDEBUGGING_MSTATS, watch for the question:

```
Do you wish to attempt to use the malloc that comes with
perl5? [y]
```

and be sure to answer it with y (yes). Perl's malloc() is very fast and should work on most systems. However, if it does not work on your system, you will have to go through the Configure ritual again, avoid the -DDEBUGGING_MSTATS flag, and answer n to this question.

After running Configure, you should run make and then make test. If the tests are successful ("skipped" is okay, but "failed" indicates a problem), you can then do a make install.

If you have installed a development version of Perl, you will probably want to update it with a newer development version from time to time. If you want to avoid being grilled by Configure each time you do this, just copy the previous config.sh file into the new source directory and edit it to update all of the release-specific answers. For example, if you are going from subversion 17 to subversion 19, this would mean searching for the string 17 in `config.sh` and replacing it with 19 wherever it is used as part of a version number. Do this manually, because numbers are used in other places in `config.sh`. You can then run `./Configure -d` and save yourself a lot of typing.

## Using a debugging version of Perl

A properly built debugging version of Perl will support both Perl's `-D` command line option and source code debugging via a debugger like `gdb`.

We won't discuss source code debugging here, although it will come in handy if you are linking other code, such as an XSUB (see Item 47), into Perl.

Perl's `-D` command line option is handy for peeking "under the hood" to examine the execution of a Perl program. You use it by appending a variety of debugging options to the `-D` option, either one or more letters like `x` (syntax tree) or `s` (stack snapshots), or a decimal number indicating which debugging bits to set (see the man pages for the list).

Here, for example, is some output from the `-Dx` command line option corresponding to the statement `$x += 1`:

```
9        TYPE = add  ===> 10
         TARG = 1
         FLAGS = (SCALAR,KIDS,STACKED)
         {
             TYPE = null  ===> (8)
               (was rv2sv)
             FLAGS = (SCALAR,KIDS,REF,MOD)
             {
7                TYPE = gvsv  ===> 8
                 FLAGS = (SCALAR)
                 GV = main::x
             }
         }
         {
8            TYPE = const  ===> 9
             FLAGS = (SCALAR)
             SV = IV(1)
         }
```

It's verbose and somewhat obscure at first glance, but what's happening here is that Perl's internal compiler has constructed four nodes representing the operations inside the expression. These "ops" are an executable representation of Perl code.

The ops are numbered. The numbers indicate the actual execution order of the ops. The first op to be executed here is 7 (gvsv), which fetches a reference to the contents of $main::x and pushes it on the stack. The next one is 8 (const), which pushes the constant 1 on the stack. The next one is 9 (add), which adds the two values on the stack. The STACKED flag indicates that the result goes into the left-hand argument, that is, the second value on the stack.

The null op is a result of Perl's peephole optimizer, which combines and/or removes nodes as it traverses the initial output of the compiler.

With a different set of options, you can see a program run. Here is a sample program and some of the output generated from the –Dtls option:

```
#!/usr/local/bin/perl –Dtls
$x = 10;
$x += 1;
```

```
% tryme
```

```
EXECUTING...

    =>
(tryme:0)      enter
Entering block 0, type BLOCK
    =>
(tryme:0)      nextstate
    =>
(tryme:5)      const(IV(10))
    => IV(10)
(tryme:5)      gvsv(main::x)
    => IV(10)  UNDEF
(tryme:5)      sassign
    => IV(10)
(tryme:5)      nextstate
    =>
(tryme:6)      gvsv(main::x)
    => IV(10)
(tryme:6)      const(IV(1))
    => IV(10)  IV(1)
(tryme:6)      add
    => PVNV(11)
(tryme:6)      leave
Leaving block 0, type BLOCK
```

The enter and leave ops indicate entry and exit of scopes at the boundaries of the program. Each Perl statement is set off by a nextstate op, which discards temporaries accumulated during the evaluation of the preceding statement and does some other bookkeeping. The other ops access variables and constants and perform arithmetic and assignments on them.

The -Dtls trace above includes running stack snapshots (the values to the right of the arrows). Notice that there are two values, 10 and 1, on the stack before the add op, and that the sum, 11, is placed there after the add executes. Note, also, that the result is a floating-point value (PVNV rather than IV). Using the integer module would force integer addition. Now that I brought it up, want to see integer addition at work?

Because the debugging options tend to produce large quantities of output, and because debugging logs are most useful when applied to small sections of code, generally you will find yourself turning debugging on and off dynamically by using the $^D special variable. Starting with debugging off is a good idea in the following example. Note that $^D requires an integer argument rather than a string—it's a little less user-friendly than the -D command line option:

*Presuming we are starting with debugging off (no -D) to avoid a whole pile of output at startup, then:*

```
use integer;                    Force integer arithmetic.
$^D = 14;                       Turn on debugging (14 = bits for
                                tls).

$x = 10;                        See integer arithmetic at work.
$x += 1;
```

## Item 39:  Test things by using the debugger as a Perl "shell."

The Perl debugger is, naturally, a handy tool for debugging Perl programs. But it is useful also for testing things out or for just fooling around. To enter the debugger, you need to supply a program. The program "0" will suffice:

```
% perl -d -e 0
Stack dump during die enabled outside of evals.

Loading DB routines from perl5db.pl patch level 0.94
Emacs support available.

Enter h or `h h' for help.

main::(-e:1):   0
  DB<1>
```

Once you're inside the debugger, your main tool for the purposes of "just testing things" will be the x command, which executes code in a list context and dumps the result in a structured way. You can also use the "Perl" command—any command that isn't recognized as a debugger command will be executed as a line of Perl. So, how does this work? Let's suppose you're curious about some bit of Perl trivia, such as whether your version of Perl allows you to delete hash slices. You start up the debugger, then type something like:

```
DB<1> %x = ( a => 1, b => 2, c => 3, d => 4 )

DB<2> x delete @x{ 'a', 'b' }
```

If you're running an older version of Perl, you'll see:

```
delete argument is not a HASH element at (eval 6) line 2, <IN>
chunk 2.
```

Oh, well. But in a newer version, you'll see:

```
DB<2> x delete @x{ 'a', 'b' }
0  1
1  2
```

The response is the return value of delete, which is a list of the deleted values.

You can examine the contents of the hash with x, but just using the direct approach won't yield a pretty result:

```
DB<3> x %x
0  'c'
1  3
2  'd'
3  4
```

The result is the hash unwound into a list, which doesn't read very well. What you actually need is:

```
DB<4> x \%x                        Print reference to %x instead.
0  HASH(0x1153b0)
   'c' => 3
   'd' => 4
```

The debugger dumps hash references in a more understandable format, as you can see.

Another useful tool inside the debugger is the otherwise little-used Perl do operator. When applied to a string, do treats the string as a filename and `eval`s the contents of that file in the current context. This provides a pleasant alternative to typing or pasting snippets of code over and over again:

*Suppose this is in the file* `tryme`:

```
@x{'A'..'J'} = 0..9;
```
*Create a table of characters and some associated numbers.*

*Now, feed it to the debugger:*

```
DB<10> do 'tryme'

    DB<11> x \%x
0   HASH(0x106c50)
    'A' => 0
    'B' => 1
    'C' => 2
    'D' => 3
    'E' => 4
    'F' => 5
    'G' => 6
    'H' => 7
    'I' => 8
    'J' => 9
```

(Hmm . . . I think we've hit a resonance in Perl's hash algorithm!)

Are you not sure exactly what variables a particular hunk of code defines? Execute it in a different package:

```
    DB<17> package foo; do 'tryme'
```

Then take a look at its symbol table:

```
    DB<18> x \%foo::
0   HASH(0x28f8bc)
    'x' => *foo::x
```

If you want to see the contents of the variables in a package, rather than just their names, use the V command:

```
    DB<19> V foo
%x = (
    'A' => 0
    'B' => 1
    'C' => 2
    'D' => 3
    'E' => 4
    'F' => 5
    'G' => 6
```

```
'H' => 7
'I' => 8
'J' => 9
```

The V command and the X command (like V but for the current package) also can be used to dump individual variables, but I think it's simpler to use x for everything, because it works for arbitrary expressions. You, of course, may use whichever you prefer. Let your imagination run wild. Perhaps you will not use the debugger to debug code. In fact, I generally don't use it—I'm an atavistic user of print statements myself. But regardless of whether you do your debugging with the debugger, keep its other uses in mind.

## Item 40:  Don't debug too much at once.

The most fundamental problem I see with students trying to fix misbehaving Perl code is one that has nothing to do with Perl at all. That problem is a lack of debugging strategy. Good debuggers (as in, programmers who are good debuggers) are made, not born. Some people seem to have a particular knack for debugging, but more often than not they are "coincidentally" very experienced programmers who learned to program in adverse environments. I've personally performed a number of feats of debugging wizardry in my time, including debugging by telephone programs I didn't write and had never seen before. There is nothing magical about this, though. I just happen to know what I am doing, just as other good debuggers do.

Good debuggers have a good debugging strategy. Such a strategy is independent of language. A good debugging strategy is something that Perl programmers can make use of just as much as programmers in other languages can. Here are three rules that should point you in the right direction. They aren't a perfect or complete strategy, but if you follow them thoughtfully, you should find that debugging Perl isn't that formidable a chore after all.

### Test your code as often as possible

Another way of saying this is: *Write a little bit at a time*.

If you are new to Perl, or are trying out features that you aren't sure of, don't type a 300-line program into your text editor and then try running it for the first time. It won't run, you will get screens full of bewildering error messages, and you will never make any meaningful progress toward getting it to work. Instead, find a way to write your program a little piece at a time.

What an appropriately sized piece of code is depends on your skill level, your familiarity with the task and the language, and how hard it is to run the program while work is "in progress."

Anecdote: I once spent several days rewriting a C++ collection class library from templates into macros (this is reverse progress, I know). The library formed the innards of a 25,000-line program, and there was no way to test it until I was done. Unbelievably, it worked *the first time* I was finally able to compile it and "flip the switch," and my hundreds of lines of mostly manual changes didn't introduce any bugs! In shock, I took the rest of the day off. In the real world, though, this almost never happens. A few hours of work usually means a few new bugs.

Perl is different from compiled languages like C and C++ in that there is no compile-link-run cycle to slow your testing down. If you are making incremental changes to a program, you should try running and testing it as often as possible. Because a Perl program generally starts running faster than you can type the command that starts it, there is very little cost to incremental testing. I usually try running a program every few minutes as I am writing it, and I try to write it in such a way that it will be at least partially functional throughout its development.

Even if you can't add small increments of functionality to your program, you can try testing small pieces of the code that you're adding. Use the Perl debugger to try out snippets (see Item 39) or write and run small programs that verify your new additions. It's a whole lot easier to put together a bunch of working parts than it is to fix a big broken mess.

## Find out where and why your program is failing

This may seem incredibly obvious, but you cannot hope to begin debugging a program of significant length without knowing exactly where it is failing. Perl helps you out by printing out the line number and filename of the file where a fatal run-time error occurred. However, the error that causes Perl to hiccup isn't necessarily the error that you are looking for. Consider a program containing code like the following:

*A program to read a hash of configuration values from a text file.*

```
open F, $config_file;
while (<F>) {                    Read a line.
  ($k, $v) = split;              Split out key and value.
  $config{$k} = $v;              Save them in hash %config.
}
```

*Then, farther down:*

```
$x_real =
  $x / $config{X_SCALE};
```
                                                    *Divide by zero error?*

This code could very well die with a divide-by-zero error at the line indicated, but the real problem is that the code lacks some important sanity checks. For one, the return status of the open at the top of the example is ignored. If $config_file does not exist, %config will contain nothing, and all of its values will appear to be undef. A proper open would look more like:

```
open F, $config_file or
  die "couldn't open $config_file: $!"
```

It would also be wise to verify the validity of the data read:

```
die "X_SCALE must be specified" unless exists $config{X_SCALE};
die "X_SCALE must be nonzero" unless $config{X_SCALE};
```

Bugs can be much stranger than this. I once saw a program that had something like the following in it:

```
use FileHandle;

sub file_func {
  my $fh = shift;
  # some stuff using $fh here ...
  return *fh;
}

open FH, "somefile.txt" or
  die "couldn't open: $!";

my $fh = file_func(\*FH);
```
                                        *At this point,* $fh *doesn't work—*
                                        *what happened?*

This program was written by someone who was trying to tackle my, type-globs, and references all at once, and who apparently broke the "test your code as often as possible" rule. His code was actually much more involved than this somewhat purified example, and the problems with it were not obvious at first.

When I got hold of the code, the first thing I noticed were the two type-globs. Passing filehandles by globref (\*FH) is sanctioned (see Item 26), but returning a typeglob is unusual. The interior of file_func was working properly—you can use filehandle globrefs just like filehandles—but the return value of file_func was apparently not a valid filehandle. Hmm. Well, in looking at the code I couldn't tell offhand exactly what sort of value it might be. I resorted to Data::Dumper and found that the value returned from `file_func` was indeed a globref to a variable named `$fh`, but `$fh` was undefined. The code obviously wasn't right but what I was seeing still didn't make any sense. After a bit of reflection it occurred to me that the `*fh` glob was referring to the global variable `$fh`, not the `my $fh` inside `file_func`. (Remember that `my` variables don't appear in the symbol table? Item 23—it's easy to forget.) Perl is tolerant of all kinds of abuses of type-globs, so there was never a run-time error that had anything to do with the actual problem.

I patched things up with the suggestion that the programmer change the `return *fh` to `return $fh`, but consider other ways of writing the program—perhaps using `FileHandle`.

## Never take anything for granted

Every once in a while a bug comes along that takes an unusually long time to exterminate. If you've been around a while you are probably familiar with the type. You may be used to finding and fixing most bugs in minutes and almost all the rest in an hour or two, but once in a blue moon you encounter a bug that is just *resistant*. These are the kinds that take hours, or even days, to fix. Often, you can't even figure out what's going wrong or where the source of the error is. For experienced programmers, most such bugs are the result of a basic human failing that has little to do with programming: *overlooking the obvious*.

I can't provide a list of "obvious" things that you shouldn't overlook, but I can provide a couple of embarrassing examples to illustrate what I'm talking about. Not that long ago, I was trying out some snippets of Perl in the debugger. I was using several different versions of Perl and, in one of them, I pasted something like:

```
%x = { foo => 1, bar => 2, baz => 3 };
```

It accepted the code without comment. I pasted the same code into the debugger in a later (development) version of Perl, and it emitted a page of gobbledygook that started out with "`Odd number of elements in hash list at (eval 3) line 2`". The page of gobbledygook struck me as a debugger problem, because most of it was nonsensical. I became fixated on this and spun my wheels for a while. It took me about an hour to notice that in addition to the debugger problem, which was real, I had also substituted braces for parentheses—which was what the very first line of the error message was telling me in a roundabout way. I should have written:

```
%x = ( foo => 1, bar => 2, baz => 3 );
```

Another more clear-cut case of overlooking the obvious comes to mind. I was trying to fix a bug in some page-layout routines in a large C++ application (the one mentioned in the Preface). It had taken me a long time to pin down the source of the bug and a while longer still to concoct a fix. I began to code the fix. When I was partially done, I did a test compile, ran the program, and noticed that I was making progress. With a sense of relief, I got up from my desk and wandered off to get a soda and take a break. When I returned, I coded some more of the fix, did another test compile, and ran the program again. Now, suddenly, the program was broken. In fact, the changes I had made earlier, before getting up, didn't seem to be there.

I went back to the source code, which was already open in another window. My changes were still visible in the editor. Very strange. I wondered if the second set of changes I had made were causing a failure with symptoms like those of the original bug. I began to sprinkle all kinds of debugging statements and sanity checks throughout the source code. They didn't seem to have any effect. In fact, they didn't even seem to be showing up in the compiled program!

Around this time, I began to have fanciful thoughts about corrupted filesystems, broken NFS servers, and whatnot. Something totally weird was happening that was preventing the changes I was saving and compiling from being realized in the executable.

After about three hours of wild speculation and increasing wonderment, I found the problem. The version of the program I was running wasn't the one I was editing and compiling. For some reason, after I had come back from my break, I had started typing my make and run commands into a shell window that had a different PATH environment than what I was used to. I had changed it in that window earlier in the day and had forgotten about it. The changes I was making were being compiled into an executable, but I wasn't running that executable!

*Don't overlook the obvious.*

# Using Packages and Modules

## Item 41: Don't reinvent the wheel—use Perl modules.

*Modules* are Perl's "Software ICs." Perl modules provide a versatile, clean means of adding functionality to Perl. At their simplest, modules define ordinary functions that can be used in Perl programs. They also can add objects and methods (see Item 49). Modules can be written entirely in Perl, as is usually the case, or they can be written with a mixture of C or C++ and Perl (see Item 47). Modules also can be written to modify the behavior of Perl's compile- or run-time phase itself, as with pragma modules like `strict` (see Item 36).

There are many, many different modules available to Perl programmers. A wide variety of common programming chores have been encapsulated in freely distributed modules available from the Comprehensive Perl Archive Network (CPAN). What's available includes e-mail, netnews, FTP, and World Wide Web (WWW) utilities; graphical and character user interface tools; Perl language extensions; and database, text-processing, mathematical, and image-processing utilities. The list goes on from there—and for quite a while!

### Getting modules from the CPAN

The CPAN is a replicated archive, mirrored on many different FTP and WWW servers worldwide. One way to get modules from the CPAN is to download and install them yourself. If you know of a CPAN site "near" you (meaning one to which you have good connectivity), you can retrieve files directly from that site via FTP. On the other hand, if you don't know where to find a CPAN site, you can use the CPAN multiplexer at `www.perl.com` to find one for you. Just access the following URL from your favorite web browser:

```
http://www.perl.com/CPAN/
```

A site will be automatically selected for you. If you omit the trailing slash, you will be presented with a list of sites to choose from. Another way to get modules from the CPAN is to use the CPAN module. The CPAN module is part of the Perl distribution as of version 5.004 and can be installed for earlier versions of the language. If you have the CPAN module installed, you can use it interactively by typing the following at a command line:

```
% perl -MCPAN -e shell
```

If this is the first time you have used the module, you will be asked a number of configuration questions. The default answers will be fine for most of them. Toward the end, you will be asked for the URL of your preferred CPAN site. You would ordinarily answer with something like:

```
We need to know the URL of your favorite CPAN site.
Please enter it here: ftp://your.site.here.com/pub/perl/CPAN/
```

If you are lucky enough to have a CPAN mirror on your own machine (not all that hard to set up, really, but beyond the scope of this book), you can use a file URL:

```
Please enter it here: file:///home/joseph/CPAN/
```

Now you will enter the interactive mode of the CPAN module. Here you can list and explore the modules that are available. You can also download, build, and install them. For example, to build and install a new version of the CPAN module, and assuming that you have the correct permissions, just type:

```
cpan> install CPAN
Running make
CPAN-1.28/
CPAN-1.28/lib/
... etc.
```

You can even restart the new version without exiting:

```
cpan> reload CPAN
Subroutine AUTOLOAD redefined at (eval 8) line 61, <GEN8> chunk
1.
Value of $term will not stay shared at (eval 8) line 92, <GEN8>
chunk 1.
... blah blah blah ...
```

## Installing Perl modules

If you are running an older version of Perl and don't have the CPAN module installed, or if you want to install a module that is not part of the CPAN (e.g., one that you are writing yourself), you need to make and install the module manually. Fortunately, the procedure is straightforward.

The module should be supplied in a tar-ed, compressed archive. It should have a name that looks something like `File-Magic-1.03.tar.Z`—if it doesn't, it may have been created without using h2xs and MakeMaker (see Item 45), and all bets as to how to install it are off. Fortunately, although "funky" modules were commonplace in the early days of Perl 5, they are rare now.

There is no `File::Magic` module (not that I'm aware of, anyway), so the example below is for illustration only. Replace `File-Magic` with the name of the module you actually want to install. Also, the output you see while building and installing a module may be somewhat different than what follows.

**Note:** If you follow the steps below, you will install a module *into your existing Perl installation*. If you do not want to do that, or do not have the necessary permissions, see later in this Item for ways to install and use a module in a different directory.

The first step is to uncompress and un-tar the package. Depending on your version of Unix, you will do something like this:

```
% uncompress File-Magic-1.03.tar.Z
% tar xvf File-Magic-1.03.tar
File-Magic-1.03/
File-Magic-1.03/Makefile.PL
File-Magic-1.03/Changes
File-Magic-1.03/test.pl
File-Magic-1.03/Magic.pm
File-Magic-1.03/MANIFEST
```

Next, cd to the newly created directory and create the module's makefile:

```
% cd File-Magic-1.03
% perl Makefile.PL
Checking if your kit is complete...
Looks good
Writing Makefile for File::Magic
```

You can now make and test the module:

```
% make
cp Magic.pm ./blib/lib/File/Magic.pm
Manifying ./blib/man3/File::Magic.3
% make test
PERL_DL_NONLAZY=1 /usr/local/bin/perl -I./blib/arch
-I./blib/lib -I/usr/local/lib/perl5/sun4-solaris/5.004
-I/usr/local/lib/perl5 test.pl
1..2
ok 1
ok 2
```

If everything went smoothly, go ahead and install the module:

```
% make install
Installing /usr/local/lib/perl5/site_perl/./File/Magic.pm
... etc.
```

For more about using Perl modules, see Item 42.

### Installing Perl modules in private or alternative directories

If you aren't the official Perl administrator on your system, or if you don't want to install a new version module into the main distribution without trying it out first, you will have to install new modules into a different directory than the default. There are several ways to install a module into a nonstandard place, but we will discuss only the one that is most straightforward: the LIB variable.

To change the place where a module is installed, you need to modify the makefile that installs it. The way you do this is by setting the value of the LIB variable when you run the Makefile.PL script. For example, say you want to cause the module to be installed in /home/joseph/perllib:

```
% perl Makefile.PL LIB=/home/joseph/perllib
```

Now, when you make, test, and install the module, it will wind up in /home/joseph/perllib rather than in the Perl tree.

To use a module installed in a nonstandard place, you will generally need to modify the module include path, @INC. The best way to do this is with the use lib pragma:

```
use lib '/home/joseph/perllib';          Add this directory to the include
                                          path.

use File::Magic qw(WaveWand);            Now we can get to File::Magic.
WaveWand glob "*.h";
```

For more about the module include path, see Item 43.

## Item 42: Understand packages and modules.

Perl modules are really a specialized form of Perl *packages*. In this Item we will discuss packages, then the specializations that make a package a module.

## Packages

A Perl package is a namespace. It's that simple. Whether or not you are familiar with packages, if you have written a Perl program, you have already used at least one: the `main` package. By default, all variables created in a Perl program are part of the `main` package.

To refer to a variable in another package, prefix its name with the package name, followed by two colons (called a "qualified name"). Two colons without any package name is shorthand for the `main` package:

```
$a = 'Testing';                         Assign to $a, a.k.a. $main::a.
print "main::a = $main::a\n";           main::a = Testing

$foo::a = 'one two three';              Assign to $foo::a.
print "$main::a $foo::a\n";             Testing one two three
print "$::a $foo::a\n";                 Testing one two three
```

The `package` directive changes the current default package. It remains effective until the end of the current block or file:

*Continued from above:*

```
{                                       Begin a new scope.
  package foo;                          foo is now the default package.

  $a = 'four five six';                 Assign to $a, a.k.a. $foo::a.
  print "$::a $a\n";                    Testing four five six
}

print "$a $foo::a\n";                   Testing four five six, since $a
                                        now means $main::a again.
```

Packages can be nested. For example, `$foo::bar::bletch` is a variable named `bletch` nested inside a package named `bar` inside a package named `foo`. However, qualified names always must appear in full—you cannot use `$bar::bletch` to refer to the above variable `bletch` even if the default package is `foo`.

Packages are implemented as symbol tables, which are just ordinary Perl hashes with a special purpose (see Item 55). The name of a package symbol table is the package name followed by two colons, for example `%foo::` and `%::` (the `main` package's symbol table). Although occasions when you should directly manipulate symbol tables are rare, you can, for example, import names from one package into another:

```
package foo;
($a, $b, $c, $d) =
  qw(testing one two three);
sub Bar { 3 };

package main;
@::{qw(a b c Bar)} =
  @foo::{qw(a b c Bar)};
print "$a $b $c ", Bar(), "\n";
```

*Define some variables in*
*package* foo.

*Define subroutine* $foo::Bar.

*Import* a, b, c *and* Bar *from* foo.

testing one two 3

A possibly unexpected side effect of this kind of manipulation is that it aliases variables in one package to another. In the example above, $main::a and $foo::a now refer to the same thing:

*Continued from above:*

```
$foo::a = 'TESTING';
```

*Change value of* $foo::a.

```
print "$a $b $c ", Bar(), "\n";
```

TESTING one two three—
$main::a *is aliased to* $foo::a.

You can see more of this type of Perl "magic" in Item 55. Remember that my variables are never in *any* package (see Item 23).

## Modules

A Perl module is a package that meets certain requirements. To be a Perl module, a package must:

- be contained in a separate file whose name ends in .pm ("Perl module"),[1]

- define an import method—usually done by subclassing the Exporter module,[2] and

- define a (possibly empty) list of symbols that are automatically exported, as well as a (possibly empty) list of symbols that can be exported on request.[3]

The purpose of a module is to implement reusable, modular functionality. Generally, modules define subroutines and/or Perl classes (see Item 49). Modules can also define variables (scalars, arrays, etc.). They can perform

---

1. Old-style "Perl libraries" were contained in files ending in .pl. You may see these used in older code from time to time. There is no reason to write or use this type of library any more, except when necessary to maintain existing software.
2. Why does the Exporter class import things? Hmm. This is another one of those Perl enigmas that it is better not to contemplate deeply.
3. This is a convention, not a requirement. But it is rarely broken.

actions at startup and can even alter language syntax or semantics (see Item 37).

Modules are generally stored in a library directory that is accessible via Perl's default include path (see Item 43). Exactly what that location is will vary depending upon your installation, but a typical location would be something like `/usr/local/lib/perl5/`.

Modules can be nested. Nested modules are stored in a nested directory/file structure. For example, given an installation whose libraries are stored in `/usr/local/lib/perl5/`, the `File::Basename` module will most likely be found in `/usr/local/lib/perl5/File/Basename.pm`.

## Using modules

It's easy to put a module to work for you. Just "use" the module—with Perl's use directive. The use directive loads a module and imports the subroutines and other symbols that are exported from that module by default:

```
use SomeModule;
```
*Load the module* SomeModule.pm *and do default imports.*

For example, suppose you have just learned about the `File::Basename` module. Suppose you would like to use the `dirname` subroutine that it defines. Here's one possibility:

```
use File::Basename;
```
*Load* File::Basename *module— exports* dirname, basename, *etc.*

```
setpwent;
while (@pwinfo = getpwent) {
  my ($usr, $sh) = @pwinfo[0, -1];
  if ($sh and
      dirname($sh) ne "/bin") {
    print "shell $sh for $usr?\n"
  }
}
```
*Loop through password info looking for shells not beginning with* /bin.

The use directive can take a list of arguments. These are passed to the module's import method, and, assuming that the module's import method has the usual semantics, this list should be a list of symbols—subroutine names and the like—that are to be imported into the current package. For example, if you wish to import only `dirname` and `basename` from `File::Basename`, you can invoke it as:

```
use File::Basename qw(dirname basename);
```

If you wish to import no symbols at all, pass an explicit empty list:

```
use File::Basename ();
```

Remember that Perl doesn't prevent you from accessing symbols (other than my variables) that are not in the current package. If you use a module but choose not to import any symbols from it, you can always refer to them with their fully qualified names:

```
use File::Basename ();
```
*Load* `File::Basename.pm` *but import no symbols.*

```
print "Gimme a pathname: ";
$file = <>;
$dir =
  File::Basename::dirname($file);
print "dir = $dir\n";
```
*Now we have to call* `dirname` *the long way.*

## Item 43:  Make sure Perl can find the modules you are using.

From Item 42 you know that Perl modules are contained in files ending with the extension .pm, and that the use directive incorporates modules into your programs. However, a question that has gone unanswered thus far is:

"How does use find my modules, anyway?"

The answer is that Perl searches the *module include path*, a list of directories stored in the global variable @INC. The default include path is built into the Perl executable when Perl is compiled. There are a number of ways to see exactly what the current include path is. One, of course, is to write a little script that prints it out. From the command line, this will do the trick:

```
% perl -e 'print "include is @INC\n" '
```

A slightly easier-to-type alternative is to check Perl's configuration with the -V command line option:

```
% perl -V
Summary of my perl5 (5.0 patchlevel 4 subversion 1)
configuration:
Platform:
    osname=solaris, osvers=2.5.1, archname=sun4-solaris
... blah blah blah ...

Characteristics of this binary (from libperl):
  Built under solaris
  Compiled at Jun 16 1997 15:37:41
  @INC:
    /usr/local/lib/perl5/sun4-solaris/5.00401
```

```
/usr/local/lib/perl5
/usr/local/lib/perl5/site_perl/sun4-solaris
/usr/local/lib/perl5/site_perl
                       .
```

No matter how you look at it, the include path lists the directories in which the `use` directive will search for Perl modules, or, in the case of nested modules like `File::Basename`, the directories in which the various module trees like `File` are rooted.

## Modifying the include path

If you have modules installed in places other than those listed in the built-in `@INC`, you will have to modify the include path to get Perl to `use` them. Under normal circumstances, this won't happen very often. When you build and install modules—either by using the CPAN module or by just unpacking and making them manually—Perl's MakeMaker module automatically generates a makefile that will put the module's `.pm` file in the correct location for your particular installation of Perl. If that's not where you want the module to go, you have to force MakeMaker to put it somewhere else (see Item 42).

But let's assume you have a module installed in a strange place, say, in the directory `/share/perl`. You might be tempted to just modify the include path in your program's source code:

```
unshift @INC, "/share/perl";        Where MyModule.pm lives.

use MyModule;                        WRONG! No effect.
```

Unfortunately, this simple approach *will not work*. The problem is that the `use` directive is a compile-time rather than a run-time feature. When `use Module` appears in your program, it actually means:

```
BEGIN { require "Module.pm"; import Module; }
```

The code inside the `BEGIN` block is executed at compile time rather than run time. This means that changes to `@INC` at run time have no effect on `use` directives. (For more information about `BEGIN`, see Item 59. For more about `require`, see Item 54.)

A rather blunt way around this is to put the change to `@INC` in a `BEGIN` block of its own:

```
BEGIN {
  unshift @INC, "/share/perl";       Where MyModule.pm lives.
}
use MyModule;                        It works now!
```

Now, the include path is set up at compile time, and `use` can find the module. Although this is a workable strategy, there is a better way to control the include path: the `lib` pragma module. The `lib` pragma was added fairly early in the development of Perl 5, and all recent versions support it. To prepend one or more directories to the include path, just supply them as arguments to `use lib`:

```
use lib "/share/perl";          Add dir /share/perl.
use lib qw(
  /xtra/perl                    Add more dirs.
  /xtra/perl5
);

use MyModule;                   Ready to go now.
```

Aside from improved readability, `use lib` has one other advantage over explicit changes to the include path. The `lib` pragma also adds a corresponding architecture-specific autoload path, if such a directory exists. This can result in improved performance if you are using a module that is autoloaded. For example, if the machine architecture is `"sun4-solaris"`, then `use lib "/share/perl"` will add:

```
/share/perl/sun4-solaris/auto
```

in addition to /share/perl, if the autoload directory exists.

There are some other ways to control the include path in those cases in which `use lib` isn't appropriate. You can use the `-I` command line option:

```
% perl -I/share/perl myscript
```

You can also use `-I` in the "pound bang" line:

```
#! /usr/local/bin/perl -I/share/perl
```

Finally, you can put one or more directory names, separated by colons, in the `PERL5LIB` environment variable.

## Modifying the include path: special cases

As I mentioned earlier, the include path is built into Perl when it is compiled. Generally, it will derive from the installation prefix specified when the `Configure` script is run:

```
Installation prefix to use? (~name ok) [/usr/local]
```

Changing the installation prefix allows you to build and install private or alternative copies of Perl for testing or perhaps debugging purposes (see Item 38).

Ordinarily the built-in modules and library files go into the subdirectory `lib/perl5` underneath the prefix directory, say, `/usr/local/lib/perl5`. It's a good idea to leave them there, but if you want them to go somewhere else, you can also control that with `Configure`:

```
Pathname where the private library files will reside? (~name
ok) [/usr/local/lib/perl5]
```

If you change the private library directory, the include path for this version of Perl will also be changed accordingly. Finally, if you are writing a Perl module, you may want to test scripts against it without actually installing the module. The `blib` (build library) pragma module is useful in these cases:

```
#!/usr/local/bin/perl

use blib "/home/joseph/Magic";          Looks for blib in
                                        /home/joseph/Magic.
```

although it is more often used from the command line:

```
% perl -Mblib my_script               Looks for blib in the current
                                       directory.
```

## Item 44: Use `perldoc` to extract documentation for installed modules.

Perl comes with a large quantity of documentation—a very large quantity. The man pages included with early distributions of Perl 5 ran to over 500 pages. The page count for the newest versions is much higher. The standard distribution also includes many modules, each of them with its own man page. There is a huge amount of useful information in the man pages, so it pays to be able to read them. There are two simple ways to read on-line documentation for Perl: `perldoc` and `man`. Of these two ways, `perldoc` is generally the best—read on to find out why.

Your site may also have documentation in HTML form. Ask the person who installed Perl whether it is available, and if so, how to get to it.

### Why `man` can't find man pages

For some operating systems, getting to the Perl man pages is *not* as simple as typing `man perl`. The problem is that the `man` command cannot always find the files containing the man pages.

Older versions of the Unix man command rely on explicit searches of the filesystem. There is a built-in "man path" that can be changed using the

MANPATH environment variable. The man command searches through the directories and subdirectories that are accessible from the man path until it finds the right file.

This is a time-consuming and resource-intensive way to find a man page. As a result, most versions of Unix now ship with versions of man that *do not* perform exhaustive searches, at least not by default. Instead, they consult a "whatis" database to find out which man pages are installed and where they are located. The problem with the whatis database is that it must be kept up-to-date by a system administrator (usually with something like the catman command). If the database is not up-to-date, recently installed man pages will not be found by the man command. [4]

There are various workarounds involving man. Most versions of the man command allow you to force an explicit search (ignoring any whatis database) and/or list directories that you want to search for man pages. This takes a lot of typing, though; furthermore, man is different from machine to machine.

Enter perldoc.

## Why perldoc *can* find man pages

The perldoc command is a Perl script that is installed along with the Perl executable and other utilities like s2p and h2xs.

The perldoc command does not search for man pages. Instead, it searches the Perl tree for perl modules (.pm) with embedded documentation, as well as documentation-only .pod files (see Item 46). This means that perldoc will search places that man often doesn't. When a matching file is found, perldoc formats the contents into a man page and displays it. For example:

```
% perldoc perldoc
PERLDOC(1)  User Contributed Perl Documentation  PERLDOC(1)

NAME
     perldoc - Look up Perl documentation in pod format.

SYNOPSIS
     perldoc [-h] [-v] [-t] [-u] [-m] [-l]
... etc.
```

---

4. If you are an administrator trying to get the Perl man pages working, bear in mind that the man pages for modules are installed beneath the private library directory—something like /usr/local/lib/perl5/man rather than /usr/local/man. The man pages for locally-installed modules will be in a different site library directory.

To get documentation on a module, supply the module name as the argument to `perldoc`:

```
% perldoc File::Basename
```

You can omit all but the last part of the module name. The `perldoc` command also will perform case-insensitive searches:

```
% perldoc basename                          Same as using File::Basename.
```

You can also get documentation on a single Perl function by using the `-f` option:

```
% perldoc -f length                         Document the length function.
```

Of course, in order for `perldoc` to work, it must be properly installed. The directory that `perl` is installed in should contain all the various Perl utilities—`perldoc`, `pod2man`, `h2xs`, and so on. The Perl installer does this automatically, but if you are using a machine onto which an administrator "manually" installed Perl by copying or linking the Perl executable from another directory, you may have problems. If `perldoc` seems broken or is inaccessible, see your administrator.

# Writing Packages and Modules

## Item 45:  Use h2xs to generate module boilerplate.

From Item 42 you know that modules are packages that follow certain conventions. There is enough nitpicky detail in these conventions to make it difficult to write a module on your own without some help. This is particularly true if you are planning to package and release a module for public use. Fortunately, help is available in the form of a utility called h2xs.

The h2xs program was originally designed to simplify the process of writing an XS module (see Item 47), but has long since been used for the broader purpose of providing a starting point for writing all Perl modules, XS or not. You should *always* use h2xs to create the boilerplate for a new Perl module. This will save you and your module's potential users many hours of grief, confusion, and frustration. Trust me on this one.

The easiest way to get started with h2xs is to try it for yourself. Let's look at an example.

### Creating a module using h2xs

Let's use h2xs to create a skeleton for a new module called File::Cmp, then flesh it out so that it works. File::Cmp will contain a function that will compare the contents of two files and return a value indicating whether they are identical. (There already is a File::Compare module that does the same thing, but, remember, this is just an example.)

The first step is to run h2xs. This will create some directories and files, so be sure to execute the command in a "scratch" directory in which it's okay for you to work. We will use the -A, -X, and -n options. The -A option tells h2xs not to generate any code for function autoloading. The -X option tells h2xs that this is an ordinary module and that no XS skeleton will be needed (see Item 47). The -n option supplies the module name. This is the usual combination of options for starting work on a "plain old module":

■ **Begin work on a module by running h2xs.**

```
% h2xs -A -X -n File::Cmp
Writing File/Cmp/Cmp.pm
Writing File/Cmp/Makefile.PL
Writing File/Cmp/test.pl
Writing File/Cmp/Changes
Writing File/Cmp/MANIFEST
```
*No XS or autoloading.*
*h2xs creates some files.*

At this point you already have a "working" module that does nothing. You could build, test, and install it just as if you had downloaded it from the CPAN (see Item 41). Before we do that, however, let's add some code so that it actually does something useful. Let's start with the file Cmp.pm, which contains the new module's Perl source code. It should look something like the following—minus the italicized annotations, of course:

● **The file Cmp.pm**

*Begin by setting the default package to* File::Cmp, *turning on* strict, *and declaring a few package variables.*

```
package File::Cmp;

use strict;
use vars qw($VERSION @ISA @EXPORT @EXPORT_OK);
```

*Use the Perl library's* Exporter *module. We can* require *rather than* use *it because this module will be* use-d.

```
require Exporter;
```

*Subclass* Exporter *and* AutoLoader. *We're not actually using* AutoLoader *in this example, so you can delete any references to it if you like. For more about subclassing and inheritance in Perl, see Item 50.*

```
@ISA = qw(Exporter AutoLoader);
```

*Here's a place to add the names of functions and other package variables that we want to export by default. When we* use *this module,* Exporter *will import these names into the calling package. You also can add names to an array called* @EXPORT_OK. Exporter *will allow those names to be exported on request.*

```
# Items to export into callers namespace by default. Do not export
# names by default without a very good reason. Use EXPORT_OK instead.
# Do not simply export all your public functions/methods/constants.
@EXPORT = qw(

);
```

● **The file Cmp.pm** (cont'd)

*A version number that you should increment every time you generate a new release of the module.*

```
$VERSION = '0.01';
```

*Insert function(s) after the next line.*

```
# Preloaded methods go here.
```

*We're not autoloading anything, so ignore this.*

```
# Autoload methods go after =cut, and are processed by the autosplit
program.
```

*Modules must return a true value to load properly (see Item 54). Make sure you don't get rid of this all-important 1.*

```
1;
__END__
```

*The stub for the built-in POD documentation (see Item 46) follows the __END__ of the source code.*

```
# Below is the stub of documentation for your module. You better edit
it!

=head1 NAME

File::Cmp - Perl extension for blah blah blah

=head1 SYNOPSIS

  use File::Cmp;
  blah blah blah

=head1 DESCRIPTION

Stub documentation for File::Cmp was created by h2xs. It looks like
the author of the extension was negligent enough to leave the stub
unedited.

Blah blah blah.

=head1 AUTHOR

A. U. Thor, a.u.thor@a.galaxy.far.far.away
```

● The file Cmp.pm (cont'd)

```
=head1 SEE ALSO

perl(1).

=cut
```

Let's add a function called cmp_file. It will compare the contents of two files, then return 0 if they are identical, a positive number if they are different, and -1 if some sort of error has occurred. Insert the following code after the line that says Preloaded methods go here:

● cmp_file: Compare contents of two files

```
sub cmp_file {                        This subroutine takes two
  my ($file1, $file2) = @_;           filenames as arguments.
  local(*FH1, *FH2);

  return -1 if !-e $file1 or !-e $file2;   See if files exist.
  return 0 if $file1 eq $file2;            Same filenames = same
                                           contents.

  open FH1, $file1 or return -1;      Open files.
  open FH2, $file2 or
      close(FH1), return -1;          Different sizes = different
  return 1 if -s FH1 != -s FH2;       contents.

  my $chunk = 4096;                   We will read one "chunk" at a
  my ($bytes, $buf1, $buf2, $diff);   time.
  while ($bytes =
        sysread FH1, $buf1, $chunk) { Read a chunk from each file
    sysread FH2, $buf2, $chunk;       and compare as strings.
    $diff++, last if $buf1 ne $buf2;
  }

  close FH1;                          close files, return status
  close FH2;
  $diff;
}
```

We will want to export cmp_file from this module automatically (see Item 42). Just add it to the @EXPORT list:

```
@EXPORT = qw(
    cmp_file
);
```

Now we need a test script. Open the file test.pl and add the following at the end:

● **Test script for `File::Cmp`**

*This script creates three files containing some random data. Two files are identical and the third is different. We start by creating the data:*

```perl
srand();
for ($i = 0; $i < 10000; $i++) {
  $test_blob .= pack 'S', rand 0xffff;
}
$test_num = 2;
```

*Do the testing inside an `eval` block (see Item 54) to make error handling easier.*

```perl
eval {
  open F, '>xx' or die "couldn't create: $!";
  print F $test_blob;

  open F, '>xxcopy' or die "couldn't create: $!";
  print F $test_blob;

  open F, '>xxshort' or die "couldn't create: $!";
  print F substr $test_blob, 0, 19999;
```

*The test files have been created. Now, use `cmp_file` to compare them.*

```perl
  if (cmp_file('xx', 'xxcopy') == 0) {
    print "ok ", $test_num++, "\n";
  } else {
    print "NOT ok ", $test_num++, "\n";
  }

  if (cmp_file('xx', 'xxshort') > 0) {
    print "ok ", $test_num++, "\n";
  } else {
    print "NOT ok ", $test_num++, "\n";
  }
};
```

*Report any exceptions from the `eval` block, tidy up, and we're done.*

```perl
if ($@) {
  print "... error: $@\n";
}

unlink glob 'xx*';
```

You also should change the line near the top of `test.pl` so that the count of tests reads correctly:

```perl
BEGIN { $| = 1; print "1..3\n"; }
```

At this point, we can build and test the module (see Item 41):

```
% perl Makefile.PL
Checking if your kit is complete...
Looks good
Writing Makefile for File::Cmp
```

```
% make test
cp Cmp.pm ./blib/lib/File/Cmp.pm
AutoSplitting File::Cmp (./blib/lib/auto/File/Cmp)
PERL_DL_NONLAZY=1 /usr/local/bin/perl -I./blib/arch
-I./blib/lib -I/usr/local/lib/perl5/sun4-solaris/5.003
-I/usr/local/lib/perl5 test.pl
1..3
ok 1
ok 2
ok 3
```

Cool.

There are still some things to be done. You will need to replace the documentation stub in Cmp.pm with something more informative (see Item 46). You also should add a description of the work you did to the log in Changes. You could add some more thorough tests to test.pl.

Once you have whipped the module into shape, you can prepare a distribution. Just make the tardist target:

```
% make tardist
rm -rf File-Cmp-0.01
/usr/local/bin/perl -I/usr/local/lib/perl5/sun4-solaris/5.003
-I/usr/local/lib/perl5 -MExtUtils::Manifest=manicopy,maniread \
        -e 'manicopy(maniread(),"File-Cmp-0.01", "best");'
mkdir File-Cmp-0.01
tar cvf File-Cmp-0.01.tar File-Cmp-0.01
File-Cmp-0.01/
File-Cmp-0.01/Makefile.PL
File-Cmp-0.01/Changes
File-Cmp-0.01/test.pl
File-Cmp-0.01/Cmp.pm
File-Cmp-0.01/MANIFEST
rm -rf File-Cmp-0.01
compress File-Cmp-0.01.tar
```

Voila! You now have a file called File-Cmp-0.01.tar.Z, which contains the source to your module. This file follows the conventions of the CPAN and is ready for distribution to the world.

If you have written a useful module, consider sharing it with the rest of the world—see Item 48.

## Item 46:  Embed your documentation with POD.

Ahh, documentation! Just what all programmers love to spend their time writing when they could be coding, or perhaps playing NetHack, or even enjoying some non-nerdlike activity like friends, family, or exercise. Given that some developers spend ten, twelve, or more hours a day just getting their code to run, it's not surprising that a lot of documentation winds up being written in a half-hearted way, or is written by non-programmers, or is not written at all.

A good many software developers, especially those working on sizable projects, work to coding standards that require them to start off function definitions with block comments that provide key information about that function—overview, inputs, outputs, preconditions, change history, and the like. If those embedded comments are formatted precisely enough, they can be parsed by scripts (probably Perl scripts!) and reformatted into documentation. A source file could thus contain (or be) its own programming reference. This is a Good Thing, because it allows developers to tweak the documentation each time they tweak the code without having to locate and edit a separate document. Sometimes this is about all the documentation that a developer can manage to do correctly.

The down side to embedded documentation, however, is that unless you're working in a language or environment that supports it, you or someone in your group has to write and maintain tools that extract the goodies from your source files and generate documentation from them. Someone also has to decide what format the comments are going to be in, and someone has to enforce it. It would be nice, of course, if your comments were formatted like those from other groups so that you could share tools, but without any standards that isn't likely to happen.

Fortunately, Perl directly supports embedded documentation. Perl does it in a standardized way that is part of the core of the language, with a feature called POD, or "Plain Old Documentation." Perl source code can contain embedded documentation in POD format. The Perl parser ignores POD sections when compiling and interpreting scripts, but other programs supplied with the Perl distribution can scan source files for documentation sections and format them as man pages, HTML, plain text, or any of a number of other formats.

### POD basics

POD is a very simple markup language designed so that documentation written in POD can be translated readily into other formats (text, HTML, etc.). POD is easily readable in raw form if worse comes to worse, too.

A POD document consists of paragraphs set off by blank lines. There are three different kinds of paragraphs:

- **Verbatim text.** A paragraph whose lines are indented will be reproduced exactly as it appears—no line wrapping, no special interpretation of escape sequences, no nothing. Translators that can display different fonts will generally reproduce verbatim text in a fixed-width font.

- **A POD command.** A command is a line beginning with the character =, followed by an identifier, then some optional text. Currently defined commands, which may not be understood by all translators, are shown below:

**POD commands**

| Command | Description | Example |
|---------|-------------|---------|
| =head1<br>=head2 | Level 1, level 2 headings. | =head1 Understand Packages and Modules.<br><br>=head2 Packages |
| =item | An item in a bulleted or numbered list. | =item 1            *A numbered item.*<br><br>=item *            *A bulleted item.*<br><br>=item B<NOTE>    *A bolded "other" item.* |
| =over *N*<br><br>=back | Indent over N spaces.<br><br>Go back from indent. | =over 4        *4 is the customary number.*<br><br>=back |
| =cut<br><br>=pod | End of POD.<br><br>Beginning of POD. | =cut<br><br>=pod |
| =for *X*<br><br>=begin *X*<br>=end *X* | Next paragraph is of format X.<br><br>Bracket beginning and end of format X. | =for html        *Next para in HTML.*<br><br>=begin text<br><br>If you can read this, you are using a text translator.<br><br>=end text |

- **Filled text.** A paragraph that isn't verbatim or a POD command is treated as ordinary text. Formatters generally will turn it into a justified paragraph, in a proportionally spaced font if possible. A number of special formatting sequences are recognized inside filled text:

**POD formatting sequences**

| Sequence | Description | Example |
|---|---|---|
| I<*text*><br>B<*text*> | Italicized text, bolded text. | `You will be I<very> lucky to have`<br>`B<John> work for you` |
| C<*text*> | Source code. | `now, add 5 to C<$d[$a,$b]>` |
| S<*text*> | Text with nonbreaking spaces. | `C< S<foreach $k (keys %hash)> >` |
| E<*code*> | A character escape (generally not needed). | `E<lt>` *Less-than sign <.*<br>`E<34>` *Double quote " (in ASCII)* |
| L<*text*> | A link or cross-reference. | `L<name>` *Man page.*<br>`L<name/ident>` *Item in man page.*<br>`L<name/"sec">` *Section in man page.*<br>`L<"sec">` *Section in this man page.* |
| F<*name*> | Filename. | `Be careful not to delete F<config.dat>!` |
| X<*text*> | Index entry. | |
| Z<*text*> | Zero-width character. | |

Note that some POD formatters will recognize function names (an identifier followed by parentheses) and other special constructs "in context" and automatically apply appropriate formatting to them. In addition, most POD formatters can convert straight quotes to "smart" matching quotes, doubled hyphens to em dashes, and so forth.

Here is an example POD file:

● **POD file**

```
=head1 My POD Example

=head2 My second-level heading

I<POD> is a simple, useful markup language for Perl programmers as
well as others looking for a way to write "Plain Old Documentation."

With POD, you can:

=over 4

=item 1
```

● POD file (cont'd)

```
Create documentation that can be readily translated into many
different formats.

=item 2

Embed documentation directly into Perl programs.

=item 3

Amaze your friends and terrify your enemies.  (Possibly.)

=back

   Author: Joseph N. Hall
   Date: 1997
```

When translated—in this case, by my pod2mif filter—it yields:

● Translated POD file

## My POD Example

### My second-level heading

*POD* is a simple, useful markup language for Perl programmers as well as others looking
for a way to write "Plain Old Documentation."

With POD, you can:

1.  Create documentation that can be readily translated into many different formats.

2.  Embed documentation directly into Perl programs.

3.  Amaze your friends and terrify your enemies. (Possibly.)

```
   Author: Joseph N. Hall
   Date: 1997
```

## Man pages in POD

Although you can use POD for many different purposes, man pages written in POD should follow certain conventions so that they will resemble
other Unix man pages. Variables and function names should be *italicized*.
Names of programs, as well as command line switches, should be **bold**.

The man page should have a proper skeleton. The first-level headings tra-
ditionally appear in CAPITAL LETTERS. The most important of the
first-level headings, in the traditional order, are:

Man page headings

| Heading | Description |
|---|---|
| NAME | Name of the program/library/whatever. |
| SYNOPSIS | Brief example of usage. |
| DESCRIPTION | Detailed description, broken into sections if necessary. |
| EXAMPLES | Show us how we use it. |
| SEE ALSO | References to other man pages, etc. |
| BUGS | Things that need a little work yet. |
| AUTHOR | Your name in lights. |

See the pod2man man page for more information about the layout of man pages.

## Item 47: Use XS for low-level interfaces and/or speed.

Recent versions of Perl have a documented interface language, called *XS*,[1] that you can use to write functions in C or C++ that can be called from Perl. Within *XSUBs*, as they are called, you have full access to Perl's internals. You can create variables, change their values, execute Perl code, or do pretty much anything that suits your fancy.

An XS module is actually a dynamically loaded shareable library.[2] Creating one is a complex process fraught with details. Fortunately, with the XS interface you get a bunch of tools that handle most of those details for you. For reasonably simple situations, you need only run x2hs to get a set of boilerplate files, add some Perl and XS code, and run make. There are make targets for building the shareable library, testing it, building a distribution kit, and installing it.

XSUBs are a handy way to add operating-system supported features to Perl—they beat the heck out of syscall. You also can use XSUBs to speed up scripts that are spending a significant proportion of their time in a small number of subroutines. And, of course, you can use XSUBs to add a Perl interface to an existing C or C++ library of your own.

---

1. Parts of XS are still under development as of this writing. XS shouldn't change radically in the near future, but don't be surprised to find some differences between your version and what's documented here.

2. If your system does not support shareable libraries, you can still use XSUBs by linking them into the Perl executable itself.

As an example of the sort of things you might write an XSUB for, let's suppose that you would like to write a subroutine that returns a copy of a list, but with all the elements in random order. In Perl, you might write something like:

```
sub shuffle1 {
  my @orig = @_;
  my @result;
  push @result, splice @orig, rand @orig, 1 while @orig;
  @result;
}
```

This isn't exactly a model of efficiency, because you have to call `splice` once for each element in the list—not good if you're planning on shuffling long lists. A more efficient approach might be:

```
sub shuffle2 {
  my @result = @_;
  my $n = @result;
  while ($n > 1) {
    my $i = rand $n;
    $n--;
    @result[$i, $n] = @result[$n, $i];
  }
  @result;
}
```

This is better, but not a lot better. There is no splicing going on, but on the other hand the swapping of values involves a lot of assignments and subscripting, which takes a surprisingly large amount of time. (See the benchmarks at the end of this Item.) In truth, shuffling is best *not* written in Perl if efficiency is a prime concern. So let's write `shuffle` as an XSUB in C.

## Generating the boilerplate

When writing XSUBs, you should always start out by using h2xs to generate a set of boilerplate files, much as you would for an ordinary Perl-only module (see Item 45). In this case, let's start by creating boilerplate for a module called `List::Shuffle`.

```
% h2xs -A -n List::Shuffle
Writing List/Shuffle/Shuffle.pm
Writing List/Shuffle/Shuffle.xs
Writing List/Shuffle/Makefile.PL
Writing List/Shuffle/test.pl
Writing List/Shuffle/Changes
Writing List/Shuffle/MANIFEST
```

This is similar to the example in Item 45. However, since we have chosen a hierarchical package name, the boilerplate files are created in a directory named `Shuffle` that is itself nested in a directory named `List`.

As before, you will also need to generate a makefile:

```
% perl Makefile.PL
```

You may want to make some changes to the boilerplate code before you begin writing your XSUB. For example, if you want to be able to call the `shuffle()` subroutine without having to prepend the package name to it, you must export its name in `Shuffle.pm`:

```
@EXPORT = qw(shuffle);
```

## Writing and testing an XSUB

The XS language that XSUBs are written in is really just a kind of C pre-processor designed to make writing XSUBs easier.

XS source code goes into files ending with ".xs". The XS compiler, `xsubpp`, compiles XS into C code with the glue needed to interface with Perl. You probably will never have to invoke `xsubpp` on your own, though, because it is invoked automatically via the generated makefile.

XS source files begin with a prologue of C code that is passed through unaltered by `xsubpp`. A `MODULE` directive follows the prologue; for example:

```
MODULE = List::Shuffle     PACKAGE = List::Shuffle
```

This indicates the start of the actual XS source, which is itself a list of XSUBs.[3]

So, how about some examples of XS?

Here is a very simple XSUB that just calls the C standard library `log` function and returns the result:

```
double
log(x)
  double x
```

The return type appears first, on a line by itself at the beginning of the line. Next is the function name and a list of parameter names. The lines following the return type and function name are ordinarily indented for

---

3. Unfortunately, a thorough description of how to write XSUBs would fill an entire book (and it probably will, one of these days), and there isn't space to explain XSUBs in great detail here. For now, for detailed information about XS, you will have to rely on the documentation shipped with Perl, notably the `perlxs`, `perlxstut`, and `perlguts` man pages.

readability. In this case, there is only a single line in the XSUB body, declaring the type of the parameter x.

In a simple case like this, xsubpp generates code that creates a Perl subroutine named log() that calls the C function of the same name. The generated code also includes the glue necessary to convert the Perl argument to a C double and to convert the result back. (To see how this works, take a look at the C code generated by xsubpp—it's actually pretty readable.)

Here is a slightly more complex example that calls the Unix realpath() function (not available on all systems):

```
char *
realpath(filename)
  char *filename
  PREINIT:
    char realname[1024]; /* or use MAXPATHLEN */
  CODE:
    RETVAL = realpath(filename, realname);
  OUTPUT:
    RETVAL
```

This creates a Perl function that takes a string argument and has a string return value. The XS glue takes care of converting Perl strings to C's char * type and back:

```
$realname = realpath($filename);
```

The CODE section contains the portion of the code used to compute the result from the subroutine. The PREINIT section contains declarations of variables used in the CODE section; they should go here rather than in the CODE section. RETVAL is a "magic" variable supplied by xsubpp used to hold the return value. Finally, the OUTPUT section lists values that will be returned to the caller. This ordinarily will include RETVAL. It can also include input parameters that are modified and returned as if through call by reference.

These examples all return single scalar values. In order to write shuffle, which returns a list of scalars, we have to use a PPCODE section and do our own popping and pushing of arguments and return values. This is less difficult than it may sound. To get things rolling, insert the following code in Shuffle.xs following the MODULE line:

● XS source code for List::Shuffle

| PROTOTYPES: DISABLE | *Turn off Perl prototype processing for the following XSUBs.* |
|---|---|

● **XS source code for `List::Shuffle` (cont'd)**

```
void                                    Declared void because we are
shuffle(...)                            returning values "manually"
  PPCODE:                               with XPUSHs.
  {
    int i, n;                           SV is the "scalar value" type.
    SV **array;
    SV *tmp;
    array = New(0, array, items, SV *); Allocate storage. New()
                                        requests memory from Perl's
                                        memory allocator.

    for (i = 0; i < items; i++) {       Copy input args.
      array[i] = sv_mortalcopy(ST(i));
    }

    n = items;
    while (n > 1) {                     Shuffle off to Buffalo!
      i = rand() % n;
      tmp = array[i];
      array[i] = array[--n];
      array[n] = tmp;
    }

    for (i = 0; i < items; i++) {       Push result (a list) onto stack.
      XPUSHs(array[i]);
    }
    Safefree(array);                    Free storage. Safefree()
  }                                     returns memory to Perl.
```

The `PROTOTYPES: DISABLE` directive turns off Perl prototype processing (see Item 28) for the XSUBs that follow.

The strategy here is to copy the input arguments into a temporary array, shuffle them, and then push the result onto the stack. The arguments will be scalar values, which are represented internally in Perl with the type `SV *`.

Instead of a `CODE` block, we use a `PPCODE` block inside this XSUB. This disables the automatic handling of return values on the stack. The number of arguments passed in is contained in the magic variable `items`, and the arguments themselves are contained in `ST(0)`, `ST(1)`, and so on.

The SV pointers on the stack refer to the actual values supplied to the `shuffle()` function. We don't want this. We want copies instead, so we use the function `sv_mortalcopy()` to make a reference counted clone of each incoming scalar.

The scalars go into an array allocated with Perl's internal New() function, and then we shuffle them. After shuffling, we push the return values on the stack one at a time with the XPUSHs() function and free the temporary storage we used to hold the array of pointers. If all this seems sketchy, which it probably does, consult the perlguts and perlxs man pages for more details.

At this point, you can save Shuffle.xs and build it:

```
% make
```

You will see a few lines of gobbledygook as Shuffle.xs compiles (hopefully) and as some other files are created and copied into their preinstallation locations. If the build was successful, you should create a test script. Open the test script template test.pl and add the following lines to the bottom:

```
@shuffle = shuffle 1..10;
print "@shuffle\n";
print "ok 2\n";
```

Now, type:

```
% make test
```

You should see something like the following at the bottom of the output:

```
ok 1
6 4 1 5 3 7 10 2 8 9
ok 2
```

Voila! Now you just need to write the documentation POD (see Item 46). This is left as an exercise to the reader.

Let's take this module and run some benchmarks. In the process we will also try out the blib pragma (see Item 43). Create a short benchmark program, called tryme as usual:

```
use Benchmark;
use List::Shuffle;
# insert shuffle1() and shuffle2() from above here
timethese(500, {
    'shuffle'  => 'shuffle 1..1000',
    'shuffle1' => 'shuffle1 1..1000',
    'shuffle2' => 'shuffle2 1..1000',
});
```

Even though List::Shuffle isn't installed, we can use it if we tell Perl how to find the copy in the build library. The usual way is to invoke the blib pragma from the command line (this assumes tryme is in the same directory as the blib directory):

```
% perl -Mblib tryme
Using /home/joseph/perl-play/xs/List/Shuffle/blib
Benchmark: timing 500 iterations of shuffle, shuffle1,
shuffle2...
   shuffle:  3 secs ( 3.31 usr  0.00 sys =  3.31 cpu)
  shuffle1: 28 secs (28.79 usr  0.00 sys = 28.79 cpu)
  shuffle2: 31 secs (30.68 usr  0.00 sys = 30.68 cpu)
```

Well, that's an improvement in speed. As you can see, the XSUB shuffle ran approximately eight times faster (on my machine, anyway) than the two versions written in Perl. With better stack handling and some other optimizations it could be made a little faster still. But we will have to leave that as another exercise for the interested reader.

## Item 48: Submit your useful modules to the CPAN.

Although the CPAN already contains many high-quality modules that do a wide variety of things, there are still many useful modules yet to be written in Perl.

If you are considering writing a module that does something of general interest, or if you have already written one, you might want to consider contributing your module to the CPAN. The process of contributing a module is a fairly simple one—which is good, because we programmers hate it when paperwork becomes more time-consuming than the constructive work it supports.[4]

### Discuss your module

The first thing you need to do, as a potential new contributor to the CPAN, is to discuss your new module(s) with some potential users. In most cases, the best thing to do is to post some sort of a "request for discussion" to comp.lang.perl.modules. Include the proposed name of the module, its key features, and if possible, a pointer to a man page and/or a sample implementation. You don't have to take all the responses to heart, but you should at least read and consider them. Some people are just naturally "bah humbuggers" while others are helpful and interested—USENET has a lot of both kinds.

The following questions are ones that you need to have answered when you proceed:

---

4. This Item relies on the PAUSE documentation available at the time of writing. The current version can be found under modules/04pause.html in the CPAN. Please check it before registering or contributing modules for the first time, as the procedure may have changed since this was written.

- Does this capability already exist?

- Is the name I have chosen for the module appropriate? (This is very important.)

- Is the interface to the module appropriate?

- Do I have the resources and technical savvy to implement the module properly?

If or when you are ready to proceed, the next step is to register yourself with PAUSE.

## Registering with PAUSE

As a new developer, you will need to register yourself with PAUSE—the Perl Authors Upload Server. You need to choose a username or "handle" for yourself—mine is JNH, my initials. You can use your first name, your favorite login, initials, or whatever, so long as it is reasonably short, and isn't already taken. For a list of current usernames and the corresponding author names, see authors/00whois.html in your favorite CPAN mirror.

The next step is to send a message to the Perl module maintainer's mailing list—currently modules@perl.org. Mailing list addresses tend to change, so check the current PAUSE document in the CPAN to verify it. The message should contain:

- Your name

- Preferred username

- E-mail address, and home page if you have one

- A description of your project

- A description of each module in "module list format"[5]

- Pointers to public discussion of the module

You soon should receive an e-mail message asking you for a password. You should respond with an encrypted password or message. If your system supports crypt, the simplest way to do this is with a short Perl script. The PAUSE document suggests the following command line (replace mysecret with your chosen password):

```
perl -MHTTPD::UserAdmin \
  -le 'print HTTPD::UserAdmin->new->encrypt(shift);' mysecret
```

You might also try a program like:

---

5. See the module listing at modules/00modlist.long.html for a description of "DSLI" and proper module listing format.

```
$salt = pack "CC", time % 26 + 65, (time >> 8) % 26 + 65;
$pass = crypt "mysecret", $salt;
print "encrypted: $pass\n";
```

(Or just pick any two letters at random for the $salt variable.)

If you don't have crypt on your system, see the PAUSE document for other alternatives. Once your password is received and acknowledged, you're ready to upload your module and join the hallowed ranks of CPAN authors.

## Uploading and maintaining modules

The easiest way to upload modules to the CPAN is to submit them via a secure CGI script that links directly to PAUSE. As of this writing, the URL is:

```
http://franz.ww.TU-Berlin.DE/perl/user/add_uri
```

I hate to repeat myself, but these things tend to change and you should verify this URL in the PAUSE document.

You can submit a file in a number of ways. You can upload it to a holding area on the PAUSE server, then identify them in the CGI script. You can specify a URL where the server can go get it. You can also upload the file directly from your browser.

Your submission should be a "packed, compressed" module as generated by make tardist (see Item 45). There are automatic scripts that take care of extracting README files and the like from it and inserting them into the CPAN. There are other CGI scripts that allow you to change your author information, delete files, and make urgent mirror requests (generally to submit emergency bug fixes).

PAUSE and the CPAN are two of the best examples of "social anarchy" contributing to the betterment of mankind—or at least programmer-kind. Contributing a useful module to the CPAN is one of the best ways you can, in turn, show your appreciation for the efforts of hundreds of programmers who have made Perl and the CPAN such a compellingly useful resource.

# Object-Oriented Programming

What is object-oriented programming? A good many books have been devoted to that topic in full, and many more, like this one, in part.

Although it isn't difficult to give a fairly short description of what object-oriented programming *is*, I believe that one learns object-oriented programming mostly by experience and necessity. This is a long, difficult, and interesting process, enough so that I will not have room in this section to bring you up to speed from scratch. This section is intended mostly for readers who are already familiar with another object-oriented language like C++ or Smalltalk. However, even if you are a complete novice, if you work your way through the examples here and experiment a little along the way, you should begin to get a feel for things.

The essence of object-oriented programming is that an object-oriented program is structured around typed data. Object-oriented programming languages have features that allow you to create *objects* (data structures) of one or more *classes* (types) and then have the type of the objects automatically determine which functions are called in a program's execution. Such functions are called *methods*.

In the good old days you might have written code like:

```
$a{'type'} = 'LogMsg';
$a{'data'} = 'some text';

# ... some intervening stuff ...

if ($a{'type'} eq 'LogMsg') {
  write_to_log($a{'data'});
} elsif ($a{'type'} eq 'ConsoleMsg') {
  write_to_console($a{'data'});
}
```

This is not object-oriented, because it contains explicit type-checking logic and so-called "type fields" that are the mortal enemy of good object-ori-

ented style. The primary distinguishing feature of object-oriented programming languages is that they allow programmers to eliminate code like
the above, leaving to the programming language the responsibility of
selecting functions based on type. In Perl 5 you could write the above as:

```perl
package LogMsg;
sub new { my ($pkg, $data) = @_; bless { data => $data } };
sub Write { my $self = shift; print LOG "$self->{data}\n" };

package ConsoleMsg;
sub new { my ($pkg, $data) = @_; bless { data => $data } };
sub Write { my $self = shift; print "$self->data\n" };

package main;
$a = new LogMsg('some text');
$a->Write();
```

Here we have defined LogMsg and ConsoleMsg classes, then created an
object, $a, of class LogMsg. Perl automatically invokes the subroutine
LogMsg::Write when we call the Write method for an object of class
LogMsg.

The advantages of this style of programming are immediately obvious to
anyone who ever has written or maintained a program that contains long
passages of code resembling the first example. The improvement is mostly
structural. If you want to add another kind of object (say, a
FlashingLightMsg), all you have to do is add the code that defines the
object and its behavior. With the non-object-oriented style of programming, you have to go picking through your source code looking for all the
places where you test the type of your data, then change the code appropriately.

The disadvantages are also obvious—the code is longer and uses conventions that are confusing to the uninitiated. These are nontrivial issues.
Object-oriented programming is not the most appropriate solution for
every problem.

The term "object-oriented" has grown to encompass a number of features
beyond simple objects, classes, and methods. For example, you will hear
discussions of constructors, destructors, inheritance, multiple inheritance, polymorphism, overloading, and of course a number of C++-isms
like templates and inlining. If you haven't experienced object-oriented programming before, it can be bewildering, expecially if you get the full treatment right off the bat. As you strive to learn what it is and how it is
practiced, keep objects, classes, and methods foremost in your mind—
they are its essence.

## Item 49:  Consider using Perl's object-oriented programming features.

Perl contains all the features needed to support object-oriented programming, including the following:

- **Classes**—In Perl, packages are classes.

- **Objects**—Perl's objects are ordinary Perl data types like hashes and arrays that have been "blessed" into a package.

- **Methods**—Perl's methods are ordinary subroutines that are called using a special method call syntax.

- **Constructors**—These are subroutines that return a reference to a newly created and initialized object.

- **Destructors**—These are subroutines that are called when an object goes out of scope or is no longer referenced by any other object.

- **Inheritance**—Perl supports class inheritance, both single and multiple. Perl does not support data inheritance, but this is not an onerous limitation (see Item 51).

- **Overloading**—Methods can be overloaded very simply in Perl, and an overload pragma module allows operator overloading along the lines of the feature available in C++.

In addition, it is possible to approximate many other quasi-object-oriented features—like templates—in Perl.

### An object-oriented example

The easiest way to approach object-oriented programming in Perl is to see an example of it. Here is a minimalist Perl class called `Timer`:

● Writing a simple class in Perl

---

*This class implements a* `Timer` *object that reports the number of seconds since it was created.*

---

*Start by setting the default package to* `Timer`:

```
package Timer;
```

*Next is the constructor for* `Timer` *objects.*

```
sub new {                              new is lowercase by convention.
  my $pkg = shift;                     First arg is package name.
  bless { created => time }, $pkg;     Return blessed hash ref
}                                      containing current time.
```

---

● Writing a simple class in Perl (cont'd)

---

*Now, a method to return the time elapsed since creation:*

```
sub Elapsed {
  my $self = shift;                        First arg is object (see below).
  return time - $self->{created};          Return difference between
}                                          "now" and "then."
```

---

Here is an example of how the `Timer` class could be used:

● Using a class in Perl

---

```
package main;
$timer = new Timer;                             Create a Timer object.
sleep 5;                                        Do some timing.
print "elapsed: ", $timer->Elapsed(), "\n";     Use the Elapsed method to see
                                                how long it took.
```

---

Although this is a very short example, it covers all of the most important aspects of object-oriented programming in Perl (except for inheritance, which is covered in Item 50). Bear this example in mind as I launch into a somewhat long-winded discussion of it below.

A class in Perl is a package (see Item 42). The concept of class in other object-oriented languages is similar, in that a separate namespace is one of the most important facilities provided by a class.

A Perl object is data that has been blessed into a package. The bless operator takes a reference (usually, but not necessarily, a hash reference) and a package name as arguments. The package name is optional—the current package is used if it is omitted. When blessed, data "knows" to which package it belongs. In PEGS, blessed data is topped off with a rounded-corner rectangle containing the package name:

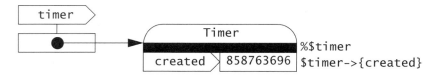

The ref operator (see Item 30) returns the package name rather than the type of data when it is applied to a blessed reference: [1]

---

1.  For the buzzword-compatible user, this is RTTI (Run-Time Type Identification)

■ **The `ref` operator returns the package name of a blessed object.**

---
*Continued from above:*

```
print "timer is a: ", ref $timer, "\n";          $timer is a Timer.
```
---

This can be handy information but it should not be overused, because a major goal of object-oriented programming is to *avoid* explicitly testing the type of an object.

It is important to realize that although the `bless` operator takes a reference as an argument, it is not blessing the reference. It is blessing *the data to which the reference points*:

■ **The `bless` operator blesses data, not references.**

---
*Continued from above:*

```
my $timer2 = $timer;                          Make a copy of $timer.
print "timer2 is a: ", ref $timer2, "\n";     $timer2 is still a Timer.
```
---

In PEGS, this looks like:

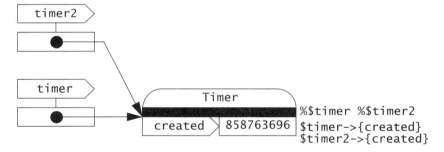

Returning to the example, the first subroutine that we define is a constructor. A constructor is a subroutine that creates and initializes a new object. In general, Perl constructors return references to anonymous hashes. This is a convention, and a convenient one, because hashes are a natural way to express "structs" or "records" in Perl (see Item 33).

Another convention is that constructors are generally named new. Unlike some other object-oriented languages, Perl has no special object-constructing or memory-allocating operator. A constructor could be named something entirely different, for example, `gimme_a_new`, and it would still work in the same way. Naming a constructor new makes object-oriented Perl look familiar to programmers who have worked in other object-oriented languages.

Constructors are methods. You will remember, from the discussion of object-oriented Perl above, that methods are ordinary subroutines that are invoked with a special method call syntax. The line

```
$timer = new Timer;
```

is an example of "indirect object" method call syntax. Perl interprets a subroutine name followed immediately by a package name in a special way—as a call to a subroutine in that package, with the package name as the first argument. So the above line is equivalent to:

```
$timer = Timer::new('Timer');
```

Methods invoked by package name are referred to as "static," "class," or "package" methods, according to your preference of nomenclature.

The second subroutine that we define, Elapsed, is also a method. Unlike the constructor, it is designed to be called via an object rather than a package. Although you can use indirect object syntax, the more common technique is to call it using the other type of method call syntax, the "arrow":

```
$elapsed = $timer->Elapsed();
```

Here, Perl uses the class of the $timer object to the left of the arrow to determine in which package to look for the subroutine Elapsed.[2] Because $timer has been blessed into package Timer, Perl calls the subroutine Timer::Elapsed. Perl also automatically uses the value to the left of the arrow as the first argument to the subroutine, that is:

```
$elapsed = Timer::Elapsed($timer);
```

Methods invoked via an object rather than a package name are referred to as "object" or "dynamic" methods.

Finally, let's look more closely at the Elapsed method itself. Most object-oriented languages have an automatically created variable called this or self that you can use inside methods. This "self" variable contains a pointer to the object that was used to invoke the method. Perl does not create a $self variable for you automatically. However, as you just saw in our discussion of new and Elapsed, Perl does supply an object or a package name as the first argument to a method. In the case of an object method like Elapsed, it is customary to shift this value off the argument list and name it $self. This is exactly what happens behind the scenes in other object-oriented languages. In the case of the Elapsed method, $self is a reference to a Timer object. This object is an anonymous hash created

---

2. Perl will accept a surprisingly large variety of things to the left (and even right) of the method call arrow as well as in the indirect object slot. This behavior is not thoroughly documented as of this writing, but feel free to experiment with things like 'Foo'->Bar() to get a feel for this extra "intelligence."

by the `Timer` constructor, and therefore `$self` is a reference to a hash (see Item 30).

## Destructors

When the last reference to an object is gone, or the object goes out of scope, the object is destroyed and its space is reclaimed for later use by Perl. For ordinary, non-blessed data, that is the end of the story. Blessed objects, however, can go out with a little more fanfare. If a package contains a subroutine named DESTROY, this subroutine, called a *destructor*, will be invoked just before a blessed object belonging to that package is destroyed:

```perl
package Foo;                            Class Foo . . .
sub new {                               Define a constructor.
  my $pkg = shift;
  bless { name => shift }, $pkg
}
sub DESTROY {                           Define a destructor.
  my $self = shift;
  print "nuke '$self->{name}'\n";
}

package main;
$a = new Foo('Bar');
{
  my $b = new Foo('Bletch');
}                                       nuke 'Bletch' (out of scope)

$a = new Foo('Baz');                    nuke 'Bar' (no refs left)
                                        nuke 'Baz' (at termination)
```

Destruction occurs when an object is no longer referenced—either because the last reference to it was overwritten (as is the case with the second assignment to $a, above) or the last reference to it has gone out of scope (as is the case with $b). Objects still in existence at program termination are destroyed in a final mark-sweep garbage collection pass, as is the case with the final contents of $a. (For more about memory allocation and garbage collection in Perl, see Item 34.)

Destructors are useful for ensuring that shareable resources like semaphores, locks, and files are released properly when the life of an object that uses them is over. For example:

■ **Use destructors to "clean up."**

> *This illustrates how you might use a destructor to make sure a temporary resource, in this case a file, is released at program termination.*

```perl
use FileHandle;
```
*Use the FileHandle object-oriented file package.*

```perl
package TmpFile;

sub new {
  my $pkg = shift;
  $uniq++;
  my $prog = (split m!/!, $0)[-1];
  my $name = "/tmp/$prog.$$.$uniq";
  my $fh = new FileHandle $name, "w+";
  die $! unless $fh;
  bless { name => $name, fh => $fh }
}
```
*Construct a TmpFile.*

*Get program name from $0.*
*Create unique filename.*
*Open file.*

*Save name and FileHandle.*

```perl
sub DESTROY {
  my $self = shift;
  close $self->{fh} or die $!;
  unlink $self->{name} or die $!;
}
```
*Destroy a TmpFile.*

*Close the file.*
*Delete the file.*

```perl
sub FH {
  my $self = shift;
  $self->{fh};
}
```
*A method to return the FileHandle of a TmpFile.*

```perl
package main;

$temp = new TmpFile;
$fh = $temp->FH;
print $fh "temp data\n";
$fh->seek(0, 0);
print $fh->getline();
```
*Create a TmpFile.*

*Write some data to it and read it back out. The file will be deleted upon termination.*

# Item 50: Understand method inheritance in Perl.

Inheritance, like many other things in Perl, is pared down to its bare essentials. Perl has direct support for method inheritance only. It does not provide a built-in mechanism for inheriting data—see Item 51.

## Method inheritance

To derive class B from class A, you add the name 'A' to class B's @ISA variable. For example:

```
package B;
@ISA = qw(A);
```

For each class, the package variable @ISA defines a list of parent classes that supply inherited methods. Inherited methods are invoked when Perl cannot find a method in the first place it looks. Remember that method calls like the following:

```
$foo = Method Class('arg1', 'arg2');
```

are translated into:

```
$foo = Class::Method('Class', 'arg1', 'arg2');
```

What if there is no Class::Method? If @ISA is empty, then the result is a run-time fatal error. However, if @ISA contains one or more class names, then Perl also looks in those classes for a subroutine named Method and, if necessary, to the parent classes of those classes, and so on, yielding a fatal error only after it has exhausted its search of the inheritance tree.

Let's see how this actually works. Here's a class hierarchy:

```
package A;                          Define a top-level class A and
sub new { bless {}, shift };        a bare-bones "all-purpose"
sub A_Method {                      constructor.
  print "A_Method\n";
}

package B;                          Define a class B derived from A.
@ISA = qw(A);
sub B_Method {
  print "B_Method\n";
}
sub Method {
  print "Method (in B)\n";
}

package C;                          Define a class C derived from B.
@ISA = qw(B);                       It also derives indirectly from A.
sub C_Method {
  print "C_Method\n";
}
sub Method {
  print "Method (in C)\n";
}
```

And here are some examples using the classes A, B, and C:

```
package main;                       All our examples are in main.

$a = new A;                         Create a new object of class A.
```

| | |
|---|---|
| `$b = new B;` | B *has no method* new, *so this calls* A::new('B') *and creates a new object blessed into class* B. |
| `$c = new C;` | *Looks for* new *in* B, *then in* A, *calls* A::new('C') *and creates a new object blessed into class* C. |
| `$c->C_Method();` | *Prints* C_Method. |
| `$c->Method();` | *Prints* Method (in C). |
| `$c->B_Method();` | *Prints* B_Method. |
| `$c->A_Method();` | *Prints* A_Method. |
| `$b->Method();` | *Prints* Method (in B). |
| `$a->Method();` | *Run-time fatal error.* |

Inheritance in Perl is a run-time mechanism. It is possible to modify @ISA at run time and thereby change the inheritance hierarchy of a program "on the fly." In most cases this would be a bad or at least a very strange idea; however, it could be useful for implementing some kind of template or dynamic loading mechanism.

## Multiple inheritance

Multiple inheritance is Considered Scary[3] in many programming languages, but in Perl it is a simple and widely used feature. The absence of data inheritance makes multiple inheritance much less confusing.

To inherit methods directly from more than one class, you add more than one class name to @ISA:

```
package A1;                          Define a top-level class A1.
sub A1_Method {
  print "A1_Method\n";
}
sub Method {
  print "Method (in A1)\n";
}
```

---

3. A feeble attempt at paraphrasing the title of Edsger W. Dijkstra's famous "Goto Statement Considered Harmful" letter from the March 1968 *Communications of the ACM*. Discussions of multiple inheritance sometimes raise the same kind of ideological arguments.

```
package A2;                           Define a top-level class A2.
sub A2_Method {
  print "A2_Method\n";
}
sub Method {
  print "Method (in A2)\n";
}

package B;                            Define a class B that derives
@ISA = qw(A1 A2);                     from both A1 and A2.
sub new { bless {} }
```

Perl searches parent classes in the order in which they are encountered in @ISA. This is a depth-first search, meaning that Perl searches the first class listed in @ISA as well as all of its parent classes before searching the second class in @ISA.

Here are some examples using the classes A1, A2, and B:

```
package main;                         All our examples are in main.

$b = new B;                           Creates a new object of class B.

$b->A1_Method();                      Prints A1_Method.

$b->A2_Method();                      Prints A2_Method.

$b->Method();                         Prints Method (in A1) — A1 is
                                      first in @B::ISA.

@B::ISA = qw(A2 A1);                  Search A2 first.
$b->Method();                         Now prints Method (in A2).

A1::Method('A1');                     Invoke A1::Method explicitly—
                                      note class name argument to
                                      conform to method calling
                                      conventions.
```

If you don't want to search the entire inheritance hierarchy for a method, you can qualify the method name with the name of the package where you want the search to start:

*Continued from above:*

```
$b->A1::Method();                     Search A1 and its parent classes
                                      (if any).
                                      Prints Method (in A1).

$b->A2::Method();                     Prints Method (in A2).
```

The special pseudo package name SUPER:: can be used to refer to the @ISA list for the *current package*:

*Continued from above:*

```
package B;
```
*SUPER:: refers to the current package, not the class of the object to the left of the arrow.*

```
$b->SUPER::Method();
```
*Search @B::ISA for Method, skipping B itself.*

The most commonly encountered use of multiple inheritance is in creating modules (see Item 45). The top-level package for most Perl modules is generally a subclass of Exporter and is often also a subclass of AutoLoader or SelfLoader.

## More about method inheritance—AUTOLOAD and UNIVERSAL

After searching @ISA for methods, Perl also tries two other special locations: an AUTOLOAD subroutine in the search path and the UNIVERSAL class.

Perl calls a package's AUTOLOAD subroutine, if one exists, whenever an attempt is made to call a nonexistent subroutine in that package. Perl will also look in all the packages in the class hierarchy for an AUTOLOAD subroutine if the original subroutine's package lists one or more parent classes in @ISA and if the subroutine was invoked using method call syntax.[4]

An AUTOLOAD subroutine is easy to write. The variable $AUTOLOAD contains the fully qualified name of the subroutine called, and the arguments to the subroutine are the ones from the original subroutine call:

```
package A;
sub new { bless {}, shift }
sub AUTOLOAD {
  print "auto $AUTOLOAD\n";
  print "@_\n";
}
```
*Define a parent class A with an AUTOLOAD subroutine.*

---

4. In earlier versions of Perl 5, the inheritance tree was searched for AUTOLOAD subroutines *whether or not* a nonexistent subroutine was called using method call syntax. When brought to the attention of the Perl maintainers, this behavior was ruled a bug. In some future release it will be changed so that the inheritance tree is searched for AUTOLOAD subroutines only in the case of method calls and not ordinary subroutine calls.

```
package B;                          Define an empty class B that
@ISA = qw(A);                       inherits from A.

package main;                       Prints:
$b = new B;                         auto B::foo
$b->foo('bar', 'baz');              B=HASH(0x116098) bar baz
```

If you try this code out yourself you will see something interesting. In addition to autoloading B::foo, this example also autoloads B::DESTROY! This may seem surprising at first, but remember that blessed objects like $b are automatically destroyed when they go out of scope or when the program terminates. When Perl attempts to invoke the destructor for $b, it uses the same search path as for any other method, and thus it autoloads the destructor.

Finally, if Perl cannot conclude its search for a missing method or subroutine via AUTOLOAD, it checks the "package of last resort"—the UNIVERSAL package. You could even combine UNIVERSAL and AUTOLOAD to write a *truly* universal subroutine:

```
package UNIVERSAL;                  Any unresolved subroutine or
sub AUTOLOAD {                      method call will wind up here.
  print "auto $AUTOLOAD\n";
}
```

## Avoid calling methods as subroutines

Method call syntax isn't *just* a fancy way to refer to a subroutine in another package. Method calls support inheritance, which means that superclasses are searched when a nonexistent method is called. You can't get the equivalent behavior with an ordinary subroutine call:

```
@Student::ISA = qw(Person);         Here's a method call.
$aStudent->drive($aCar);

Student::drive($aStudent, $aCar);   An equivalent call if drive is in
                                    Student.

Person::drive($aStudent, $aCar);    But this is the equivalent if
                                    drive is not found in Student,
                                    but in its parent class, Person.
```

If you call the subroutine Student::drive subroutine directly, and it doesn't exist, you'll get an error. The method call would have searched both Student and Person, finding it in Person. And you especially don't want to call a method directly without passing the initial class or instance parameter, because that would very likely confuse the method.

## Item 51: Inherit data explicitly.

As mentioned earlier, Perl has no built-in facilities for data inheritance. By and large, this isn't a problem at all. Consider the following:

- Perl objects do not have predeclared members or sizes. Typically, Perl objects are represented using references to anonymous hashes. The members of an object are key-value pairs in a hash. There is no need for a member to be declared, and consequently there is no need for a subclass to inherit declarations from a parent class.

- Perl constructors are inheritable and can be very "thin" and general. A single parent class constructor can serve the needs of a whole family of derived classes. (See the "generic, inheritable" constructor immediately below.)

Let's look at a simple class hierarchy:

```
package Person;
sub new {                        The basic generic, inheritable
  my $pkg = shift;               constructor.
  bless { @_ }, $pkg;
}

package Student;                 A subclass of Person, inheriting
@ISA = qw(Person);              Person's constructor.

$joseph = new Person(            Create a new Person.
  first => 'Joseph',
  last => 'Hall'
);

$merlyn = new Student(           Create a new Student by
  first => 'Randal',            inheriting Person::new.
  last => 'Schwartz',
  id => 7777
);
```

Because of the way Perl works, in many cases there is no requirement for any kind of data inheritance. Objects have the members they are assigned. Their class is irrelevant.

### Data inheritance and complex constructors

When constructors become more complex, however, some form of data inheritance may be necessary. A good example is when subclass constructors add default values for some members. Let's consider a class hierarchy of objects representing shapes in a graphics window—circles, rectangles, polygons, text, and so on. Generally, a hierarchy like this is derived from a single parent class—we will call ours `Graphic`. Suppose the `Graphic` constructor sets some default values for line width and color:

● **The `Graphic` class**

```
package Graphic;

sub new {
  my $pkg = shift;
  bless {
    pen => 1,
    color => 'black',
    @_
  }, $pkg;
}
```

*A generic constructor for `Graphic` objects.*

*Supply some default values for members in case they are not supplied in @_.*

Now, suppose we want to derive a class, `Text`, from `Graphic`. Our constructor for `Text` also will need to set some default values, but these will be peculiar to `Text` objects. We will have to write the constructor for `Text` objects so that it invokes the `Graphic` constructor. However, we also have to be careful to write it so that the constructed object gets the `Text` default values. It must also wind up blessed into class `Text`:

● **The `Text` class**

*This example defines a constructor for `Text`, a subclass of `Graphic`. The constructor would be called like this:*

```
$text = new Text (color => 'blue', font => 'courier');
```

```
package Text;

@ISA = qw(Graphic);

sub new {
  my $pkg = shift;
  SUPER::new $pkg (
    font => 'times',
    size => 12,
    @_ );
}
```

*Subclass of `Graphic`.*

*Call superclass constructor, passing in our own defaults.*

The tricky part in this example is the way in which the `Graphic` constructor is called. `SUPER::new $pkg ()` invokes the inherited constructor (see Item 50 for more information about SUPER), but passes `'Text'`, not `'Graphic'`, as the constructor's class argument. You might be tempted to write a slightly simpler Text constructor, eschewing the fancy SUPER keyword:

▼ **The Text class—the wrong way**

```
package Text;

@ISA = qw(Graphic);

sub new {
  my $pkg = shift;
  new Graphic (                       Call the Graphic constructor—
    font => 'times',                  but what class is the object?
    size => 12,
    @_ );
}
```

This does the right thing by calling the parent class constructor, but unfortunately, this Text constructor creates and returns Graphic objects. You will have to re-bless them into Text at the end of the constructor:

```
sub new {
  my $pkg = shift;
  bless new Graphic (               Call the Graphic constructor—
    font => 'times',                but what class is $self now?
    size => 12,
    @_ ), $pkg;                      OK, make it a Text (or
}                                    whatever).
```

This is okay, but you'll be better off using SUPER. Among other things, using SUPER::new means that you do not have to modify the subclass constructor if the name of the parent class changes.

## Item 52: Create invisible interfaces with tied variables.

Let's end our discussion of object-oriented programming with an example. A *tied variable* in Perl is a variable that has been given magical properties via the tie operator. A tied variable is bound to a Perl object. All of the operations on that variable, such as assignment to it, reading its value(s), iterating over its values, and so on, are translated into method calls for that object. Perl supports tying the following types of variables:

- **Scalars**—Tied scalars let you create your own magic variables along the lines of $!.

- **Arrays**—The implementation for arrays is incomplete as of this writing, but it is somewhat usable in its current form.

- **Hashes**—The implementation for hashes is complete and robust, largely because the first tied variables were Perl 4 DBM hashes.

- **Filehandles**—Recent versions of Perl support tied filehandles.

Let's just dive right in and look at an example. I've tried to explain it reasonably thoroughly on the fly, but this isn't intended to be a complete description of how to write a tied class. For that you should consult the `perltie` man page.

## A tied hash

We will create a class called `FileProp` that allows you to access certain properties of a file by accessing the elements of a hash. To keep things simple, let's support just the following:

- `name` (read/write)—the name of the file

- `contents` (read/write)—the contents of the file

- `size` (readonly)—the size of the file

- `mtime` (read/write)—the modification time of the file, in Unix seconds since the epoch

- `ctime` (readonly)—the "change time" of the file

There are nine methods to write for a tied hash: TIEHASH, FETCH, STORE, DELETE, CLEAR, EXISTS, FIRSTKEY, NEXTKEY, and DESTROY. You don't have to write all of them if you will be using only some of the functionality of a hash (see Item 58 for an example of this), but you should go the full Monty if you are writing a tied hash class for general use.

The first step is to create a constructor—the TIEHASH method—for the `FileProp` class:

● The `FileProp` prologue and constructor

```
#!/usr/local/bin/perl -w          We'll put everything in one file
package FileProp;                  for convenience.
use Carp;                          The Carp module adds the
                                   croak function, which reports
                                   errors at the point our package
                                   was called, rather than from
                                   within the package.

my %PROPS = (                      The PROPS hash contains
  name => 1, size => 0, mtime => 1,    property names and a flag
  contents => 1, ctime => 0        indicating whether they are
);                                 read/write.
my @KEYS = keys %PROPS;            KEYS will help with iterators.
```

● The `FileProp` prologue and constructor (cont'd)

```
sub TIEHASH {
  my ($pkg, $name) = @_;
  unless (-e $name) {
    local *FH;
    open FH, ">$name" or
      croak "can't create $name";
    close FH;
  }

  bless {
    NAME => $name, INDEX => 0
  }, $pkg;
}
```

*The TIEHASH method constructs a new "shadow object" that underlies the tied variable.*

*Our shadow object is a hash containing the filename and a numeric iterator index.*

You tie variables to the `FileProp` class using the `tie` operator:

```
tie %data, FileProp, "new.data";
```

Then `tie` makes a class method call to TIEHASH:

```
FileProp::TIEHASH "FileProp", "new.data";
```

TIEHASH returns a Perl object (in this case, a blessed hash ref), which `tie` magically binds to the tied variable (%data, above). Now, all accesses to the variable %data will invoke `FileProp` methods. Let's write some of those methods.

The FETCH method is called when a value is retrieved from the tied variable:

● The `FileProp` FETCH method

```
sub FETCH {
  my ($self, $key) = @_;
  my $name = $self->{NAME};
  unless (exists $PROPS{$key}) {
    croak "no property $key for $name";
  }

  if ($key eq 'size') {
    -s $name
  } elsif ($key eq 'name') {
    $name
  } elsif ($key eq 'mtime') {
    (stat $name)[9]
  } elsif ($key eq 'ctime') {
    (stat $name)[10]
```

*FETCH is called when a value is read from the tied hash.*
*Get filename for convenience.*
*Do we grok this property?*

*File size in bytes.*

*Filename.*

*Mod time, seconds since the epoch.*

*Change time, seconds since the epoch.*

● The `FileProp` FETCH method (cont'd)

```
  } elsif ($key eq 'contents') {          Contents of the file. Open it
    local $/, *FH;                        and read it in.
    open FH, $name;
    my $contents = <FH>;
    close FH;
    $contents;
  }
}
```

With the FETCH method in place, you can say:

```
print "size of data = $data{size}\n";
```

and the size of the file "new.data" will be displayed. Next up is the STORE method. The STORE method is called when a value is assigned to the tied variable:

● The `FileProp` STORE method

```
sub STORE {                               Called whenever a value is
  my ($self, $key, $value) = @_;          stored into the tied hash.
  my $name = $self->{NAME};
  unless ($PROPS{$key} and -w $name) {    Can we write this property
    croak "can't set prop $key for $name"; (and write to this file)?
  }

 if ($key eq 'name') {                     Change filename.
    croak "file $key exists" if -e $key;    Safety feature.
    rename $name => $key;                   Rename the file.
    $self->{NAME} = $key;                   Update internal filename.
  } elsif ($key eq 'mtime') {             Change mod time.
    utime((stat $name)[8], $value, $name);  Change only mtime.
  } elsif ($key eq 'contents') {          Change contents.
    local *FH;
    open FH, ">$name" or die;
    print FH $value;
    close FH;
  }
}
```

With the STORE method working, you can say:

```
$data{contents} = "Testing one two three\n";
```

and the contents of the file will be overwritten with the string "Testing one two three\n". Or, perhaps you would like to change the modification time to two minutes ago:

```
    $data{mtime} = time - 120;
```

It gets simpler from here. Let's define the methods used to test and iterate over keys:

● The `FileProp` EXISTS, FIRSTKEY, and NEXTKEY methods

```
sub EXISTS {                          Called when exists is used on
  my ($self, $key) = @_;              a key of the tied hash.
  exists $PROPS{$key};
}

sub FIRSTKEY {                        Called by keys and each to get
  my $self = shift;                   the first key from the tied hash.
  $self->{INDEX} = 0;                 We have to maintain some sort
  $KEYS[$self->{INDEX}++];            of index of where we are on a
}                                     per-object basis, thus the INDEX
                                      member.

sub NEXTKEY {                         Called by keys and each to get
  my $self = shift;                   succeeding keys from the tied
  my $key = $KEYS[$self->{INDEX}++];  hash.
  $self->{INDEX} = 0 unless defined $key;
  $key;
}
```

Now you can find out what properties are supported by `FileProp`:

```
    print "properties: ", join(" ", keys %data), "\n";
```

which will give you:

```
    name ctime size mtime contents
```

Finally, although they don't make a lot of sense for our application, we have to define methods for deleting and clearing the tied hash. We will just have them produce errors:

● The `FileProp` DELETE and CLEAR methods

```
sub DELETE {                          Called when delete is used on
  croak "can't delete properties"     a key of the tied hash.
}

sub CLEAR {                           Called when the hash is
  croak "can't clear properties"      cleared, as when assigned an
}                                     empty list.
```

A destructor (the DESTROY method) is not necessary for this example.

Let's demonstrate the completed class. First, some driver code (just add it to the end of the file):

```
package main;

tie %data, FileProp, "new.data";
$data{contents} = "Demo data";

foreach (sort keys %data) {
  print "$_: $data{$_}\n";
}
```

When run, this should produce output similar to the following:

```
% tryme
contents: Demo data
ctime: 873187477
mtime: 873187477
name: new.data
size: 9
```

That's all there is to it!

For another tied variable example, see Item 58.

# Miscellany

## Item 53: Use pack and unpack for data munging.

Perl's built-in pack and unpack operators are two of the bigger, sharper blades on the "Swiss Army Chainsaw."[1] Perhaps they were originally intended as a ho-hum means of translating binary data to and from Perl data types like strings and integers, but pack and unpack can be put to more interesting and offbeat uses.

The pack operator works more or less like sprintf. It takes a format string followed by a list of values to be formatted, and returns a string:

```
pack("CCCC", 80, 101, 114, 108)         "Perl"—pack 4 unsigned chars.
```

The unpack operator works the other way:

```
unpack("CCCC", "Perl")                  (80, 101, 114, 108)
```

The format string is a list of single-character specifiers that specify the type of data to be packed or unpacked. Here is the current list of specifiers:

### Format specifiers for pack and unpack

| Format | Description | Example | Result |
|--------|-------------|---------|--------|
| A | ASCII string, space padded | pack "A2A3", "Pea", "rl" | "Perl " |
| a | ASCII string, null padded | pack "a2a3", "Pea", "rl" | "Perl\0 " |

---

1. One of the many obliquely complimentary names Perl has been given.

Format specifiers for **pack** and **unpack** (cont'd)

| Format | Description | Example | Result |
|---|---|---|---|
| B | bit string, descending order | pack "B8", "00110000" | "0" |
| b | bit string, ascending (vec) order | pack "b8", "00001100" | "0" |
| H | hex string, high nybble first | pack "H*", "5065726c" | "Perl" |
| h | hex string, low nybble first | pack "h2h2h2h2", "05", "56", "27", "c6" | "Perl" |
| C | unsigned char | unpack "C*", "\377\1\2\376" | 255, 1, 2, 254 |
| c | signed char | unpack "C*", "\377\1\2\376" | -1, 1, 2, -2 |
| S | 16-bit unsigned integer | unpack "S2", "\377\1\2\376" | 65281, 766† |
| s | 16-bit signed integer | unpack "s2", "\377\1\2\376" | -255, 766† |
| L | 32-bit unsigned integer | unpack "L", "\377\1\2\376" | 4278256382† |
| l | 32-bit signed integer | unpack "l", "\377\1\2\376" | -16710914† |
| I | "native" unsigned integer, at least 32 bits | unpack "I", "\377\1\2\376" | 4278256382† |
| i | "native" signed integer, at least 32 bits | unpack "i", "\377\1\2\376" | -16710914† |
| N | 32-bit integer in "network" (big-endian) order | unpack "N", "\377\1\2\376" | 4278256382 |
| n | 16-bit integer, network order | unpack "n2", "\377\1\2\376" | 65281, 766 |
| V | 32-bit integer in "VAX" (little-endian) order | unpack "V*", "\377\1\2\376" | 4261544447 |
| v | 16-bit integer, VAX order | unpack "v2", "\377\1\2\376" | 511, 65026 |
| u | uuencoded string | unpack "u*", '$4&5R;```' | "Perl" |
| w | BER (Basic Encoding Rules) encoded integer | unpack "ww", "\177\377\177" | 127, 16383 |
| X | back up 1 byte | pack "A4XXA2", "Peat", "rl" | "Perl" |

**Format specifiers for pack and unpack (cont'd)**

| Format | Description | Example | Result |
|--------|-------------|---------|--------|
| x | null byte | unpack "L", pack("Cxxx", 1) | 16777216[†] |
| @ | null fill to absolute position | unpack "H*", pack('@3C', 1) | "00000001" |

[†] *Depends on platform endian-ness—this table was constructed on a big-endian machine.*

Each specifier may be followed by a repeat count indicating how many values from the list to format. The repeat counts for the string specifiers (A, a, B, b, H, and h) are special—they indicate how many bytes/bits/nybbles to add to the output string. An asterisk used as a repeat count means to use the specifier preceding the asterisk for all the remaining items.

The unpack operator also can compute checksums. Just precede a specifier with a percent sign and a number indicating how many bits of checksum are desired. The extracted items then are checksummed together into a single item:

```
unpack "c4", "\1\2\3\4";              1, 2, 3, 4

unpack "%16c4", "\1\2\3\4";           10

unpack "%3c4", "\1\2\3\4";            2
```

## Sorting with pack

Suppose that you have a list of numeric Internet addresses—in string form—to sort, something like:

```
11.22.33.44
1.3.5.7
23.34.45.56
```

You would like to have them in "numeric" order. That is, the list should be sorted on the numeric value of the first number, then subsorted on the second, then the third, and finally the fourth. As usual, if you try to sort a list like this ASCIIbetically, the results are in the wrong order (see Item 14). Sorting numerically won't work either, because that would only sort on the first number in each string. Using pack provides a pretty good solution:

```
@sorted_addr =
  sort { pack('C*', split /\./, $a) cmp
         pack('C*', split /\./, $b) } @addr;
```

For efficiency, this definitely should be rewritten as a Schwartzian Transform (see Item 14):

```
@sorted_addr =
  map { $_->[0] }
  sort { $a->[1] cmp $b->[1] }
  map { [$_, pack('C*', split /\./)] }
  @addr;
```

Notice that the comparison operator used in the sort is cmp, not <=>. The pack function is converting a list of numbers (e.g., 11, 22, 33, 44) into a 4-byte string ("\x0b\x16\x21\x2c"). Comparing these strings ASCIIbetically produces the proper sorting order. Of course, you could also use Socket and write:

```
@sorted_addr =
  map { $_->[0] }
  sort { $a->[1] cmp $b->[1] }
  map { [$_, inet_aton($_)] }
  @addr;
```

but obviously pack provides a more general capability.

## Manipulating hex escapes

Because pack and unpack understand hexadecimal strings, they can be useful in manipulating strings containing hex escapes and the like.

For example, suppose you are programming for the World Wide Web and would like to "URI unescape" unsafe characters in a string. To URI unescape a string, you need to replace each occurrence of an escape—a percent sign followed by two hex digits—with the corresponding character. For example, "a%5eb" would be decoded to yield "a^b". You can write a Perl substitution to do this in one line:

```
$_ = "a%5eb";
s/%([0-9a-fA-F]{2})/pack("c",hex($1))/ge;
```

This particular snippet is widespread in some older handrolled CGI scripts. However, it's somewhat obscure looking, and as is the case for many commonly performed tasks in Perl, there is a module designed specifically for the job:

```
use URI::Escape;
$_ = uri_unescape "a%5eb";
```

## UUencoding/decoding

Have you ever tried to write a program to uudecode a file? It's easy in Perl, thanks to the uuencode/decode support built into pack and unpack:

● A uudecode program

```
while (<>) {                          Skip to the start of the
  last if ($mode, $filename) =        uuencoded data.
    /^begin\s+(\d+)\s+(\S+)/i;
}
if ($mode) {                          Assuming we got started:
  open F, ">$filename" or             Create output file.
    die "couldn't open $filename: $!\n";
  chmod oct($mode), $filename or      Set the mode.
    die "couldn't set mode: $!\n";
  print "$mode $filename\n";          Read a line of data, uudecode
  while (<>) {                        it, print it, until done.
    last if (/^(`|end)/i);
    print F unpack('u*', $_);
  }
}
```

## Item 54: Know how and when to use eval, require, and do.

One of the advantages that Perl shares with certain other interpreted languages is the ability to compile and execute code at run time. The basic mechanism for run-time compilation is the string form of the eval operator, which takes a string argument containing source code. For example:

```
$varname = 'some_var';
$val = eval " \$$varname ";          $val gets whatever $some_var
                                     contains.
```

The contents of the string are compiled and then run in the context of the caller—in the current package, with package and local variables (even my variables) available to it. The string is compiled *each time* the eval is executed. The result of eval is the value of the last expression evaluated inside the eval, similar to the way subroutines work. Should the code fail to compile, or suffer a run-time exception (as from die, divide-by-zero, etc.), execution of the eval-ed code ends and an error message is returned to the calling context in the special variable $@:

■ Handle exceptions (inefficiently) with string eval.

```
eval q{                              Single-quoting with q{}.
  open F1, $fname1 or die "$!";       Try to open some files.
  open F2, $fname2 or die "$!";
  # some other stuff ...
};                                   Note closing semicolon!
```

■ Handle exceptions (inefficiently) with string **eval**. (cont'd)

```
if ($@ ne '') {                                    Exceptions come here.
  warn "error in eval: $@\n";
  # clean up ...
}
```

The exception-handling abilities of eval are very handy. However, if all you need to do is add exception handling to an unchanging hunk of code, you should not be using the string form of eval. You should be using the block form.

### Exception handling with eval

The block form of eval takes a block as its argument. The block form is used solely for exception handling, because the block is compiled *only once*, at the same time as the surrounding code:

■ Handle exceptions with block **eval** (preferred).

```
eval {                                          A block instead of a string.
  open F1, $fname1 or die "$!";                 Now, compiled with the
  open F2, $fname2 or die "$!";                 surrounding code rather than
  # some other stuff ...                        when eval is encountered at
};                                              run time.

if ($@ ne '') {                                 Exceptions come here—same
  warn "error in eval: $@\n";                   as with string form.
  # clean up ...
}
```

The block form of eval turns out to be more useful than the string form. Occasions to use the string form are rare (but see the example later in this Item). Although both forms of eval will catch exceptions, neither will catch signals, panics, or other types of "really fatal" errors. They also cannot "bring you back" from an exec or something similar. You can, however, benefit by adding signal handlers to eval blocks:

■ Use **eval** with signal handlers.

```
eval {
  local $SIG{INT} = sub {                       Install a signal handler to catch
    die "caught an interrupt"                    control-C (or whatever).
  };
  my $foo = <>;                                 Wait for some input.
};
```

■ **Use** eval **with signal handlers. (cont'd)**

```
if ($@) {
  print "error in eval: $@\n";
}
```
*Control goes here if the user hits control-C while the program waits for input above.*

## Incorporating source files at run time with require

Although the string form of eval is rarely used, it forms the basis for a very important "file" form of run-time compilation, require.

The require directive takes a numeric or string argument. The numeric form of require causes a fatal error if the current version of Perl is not equal to or greater than the numeric argument:

```
require 5;
```
*Fatal error unless running at least version 5.000.*

```
require 5.004;
```
*Fatal error unless running at least version 5.004.*

The string version, which is the one more relevant to the current discussion, reads in Perl source code at run time and executes it. In other words, it evals the contents of a file:

● **Loading and executing source code at run time with** require

| *File* foo.pl | |
| --- | --- |
| print "loading foo!\n"; | *Will be executed when* require-d. |
| sub bar { print "sub bar\n" } | *Define a subroutine.* |
| 1; | *Indicate successful loading.* |
| *Main program* | |
| #!/usr/local/bin/perl | *Wherever Perl is.* |
| require "foo.pl"; | *Prints* loading foo! |
| &bar(); | *Prints* sub bar |

Unlike eval, require uses the last expression evaluated in the included source file to determine whether the inclusion was successful. If the value is false, the load is deemed unsuccessful and require produces a fatal exception. This is why Perl module and library source files often end in "1;" on a line by itself.

In the good old days of Perl 4, require was the primary mechanism used to support Perl libraries. Library source files would typically define subroutines and (possibly) run some initialization code, much as in the example above. The use directive has largely supplanted require, although use is built on require (see Item 42).

Now, what require does is actually a little more sophisticated than reading source code and eval-ing it. (See do, discussed later, for the bare bones version.) First, require only loads a file once. Attempts to require a file more than once are ignored. Second, require searches the module include path for the specified filename. (The include path would ordinarily include the current directory.) See Item 43 for more about the module include path. Finally, if the argument to require is a bareword (an unquoted identifier), require automatically adds the extension .pm ("Perl Module") to the argument and searches for a file by that name. This is part of require's support for the use directive.

## Doing things with do

We have seen how eval has two somewhat different meanings (string and block form) and how require also does (Perl version and source file inclusion). We are about to discuss Perl's do operator, and you might wonder whether it too has more than one meaning.

Of course it does.

The file form of do is similar to require, but has fewer frills. It returns the value of the last statement evaluated in the included file, and it makes no difference whether this value is true or false. Neither does the file form of do presume a .pm suffix in the case of a bareword argument. The file form of do does, however, use the module include path. The file form of do can be useful at times. It is a handy way to load a "configuration file" of data, if the data can be written as Perl source:

● Loading configuration files with require

| *File* config.dat | |
|---|---|
| `$ROWS = 25;`<br>`$COLS = 80;` | *Some configuration values.* |
| *Main program* | |
| `#!/usr/local/bin/perl`<br>`die "where is config.dat? "`<br>`  unless -e "config.dat";`<br><br>`do "config.dat";` | *See if our file is there.*<br><br><br>*Read in some data.* |

It is also useful in combination with `Data::Dumper` (see Item 37) and other modules that generate Perl code.

The other form of do, the block form, has nothing to do with either files or `eval`, but we might as well cover it here. The block form returns the value of the last statement evaluated in its argument block:

```
$max = do {                           Returns the greater of $a
  if ($a > $b) {                      and $b.
    $a
  } else {
    $b
  }
};
```

The block form is hacked so that if it is used as the expression argument to a statement modifier, it is always evaluated once before the modifier's condition is tested. This allows you to write do `{...}` `while` loops in Perl:

```
do { $i *= 2 } while $i <= 1024;       Multiply $i by 2 at least once.
```

## Creative uses for string `eval`

The only occasions in which the string form of `eval` is really worthwhile is when there is a need to read or generate, then execute, Perl code on the fly. You might, for example, allow a user to type in a function, then compile it so that it could be plotted or analyzed for roots, minima, maxima, or whatever. Hopefully this will be a trusted user who will stick to typing in mathematical functions; otherwise you should check out the `Safe` module.

You can also use string `eval` to generate boilerplate functions automatically. Here is a slightly contrived example along those lines. The following code automatically generates "get" and "set" functions for Perl objects:

● **Generating class boilerplate with string** `eval`

*The code below allows you to declare a Perl class and its member variables with a* class *function, using syntax like:*

```
class MyClass qw(Member1 Member2 Member3);
```

*The* class *function automatically defines a constructor for* MyClass, *as well as methods to set and get the values of each member, for example:*

```
$myObj = new MyClass;
$myObj->Member1($some_val);
$val = $myObj->Member2();
```

● **Generating class boilerplate with string eval** (cont'd)

| | |
|---|---|
| ```perl
package UNIVERSAL;
sub AUTOLOAD {
  my ($pkg, $func) =
    ($AUTOLOAD =~ /^(.*)::(.*)$/);
  return if ($func eq 'DESTROY');
  if ($func ne 'class') {
    die "No such function $AUTOLOAD";
  }

  my $class = shift;
  my @members = @_;
``` | *To make the nice declaration syntax below work, we have to define a* UNIVERSAL AUTOLOAD *function (see Item 50). It will catch calls to functions named* class, *in any package.*

*When called with indirect object syntax (see Item 50),* $class *and the package name (from* $AUTOLOAD*) will be the same, so we just ignore* $class *below.* |
| ```perl
  eval qq{
    package $pkg;
    sub new {
      my \$self = { };
      bless \$self, '$pkg';
    }
  };
``` | *Double-quote with* qq{}. *Must set the proper package. This* eval *creates a constructor for the class. Note backslashes in front of* $self, *in honor of* qq{}. |
| ```perl
  foreach $member (@members) {
    eval qq{
      package $pkg;
      sub $member {
        my \$self = shift;
        if (\@_) {
          \$self->{$member} = shift;
        } else {
          \$self->{$member};
        }
      }
    }
  }
}
``` | *Now, for each of the members listed:* *Set the package again. This* eval *creates a function that returns the value of the member if no arguments are supplied, or that sets the value of the member with the first argument.* |
| ```perl
package main;

class Student qw(firstname lastname id);
``` | *Get back to* main.

*Here's our declaration syntax at work—this will create a constructor for class* Student, *as well as get/set functions for it.* |

● Generating class boilerplate with string eval (cont'd)

| | |
|---|---|
| ```$student = new Student;```<br>```$student->firstname('Joseph');```<br>```$student->lastname('Hall');```<br>```$student->id('7777');``` | *Let's use the constructor.*<br>*Now set first name,*<br>*last name,*<br>*and id.* |
| ```print "Name = ", $student->firstname(),```<br>```   " ", $student->lastname(), "\n";```<br>```print "Id = ", $student->id(), "\n";``` | ```Name = Joseph Hall```<br><br>```Id = 7777``` |

It might seem that this sort of application absolutely requires the use of string eval, but it doesn't. You can achieve the same effect by using closures (see Item 29), along with assignments to typeglobs to give them globally visible names. Closures are a more difficult mechanism for most programmers to understand, though, and in this case eval is probably the best way to go.

For a real module providing this kind of functionality, check out Class::Template.

## Item 55: Know when, and when not, to write networking code.

One of the many features that makes Perl an attractive programming language is its built-in support for TCP/IP programming. Perl and TCP/IP mix especially well because Perl's powerful text processing capabilities are very helpful in dealing with text-based Internet protocols like SMTP, NNTP, and HTTP.

Perl's support for network programming is so complete that you can write any conceivable type of Internet network application in it. Anything that you can express in C also can be expressed in Perl. You can write a web server or a news client from the ground up if you like. You can write a DNS server. You could even rewrite *sendmail*. The necessary capabilities are all there.

### Don't write low-level code when you can use modules instead

While it's certainly possible to write network applications from the ground up, you should consider using existing modules to support your efforts. For example, if you want to fetch a Web page, the following will suffice:

```
use LWP::Simple;
$page = get 'http://www.effectiveperl.com/';
```

(Yes, that's right—two lines!)

Of course, you could always start out with calls to socket, bind, connect, bone up on HTTP, and so on, but I think you'll agree that this is easier. HTTP is particularly well served by Perl modules, but there are also modules for working with FTP, NNTP, SMTP, and many other Internet protocols and standards. If you want to learn more about Perl's Internet modules, you should begin by looking at libwww-perl (the World Wide Web library, also called LWP) and libnet (a collection of Internet protocol modules).

## When you do write low-level networking code, don't use anachronisms

Of course, your application may be one where you are forced to write low-level networking code. For example, you might be working on a CGI script that connects to and exchanges data with a server application (possibly also written in Perl) via TCP/IP.

Networking or "sockets" code isn't easy to understand the first time you encounter it. To avoid starting from scratch, you will be tempted to look for an example to use as a starting point. This is a good idea, but you should be careful to work from an up-to-date example. Many of the older examples of sockets code in Perl that are floating around the net have various limitations, inefficiencies, and/or bugs. Let's discuss some of these problems, and how to avoid them.

First, you should always use the Socket module, or perhaps IO::Socket.[2] Among other things, the Socket module defines constants for protocol numbers and the like that will be correct for your environment. Older code may contain something like this:

```
$pf_inet = 2;
$sock_stream = 1;
$tcp_proto = 6;
```

These hard-coded values worked for many programmers for a long time, but once large numbers of people started using Perl on Solaris (System V) machines, network applications written in this manner began failing with mysterious "protocol not supported" messages. These values do not work

---

2. IO::Socket provides an object-oriented interface to the built-in socket functions as well as to some of the Socket module. This example could be rewritten to use IO::Socket, but it would not look dramatically different. IO::Socket was somewhat new at the time this example was written, so I've stuck to plain old Socket for now.

on all operating systems. The right way to write this code is to use the functions defined by the Socket module:

```
my $proto = getprotobyname 'tcp';
socket SERVER, PF_INET,
  SOCK_STREAM, $proto                    Establish a socket with the
  or die "socket: $!";                   filehandle SERVER.
```

Thus, we get the constant for the inet domain from the "constant" function PF_INET, the constant for the stream type from the function SOCK_STREAM, and the protocol number from the function getprotobyname. Another thing you may see in older code is the use of the pack operator to create the binary addresses that the various sockets functions require:

*The old way:*

```
$port = 2345;
$addr = pack 'S n a4 x8',
$pf_inet, $port, "\0\0\0\0";             This isn't exactly easy to read
bind SERVER, $addr or                    or remember.
  die "bind: $!\n";
```

The Socket module defines functions that do this for you in a more readable and maintainable way:

*The new way:*

```
$port = 2345;
bind SERVER,                             No more mysterious pack
  sockaddr_in($port, INADDR_ANY)         strings.
  or die "bind: $!";
```

Server applications are often written so that they spawn child processes to handle incoming connections. Any time you create child processes you need to do something to ensure that they do not become "zombies." One way to do this is to set up a SIGCHLD (child died) signal handler in the parent process. Whenever a child process exits, control transfers to the signal handler, which should then call wait to get rid of the zombie. You may have seen a variety of versions of this code, but one reasonably safe version looks something like this:

*This is a slightly overblown signal handler:*

```
sub REAPER {
  $SIG{CHLD} = \&REAPER;                 Reinstall if System V.
  wait;
}
$SIG{CHLD} = \&REAPER;                    Install handler.
```

It isn't necessary (or recommended) to reinstall the handler within the handler subroutine itself so long as you are on a BSD system or one that is POSIX-compliant. Nowadays the news here is likely to be good. Try the following:

```
use Config;
print "handlers stay put\n" if
  $Config{d_sigaction} eq "define";
```

You should skip reinstalling the handler if you believe your scripts will be run only on systems with POSIX signals (generally a safe bet):

```
sub REAPER { wait }
$SIG{CHLD} = \&REAPER;
```

Or, even more succinctly:

```
$SIG{CHLD} = sub { wait };          A really short version!
```

The reason to avoid the assignment to %SIG within the handler is that Perl does not yet have "safe" interrupts and may not have them for some time to come.[3] So long as this is true, the less that goes into a signal handler, the better. You may have considered using:

```
$SIG{CHLD} = 'IGNORE';              Bad, bad, BAD!
```

Please don't. It works on some System V machines but you will be experiencing "Night of the Living <defunct>" on other platforms.

## An example

Let's develop a pair of simple TCP/IP applications. We will write a server called psd that will run the ps command locally. The result will be returned to a client called rps. If you have to write both a client and a server, it's usually easiest to start writing the server, because you can probably test it using telnet as a client. Here is a bare-bones, slightly buggy first cut at psd:

● **psd: A ps daemon**

```
use strict;
use Socket;
```

---

3. Maybe I spoke too soon. As this book goes to press, a version of Perl with a safe exception-handling thread is being tested. This is "exceptionally" good news!

● **psd: A ps daemon** (cont'd)

```
my $port = 2001;
my $proto = getprotobyname 'tcp';
my $ps = '/usr/ucb/ps';                            Or wherever it is.

socket SERVER, PF_INET, SOCK_STREAM, $proto        Create a socket with filehandle
  or die "socket: $!";                             SERVER, family INET, type
                                                   STREAM, protocol TCP.
bind SERVER, sockaddr_in($port, INADDR_ANY)        Bind socket to port 2001,
  or die "bind: $!";                               allowing connections on any
                                                   interface.
listen SERVER, 1 or die "listen: $!";              Begin queueing connections.
print "$0 listening to port $port\n";

for (;;) {
  accept CLIENT, SERVER;                           Take a connection from the
                                                   queue. It become the
                                                   bidirectional filehandle CLIENT.
  print CLIENT `$ps`;                              Run ps and send the output
                                                   to the client.
  close CLIENT;                                     Close down the connection and
}                                                  get another one.
```

You can test this version of psd by running it in the background from the command line, then telnet-ing to the assigned port:

```
% psd &
[1] 29321
psd listening to port 2001
% telnet localhost 2001
Trying 127.0.0.1...
Connected to localhost.
Escape character is '^]'.
  PID TT       S  TIME COMMAND
 10582 pts/7   S  0:01 -tcsh
   ... blah blah blah ...
Connection closed by foreign host.
%
```

There are a couple of problems with this code that we ought to fix. If you start this version of psd, connect to it at least once, then kill it (with Control-C), and then try to restart it immediately, it may die with an error message along the lines of "address already in use." If you wait a while, though, it will run fine. What is happening is that one or more closed connections in the TIME_WAIT state (a perfectly normal condition) are preventing the call to bind from succeeding, because bind will not by default allow more than one socket to use the same name (address and port number) at the same time. After a few minutes, the closed connections time out completely and the name becomes available for reuse again.

Another problem is that this server will accept only a single connection at a time. The easy and customary way to have a server accept multiple simultaneous connections is to spawn a new child process to handle each incoming connection.

We will get back to the server shortly. Let's take a look at our client, rps:

● **rps: A remote ps client**

```
use strict;
use Socket;

my $remote_host = shift or
  die "$0: no hostname\n";
my $port = 2001;

my $ip = inet_aton $remote_host        Translate hostname into
  or die "unknown host: $remote_host"; numeric address.
my $proto = getprotobyname 'tcp';      Get TCP protocol number.
socket PSD, PF_INET, SOCK_STREAM, $proto   Create a socket with filehandle
  or die "socket: $!";                 PSD, family INET, type STREAM,
                                       protocol TCP.

connect PSD, sockaddr_in($port, $ip)   Establish a connection to the
  or die "connect: $!";                supplied port and address
                                       using socket PSD.
print while <PSD>;                     Read from remote psd.
close PSD or die "close: $!";          All done.
```

You can now use rps instead of telnet to talk to psd (kind of a mouthful of Unix, isn't it?):

```
% psd &
[2] 29678
psd1 listening to port 2001
% rps localhost
  PID TT        S  TIME COMMAND
 10582 pts/7    S  0:01 -tcsh
  ... blah blah blah ...
%
```

Extra features are nice, up to a point, so let's add one. Let's allow the user to specify a ps option as an argument on the command line, which rps will pass on to psd. First, at the top of the file, add:

```
use FileHandle;
```

Then, before my $remote_host..., add:

```
my $option = shift if @ARGV[0] =~ /^-/;
```

Next, we have to send the option to the server. This will require changes to both rps and psd. The change to rps is simple. Before print while <PSD>, insert the following:

```
PSD->autoflush(1);  # prettier than SELECT(PSD) and $| = 1
print PSD "$option\n";
```

We want to make sure that the option string we are sending gets sent; otherwise the server will hang. Here's psd, rewritten to incorporate an option string sent from rps and to support multiple connections:

● **psd**: A revised **ps** daemon

```
use strict;
use Socket;

my $port = 2001;
my $proto = getprotobyname 'tcp';
my $ps = '/usr/ucb/ps';
$SIG{CHLD} = sub { wait };              Dispose of zombies.

socket SERVER, PF_INET, SOCK_STREAM, $proto    Create a socket with filehandle
  or die "socket: $!";                         SERVER, family INET, type
                                               STREAM, protocol TCP.
setsockopt SERVER, SOL_SOCKET,                 Set SO_REUSEADDR so that
  SO_REUSEADDR, 1 or die "setsockopt: $!";     we can establish multiple
                                               connections to this socket.
bind SERVER, sockaddr_in($port, INADDR_ANY)    Bind socket to port 2001,
  or die "bind: $!";                           allowing connections on any
                                               interface.
listen SERVER, 5 or die "listen: $!";          Begin queueing connections.
print "$0 listening to port $port\n";

for (;;) {
  my $addr = accept CLIENT, SERVER;            Take a connection from the
  my $client_host = gethostbyaddr(             queue into CLIENT.
    (unpack_sockaddr_in $addr)[1],
    AF_INET);
  print "connection from $client_host\n";

  die "can't fork: $!"                         Fork after accepting.
    unless defined (my $kid = fork());
  if (not $kid) {                              Child here.
    my $option = <CLIENT>;                     Read option, then excise any
    $option =~ tr/a-zA-Z//cd;                  unsafe stuff in it.
    $option = "-$option" if $option;
    print CLIENT `$ps $option`;
    exit;                                      Exit, lest child start accept-ing.
```

● **psd: A revised ps daemon (cont'd)**

```
    } else {                              Parent here. We don't want
      close CLIENT;                       to mess with CLIENT.
    }
}
```

We've added a call to setsockopt that allows us to establish multiple connections on the same socket. This also will put an end to the TIME_WAIT behavior you may have observed before. The second parameter to listen has been increased to 5, which will allow us to have up to five connections queued up at once, that is, five connections that haven't yet been answered by accept.[4]

We now print out the hostname of the connecting machine and then fork a child process. The child process, which executes the code inside the first block of the if statement, reads the option sent by the client and tidies it up so that nothing bad will happen if someone sends an option like '; rm *'. There is also a SIGCHLD handler so that we don't create zombies.

Obviously, you can go a lot farther in network programming than this simple example does. Perl supports all of the Unix networking features accessible from C, including other TCP/IP features (e.g., UDP) and Unix domain networking. As I pointed out earlier, Perl is especially convenient for dealing with text-based protocols because of its string handling and pattern matching features. In any event, as you embark on your next network programming project, remember to check the CPAN to see whether what you need has already been written. The code that you need may be there already, and if it is, it is likely to be reasonably well thought out and implemented.

## Item 56:  Don't forget the file test operators.

One of the more frequently heard questions from newly minted Perl programmers is, "How do I find the size of a file?" If this question is asked on the Perl newsgroup comp.lang.perl.misc, almost invariably there will be be one response like the following:

```
($dev,$ino,$mode,$nlink,$uid,          Poster must have been reading
  $gid,$rdev,$size,$atime,$mtime,      the stat man page.
  $ctime,$blksize,$blocks) =
    stat($filename);
```

---

4.  The value 5 is a maximum in some operating systems. It is the "customary" value for the second argument to listen.

Or, perhaps:

```
($size) = (stat $filename)[7];          Poster read man page and
                                         "optimized" it.
```

But the short answer is:

```
$size = -s $filename;
```

I'm not sure why, but many people overlook Perl's file test operators. This is a shame, because they are succinct and efficient, and tend to be more readable than equivalent constructs written using the stat operator.

File tests fit into loops and conditions very well. Here, for example, is a list of the text files in a directory:

```
@textfiles =                             Tests use $_ by default.
   grep { -T } glob "$dir_name/*";
```

It's much easier to check permissions on a file using file test operators than it is to mask the mode value from stat:

```
print "$f is: ";                         Special pseudo-filehandle
print "writeable " if -w $f;             _ refers to the result of the
print "readable " if -r _;               last stat or lstat.
print "executable " if -x _;
```

This example uses the special pseudo-filehandle _, which the file test operators can use to refer to the result of the last stat performed, whether by an explicit call or as the result of a recent use of a file test operator. Because stat is slow (generally requiring a disk access), this is a worthwhile optimization.

## Item 57:  Access the symbol table with typeglobs.

In the present implementation of Perl (and probably—but you never know—in all future implementations) there is a symbol table entry for each unique identifier in a package. That entry contains slots for one of each of the possible types of values—scalar, array, hash, filehandle, and so on. To a certain extent, you can directly manipulate the contents of the symbol table. One way to do this is with a construct called a typeglob. A typeglob is an identifier preceded by an asterisk, for example, *a. It represents the symbol table entry that contains *all* of the different types of values stored under that identifier.

A warning to the uninitiated: Typeglobs are generally considered to be an obscure feature. For that reason, you should avoid using them unnecessarily. Furthermore, you should avoid using typeglobs for tasks that could be handled with references (see Item 30), because references are far more efficient. With that admonition out of the way, let's move on.

You can use typeglobs to alias names:

```
*ren = *stimpy;
```
*Make* $ren *an alias for* $stimpy,
@ren *an alias for* @stimpy,
*and so on.*

```
*main::ren = *main::stimpy;
```
*Same thing, explicit package name.*

Typeglobs can be localized:

```
local *ren = *stimpy;
```
$ren, @ren, *etc. are local.*

A similar effect, but with run-time symbol table lookup, is available using the symbol table hash directly. Here is an example that manipulates the main package's symbol table:

```
$::{'ren'} = $::{'stimpy'};
```
%:: *is the main package's symbol table.*

```
local $::{'ren'} = $::{'stimpy'};
```
*Can be localized.*

You can pass typeglobs as arguments to subroutines, or store them like scalar values:

```
@g = (*a, *b);
($a, $b) = ("ren", "stimpy");
```
*Storing typeglobs in an array.*

```
*s = $g[0];
*t = $g[1];
print "$s and $t\n";
```
*Using them.*
*Or just* (*s, *t) = @g.
*Prints* ren *and* stimpy.

You also can alias a single kind of variable, such as an array or subroutine only, by assigning a reference of the appropriate type to a typeglob:

```
sub world { "world\n" }
*hello = \&world;
```
*Alias the name* &hello *to the subroutine* &world.

```
$hello = "hello";
print $hello . ", " . &hello;
```
*Prints* hello, world.

You can use typeglobs to localize filehandles and directory handles (see Item 26):

```
sub some_file_thing {
  local *FH;                          FH is local to this subroutine.
  open FH, "foo";
  ...
}
```

You also can use typeglobs in places in which you would ordinarily use references (but avoid doing so unless you have to):

```
sub yo { print "yo, world\n" };
&{*yo}();                             Prints hello, world.
```

A recent addition to the language is the *FOO{BAR} or "typeglob subscript" syntax, which allows you to extract individual references from a typeglob:

```
$a = "testing";
@a = 1..3;
$sref = *a{SCALAR};
$aref = *a{ARRAY};
print "$$sref @$aref\n";              Prints testing 1 2 3.
```

Many of the things typeglobs were once used for now can be done more sensibly with references (see Item 30), packages, and/or object-oriented programming. However, you're likely to encounter them from time to time in older Perl code, so you should be aware of what they look like and what they do.

## Item 58: Use @{[...]} or a tied hash to evaluate expressions inside strings.

Double-quote interpolation works just fine for variables, slices, and the like:

```
$name = "Bingo";                      Prints:
print "$name was his name-o\n";       Bingo was his name-o
```

```
@n = 0..10;                           Prints:
print "Fahrenheit @n[5, 6, 2]\n";     Fahrenheit 4 5 1
```

It even works for reference syntax and objects:

```
$who->{f} = 'Tiger';
$who->{l} = 'Woods';                  Prints:
print "I'm $who->{f} $who->{l}\n";    I'm Tiger Woods
```

However, double-quote interpolation does not work for subroutine calls and other types of expressions. For example, after seeing the above work, you might try:

```
package golf;
sub new { bless {} };
sub name { 'Tiger Woods' };

package main;
$golfer = new golf;
$name = $golfer->name;
print "I'm $name\n";
print "I'm $golfer->name\n";
```

*Prints:*
```
I'm Tiger Woods
I'm golf=HASH(0xabc50)->name
```

Here, only the scalar variable part, $golfer, of $golfer->name is interpolated into the double-quoted string, and the result is probably not what was desired. You can work around this with a strange bit of Perl syntax. Just combine the anonymous array constructor [...] with the dereferencing syntax for arrays:

*Continued from above:*

```
print "I'm @{[$golfer->name]}\n";     I'm Tiger Woods
```

It's U.B.E.: Ugly But Effective.

Even if the syntax is ugly, this construct can be very helpful when you are trying to put together a long here doc string, but discover that you need to interpolate some sort of expression in the middle of it:

```
$a = 2; $b = 3;
print <<EOT;
Here are the answers:
$a + $b is @{[$a + $b]}
$a * $b is @{[$a * $b]}
EOT
```

This isn't a particularly inspired example, but if you've ever used a here doc string to generate HTML in CGI script, you've probably come across a more compelling situation.

There is another alternative, which may or may not seem simpler to you. It does, however, eliminate some more punctuation. You can use a tied hash (see Item 52):

```
sub Print::TIEHASH
  { bless \ my $thingy, shift() }
sub Print::FETCH
  { $_[1] }
```

```
tie %print, Print;

$a = 2; $b = 3;
print <<EOT;
Here are the answers:
$a + $b is $print{$a + $b}
$a * $b is $print{$a * $b}
EOT
```

Note that in this case the inside of $print{} is a scalar context. You also can use a list inside @print{}, in which case the output will be separated by spaces, as usual. So what happens if you have a list to print, but you don't want spaces between the items? One possibility is changing the value of the $" special variable. I don't recommend this, but if you decide to go this route anyway, be sure to localize the damage, er, change:

```
@digits = (1, 2, 3);
{
  local $" = "";              Output separator is "" now.
  print "Testing @digits\n";  testing 123 — no spaces.
}
```

If you don't mind a more complicated syntax, you can return to the tied variable. Let's modify the example so that we can specify a "glue" string. We have to use a reference to an array as a subscript to make this work, so we're back to the anonymous array constructor again:

```
sub SepPrint::TIEHASH {
  my $class = shift;
  bless {sep => shift}, $class
}
sub SepPrint::FETCH {
  my $self = shift;
  join $self->{sep}, @{shift()}
}

tie %comma, SepPrint, ", ";
tie %colon, SepPrint, ":";

print <<EOT;
Here are the answers:
Testing $comma{[1, 2, 3]}       Testing 1, 2, 3
Testing $colon{[1, 2, 3]}       Testing 1:2:3
EOT
```

## Item 59: Initialize with BEGIN; finish with END.

Often you will need to initialize subroutines and/or packages before they are first used. Perl provides a mechanism, BEGIN blocks, that allows you to execute initialization code at program start-up. Perl also provides a complementary mechanism, END, that allows you to execute code just before program termination.

### BEGIN

A BEGIN block encloses code that is to be executed immediately after it is compiled—before any following code is compiled. For example, you can use BEGIN to initialize a variable that a subroutine later will use:

■ Use BEGIN blocks to enclose initialization code.

```
BEGIN {
  @dow = qw(Sun Mon Tue Wed Thu Fri Sat);        Initialize @dow at start-up.
}
sub dow {
  $dow[ $_[0] % 7 ];
}
```

Because the contents of BEGIN blocks are compiled and executed before any "normal" code, it generally does not matter where a BEGIN block goes. In many cases, the best place to put a BEGIN block is inside the subroutine or other code that needs it:

■ Place BEGIN blocks where they are most convenient.

```
sub dow {                             It doesn't matter where the
  BEGIN {                             BEGIN block goes—it still gets
    @dow = qw(Sun Mon Tue Wed Thu Fri Sat);   executed first (and only once).
  }                                   Now you can cut and paste the
  $dow[ $_[0] % 7 ];                  subroutine without fear of
}                                     misplacing the BEGIN block.
```

BEGIN blocks can also be used in combination with my to create private static variables like those in C (see also Item 29):

■ Use my and BEGIN blocks to create static variables.

```
BEGIN {
  my @dow =                           @dow is local to this block—and
    qw(Sun Mon Tue Wed Thu Fri Sat);  is initialized at compile time.
```

■ **Use my and BEGIN blocks to create static variables. (cont'd)**

```
  sub dow {
    $dow[ $_[0] % 7 ];
  }
}
```
*Only the subroutine* dow *has access to* @dow—@dow *is invisible to the rest of the program.*

You can even create shared static variables:

■ **Create shared static variables with my and BEGIN blocks.**

```
BEGIN {
  my $static = 10;
  sub inc_static {
    ++$static;
  }
  sub dec_static {
    --$static;
  }
}

print "inc_static = ", inc_static, "\n";
print "dec_static = ", dec_static, "\n";
```
*$static is shared between* inc_static *and* dec_static. *It is not visible to any other part of the program.*

```
inc_static = 11
dec_static = 10
```

Because code in a BEGIN block is compiled and executed immediately as it is encountered during the compile phase, code in a BEGIN block can alter compile-time semantics. In particular, a BEGIN block can create and define functions that work as list operators—just as though they had been declared in the program text (also see Item 10):

```
eval q{
  sub func_1 {print "f1: @_\n"}
};
```
*Define* func_1 *at run time.*

```
BEGIN {
  eval q{
    sub func_2 {print "f2: @_\n"}
  };
};
```
*Define* func_2—*in an* eval *block, but as the code is being compiled.*

```
func_1(1..4);
```
*Parenthesized syntax is fine (also* &func_1() *is fine).*

```
func_2 1..4;
```
*List operator is OK, because* func_2 *was defined before this line was compiled.*

```
        func_1 1..4;
```
*List operator NOT OK, because* `func_1` *was **not** defined before this line was compiled.*

Because `require` (see Item 54) is basically a form of `eval`, we can use `BEGIN` blocks to "import" functions from files containing Perl source code:

● **Combining `BEGIN` with `require`**

| *File* `func1.pl` | |
|---|---|
| `sub func_1 {`<br>`  print "func_1\n"`<br>`}`<br>`1;` | *Same as in example above, but now the sub is defined in a separate file.* |
| *Main program* | |
| `#!/usr/local/bin/perl` | *Or wherever Perl is.* |
| `BEGIN {`<br>`  require "func1.pl";`<br>`}` | *eval contents of* `func1.pl`, *but at compile time.* |
| `func_1;` | *Because we wrapped* `require` *in* `BEGIN`, *list operator syntax is OK.* |

In fact, this is the mechanism employed by Perl's `use` directive, and it is the basis for writing modules in Perl 5:

```
    BEGIN {
      require "Module.pm";          Same as use Module.
      import Module;
    }
```

See Item 42 for more about Perl modules.

## END

END blocks enclose code that will be executed just as a Perl program terminates. END blocks are useful for cleaning up—getting rid of lockfiles, releasing semaphores, and so forth:

■ **Use `END` blocks to enclose program clean-up code.**

```
END {
  unlink glob "/tmp/$prog_name.*";          Remove scratch files.
}
```

END blocks are executed during any "planned" termination—the end of the script, exit, die, and so on. Multiple END blocks are executed in reverse of the order in which they were encountered during compilation.

END blocks are not executed in other cases—uncaught signals, Perl panics, before exec, et cetera.

## Item 60:  Some interesting Perl one-liners.

You can pack a lot of meaning into a single line of Perl. In this Item, I've selected and explained a few interesting Perl one-liners for you. Study them to get a feel for the kinds of complicated and/or unusual things you can accomplish in a single line of Perl.

### select((select(SOCK), $|=1)[0])

What's a convenient way to turn off filehandle buffering?

This is a hoary old standby, probably due to Randal, that does a fair job of demonstrating the lengths that Perl programmers will go to in order to avoid creating temporary variables. This snippet of code is actually useful, and it has appeared in production code from time to time. A long, boring version of this one-liner would look something like:

```
{
  my $old = select SOCK;          Save current fh, select SOCK
  $| = 1;                         Turn off buffering.
  select ($old);                  Reselect previous filehandle.
}
```

### [ $a => $b ] -> [ $b <= $a ]

This wonderfully symmetrical one-liner contributed by Phil Abercrombie returns the lesser of $a and $b.

It can be written with less wasted technology, but then it isn't nearly as pretty:

```
($a, $b)[$b <= $a]
```

### s/\G0/ /g

Once upon a time in 1996, someone asked comp.lang.perl.misc if there was a way to replace leading zeros in a string with spaces. This was Randal's response.

This substitution uses the \G anchor, which works with the /g pattern match flag. The \G anchor refers to either the beginning of the string or the end of the previous /g match for that pattern. When the pattern match starts up, /\G0/ matches a 0 at the start of the string. If the match is successful, /\G0/ will match another 0 if it immediately follows the first one. The pattern will continue matching until it encounters a character that isn't a 0. While this is going on, the 0s are being replaced with spaces.

## /^(?=.*?this)(?=.*?that)/

The question often arises, "How can I match one thing *and* another thing with a regular expression?" Assuming the person asking isn't too confused, the right answer usually looks like:

```
/this/ and /that/
```

In other words, use *two* match operators. However, shortly after Perl's positive lookahead pattern match feature (?=…) was introduced, Randal came up with this showy alternative.

The zero-width positive lookahead operator, (?=foo), matches if the contents enclosed by the operator (in this case, foo) appear immediately to the right of the current position in the pattern match. The contents do not, however, become part of the match itself. Now, obviously (obviously?), if the beginning of the string is followed by something matching .*?this and something matching .*?that, the string must contain both this and that.

## [^\D5]

Here's the answer to the question, "How do I match any digit except 5?" This character set [\D5] is the digit 5 plus everything that isn't a digit. Its complement (^) is any digit that isn't 5.

This same principle is useful for creating patterns like [^\W\d]—any word character that isn't a digit. This is especially helpful in the presence of use locale.

## @uniq = sort keys %{ { map { $_, 1 } @list } }

What's a good way to eliminate all the duplicates from a list? All of the good (meaning, efficient) answers to this question will involve creating a hash. If we unroll this somewhat, we have:

```
{
  my %h = map { $_, 1 } @list;      Create hash with elems of
  @uniq = sort keys %h;             @list as keys, then sort the
}                                    keys.
```

What makes this mildly nifty (or maybe just confusing) is the use of the anonymous hash constructor { } to hold the temporary result. Interestingly, each pair of braces appearing here has a different function:

| | |
|---|---|
| `map { $_, 1 } @list` | *A list suitable for initializing a hash—*($list[0], 1, $list[1], 1, ...). |
| `{ map { $_, 1 } @list }` | *A reference to an anonymous hash initialized with those values.* |
| `%{ { map { $_, 1 } @list } }` | *The "name" of the dereferenced hash—suitable as an argument for* keys. |

### @rank[sort {$x[$a] cmp $x[$b]} 0..$#x] = 0..$#x

Suppose that you have a list of items that are not in sorted order. You would like to know, for each item in the list, what position that item would have in the list if it were sorted—call this the "ranks" of the elements. For example, suppose your list is:

```
qw(jane elroy george judy)
```

Then the desired output is:

```
2 0 1 3
```

This corresponds to the positions of jane, elroy, george, and judy in a sorted list:

```
elroy george jane judy
```

The string jane has a rank of 2 because it sorts third, the string elroy has a rank of 0 because it sorts first, and so on.

It seems like this problem ought to have a simple answer, but most people lapse into some serious headscratching after starting to work on it. (This includes me—I had to ponder it for a few hours.) Let's start working toward a solution by just sorting the list:

```
@x = qw(jane elroy george judy);
@x_sorted = sort @x;                         elroy george jane judy
```

Well, that's okay, but what we actually need to sort is a list of element indices:

```
@i_sorted =                                1 2 0 3
  sort {$x[$a] cmp $x[$b]} 0..$#x;        First sorted is $x[1] = elroy,
                                          second is $x[2] = george, etc.
```

The value associated with each of the elements in the sorted list is the index of the element in the original, unsorted list. The string "elroy" is element 1 in the original list, the string "george" is element 2, and so on. We can use these indices to construct the list of ranks. The string "elroy" was element 1, and since it is the first element in the sorted result, it has rank 0. We can say:

```
$rank[1] = 0;                             The rank of elroy (element 1 in
                                          the original list) is 0.
```

For "george", which was element 2 with rank 1, we have:

```
$rank[2] = 1;                             The rank of george (element 2
                                          in the original list) is 1.
```

Or we can write the whole process out as a slice:

```
 @rank[1, 2, 0, 3] = 0..3;
```

Replacing the constants with the expressions that derived them gives us our final answer:

```
 @rank[sort {$x[$a] cmp $x[$b]} 0..$#x] = 0..$#x;
```

Tricky.

This one was due to Randal (but of course).

## "$_ is string\n" if (~$_ & $_) ne '0'

Perl values can contain either strings or numbers, or both (see Item 6). Suppose you would like to find out whether a value in $_ is a string. Although modules like Devel::Peek (see Item 37) can reveal what the internal structure of a value is, you can get a glimpse of Perl's innards without using special modules at all.

The bitwise operators ~ and & operate differently on numbers and strings—bytewise when applied to strings, and on the bits of integers when applied to numbers. You can take advantage of this to distinguish between numeric and string values, because the expression ~$_ & $_ will yield a string of zero or more nulls if $_ contains a string value. On the other hand, if $_ contains a number, it yields the number 0. Distinguishing between the number 0 and a possibly empty string of nulls is a little tricky—making a string comparison against '0' is the simplest.

### perl -pe 's/\n/" " . <>/e' data

Randal posted something like this in reponse to a request for a program that would take lines from a file and join them together in pairs. For example, here's an input file:

```
Testing
one
two
three
```

This one-liner turns the input into the following:

```
Testing one
two three
```
*Each line is two of the old lines joined together with a space.*

The -pe command line option used above (a combination of -p and -e) yields a program that acts like the following:

```
while (<>) {
  s/\n/" " . <>/e;
  print;
}
```

I sputtered a bit when I saw this one-liner for the first time because I had never thought of using <> in a substitution. But it is fairly straightforward otherwise. Note that you have to substitute for \n. Nothing else—for example, the $ anchor—will work.

# Appendix A: sprintf

For whatever reason, most Perl books don't actually document the sprintf and printf operators. Instead, they say something like "check the man page for sprintf(3)." I've always thought it would be handy if at least one of the Perl books on my shelf contained a quick reference to sprintf, though—so here it is.

The arguments to Perl's sprintf operator are a format string and a list of values to be formatted. The format string contains conversion specifiers, which begin with the percent sign character % and end with one of several characters like d, f, or x. The specifiers are replaced with their corresponding formatted values, and the result is a string:

| | |
|---|---|
| `$str = sprintf '%d', 3.1416;` | 3.1416 *formatted as decimal integer:* "3". |
| `$str =`<br>`  sprintf 'TOTAL: $%7.2f', 49.95;` | 49.95 *in seven-character wide field, right-justified:*<br>"TOTAL: $  49.95" |
| `$str = sprintf '0%o 0x%x', 15, 15;` | *Hex and octal integers:*<br>"017 0xf" |

The printf operator works like sprintf, except that it sends the formatted string to standard output, or to some other filehandle if specified:

| | |
|---|---|
| `printf 'TOTAL: $%7.2f', 49.95;` | *Prints to standard output:*<br>"TOTAL: $  49.95" |
| `printf STDERR`<br>`  'elapsed: %.1f min', $time/60;` | *Note: no comma after filehandle, as usual.* |

That's all there is to it, except for a description of sprintf's conversion specifiers. The rest of this Appendix is a summary of the conversion specifiers and their features.

## Conversion Specifiers for `sprintf`

### Parts of a specifier

A conversion specifier consists of the following parts, in the given order:

- A percent sign %.
- One or more flags (optional).
- A numeric minimum field width (optional).
- A numeric precision (optional). The precision, if present, begins with a period.
- A conversion character, which determines the type of conversion that will take place, as well as the interpretation of the other parts of the conversion specifier.

The - (minus) flag specifies left-justified output. By default, converted values are right-justified.

If a numeric field (width or precision) is replaced with an * (asterisk), the value of the field is taken from the next argument in the argument list.

### Integer specifiers

| Specifier | Description | Notes |
|-----------|-------------|-------|
| d, i | Signed decimal | + (plus) flag adds leading + to positive values. ' ' (space) flag adds a leading space if the first character of the converted value is not a + or -. |
| u | Unsigned decimal | |
| o | Unsigned octal | # flag forces leading 0. |
| x, X | Unsigned hexadecimal | x specifier outputs a-f; X outputs A-F. # flag forces leading 0x. |

For all integer specifiers, numbers are padded with leading 0s to the length specified by the precision. The 0 (zero) flag pads to the field width with 0s.

The flag l before an integer specifier indicates that the value is to be converted as a C `long` or `unsigned long` type. The flag h before an integer specifier indicates that the value is to be converted as a C `short` or `unsigned short` type. The flag V indicates that the value is to be converted as a Perl integer type.

## String specifiers

| Specifier | Description | Notes |
|-----------|-------------|-------|
| s | String | Precision specifies maximum number of characters output; assumed infinite if omitted. |
| c | Character | Value is converted to unsigned decimal and then output as a character. |

## Floating-point specifiers

| Specifier | Description | Notes |
|-----------|-------------|-------|
| f | Fixed-point | For all floating-point specifiers, the precision specifies the number of digits to the right of the decimal point (6 by default). The # flag forces a decimal point. |
| e, E | Exponential notation | Value is converted to exponential notation, e.g. 1.234e-03. E specifier gives uppercase E. |
| g, G | Fixed-point or exponential | Value is converted as per f or e (E in case of G). e is used if the exponent resulting from the conversion is less than –4 or greater than or equal to the precision. Trailing zeros after the decimal point are discarded. |

The rule for the g (or G) specifier may seem complicated, but basically all it means is to use whichever of f or e (or E) looks better.

## Other specifiers

| Specifier | Description | Notes |
|-----------|-------------|-------|
| % | Percent sign | Outputs a %. |
| p | Pointer | Address of Perl value is output in hexadecimal. |
| n | Count | Outputs a count of the number of characters generated in the output so far *into* the next variable in the argument list. |

The -w command line option can be helpful in debugging `sprintf` or `printf` formats that don't work.

# Appendix B: Perl Resources

The most important resource for Perl programmers is the *Comprehensive Perl Archive Network*, or simply *CPAN*. The CPAN is a replicated archive of Perl modules, documentation, scripts, ports, development releases, and just about anything else you can think of that relates to Perl. The CPAN can be found in many major FTP archives. It can also be accessed via the World Wide Web.

There are many other notable Perl resources on-line. The *Effective Perl Programming* page at `www.effectiveperl.com` contains documentation, examples, and scripts, as well as errata and other information about this book. Randal's home page, `http://www.stonehenge.com/merlyn/`, contains links to many articles and source code examples. O'Reilly's `www.perl.com` page contains a CPAN mirror and links to a large number of other Perl resources. You should also check out the Perl Institute's home page at `www.perl.org`.

There are many books written about Perl, many of them concentrating on Perl's use as a CGI scripting language for the World Wide Web. Quality varies; however, the official language reference, *Programming Perl*, by Larry Wall, Tom Christiansen, and Randal Schwartz, is solid. Randal's *Learning Perl* is an excellent introduction to the language and has served well as a backbone for our classes. Jeffrey Friedl's *Mastering Regular Expressions* is a must-read for anyone with a serious interest in regular expressions, in Perl or otherwise.

Perl training is available from a variety of sources, including Randal's Stonehenge Consulting Services, on-line at `www.perltraining.com`.

Answers for your Perl questions can be found by posting questions to the appropriate Perl group on USENET—generally `comp.lang.perl.misc`. Bug reports can be submitted with the `perlbug` program (part of the standard Perl installation). Technical questions concerning porting or design can be addressed to the Perl 5 Porters List.

# Index

## Symbols

#! *See* pound bang line
$ *See* regular expression: $ atom
$! *See* system error variable
$" *See* list separator variable
$# *See* last array element
$# *See* output format for printed numbers
$& *See* pattern match variable
$' *See* after-match variable
$/ *See* input separator variable
$@ *See* eval error variable
$^D *See* debugging switch variable
$^W *See* warnings variable
$_ *See* default variable, the
$` *See* before-match variable
$1, $2, $3 *See* memory variables
$AUTOLOAD *See* autoload subroutine name variable
%SIG *See* signal handler hash
() *See* empty list
(?:...) *See* memory-free parentheses
(?=...) *See* positive lookahead operator, 246
(...) [...] *See* literal slice
*FOO{BAR} *See* typeglob subscript
, *See* comma operator
. *See* regular expression: . atom
.. *See* range operator
<< *See* here doc
<=> *See* spaceship operator
<> *See* diamond operator
<*filehandle*> *See* line input operator
=> *See* arrow (equals) operator
-> *See* arrow (minus) operator
@_ *See* argument list variable
@ARGV *See* command line argument variable
@EXPORT *See* module export list
@INC *See* module include path
@ISA *See* inheritance list variable
[...] *See* anonymous array constructor
\ *See* reference operator
\A *See* regular expression: \A anchor
\b *See* regular expression: \b anchor
\G *See* regular expression: \G anchor
\Q *See* quotemeta escape
\s *See* regular expression: \s atom
\w *See* regular expression: \w atom
\Z *See* regular expression: \Z anchor
^ *See* regular expression: ^ anchor
_ *See* underscore pseudo-filehandle
||= *See* or-equals operator

## A

address already in use
    error message, 233
alias
    creating with symbol table, 168
    creating with typeglob, 238
    elements of @_, 96
    single kind of variable, 238
all-at-once input, 36
alternation
    instead of character class, 82
    count left parentheses rule and, 56
    in regular expression, 52–53, 83
and operator
    omitting parentheses with, 34
anonymous array constructor
    assigning result to array variable, 126
    creates reference to unnamed array, 119